ŚAṂKARA ON RIVAL VIEWS

A ŚAṂKARA SOURCE-BOOK

VOLUME IV

by

A.J. ALSTON

SHANTI SADAN
29 Chepstow Villas
LONDON

First published in 1989 by Shanti Sadan

British Library Cataloguing in Publication Data
Śaṅkarācārya
Śaṃkara on Rival Views—(A Śaṃkara Source Book; v.4)
1. Advaita Vedanta
I. Title
II. Alston, A.J. (Anthony John) 1919-
III. Series
181'.482

ISBN 0 85424 036 5

Printed and bound by Baker Brothers (Litho) Ltd, Pontefract, West Yorkshire.

P R E F A C E

This is the fourth of a six-volume series forming a Source-Book presenting the most important texts of the classical philosopher of Advaita Vedanta, Śaṃkara, as an ordered whole. It appears after a regrettable delay due to unforeseen circumstances.

The first three volumes covered Śaṃkara's teachings on the Absolute, on the Creation and on the Soul. The present volume, somewhat bulkier, covers his refutation of rival views in two long chapters, Chapters X and XI of the Source-Book. Chapter X deals with wrong or incomplete theories of those who accepted Vedic revelation as their starting-point, or, in the case of the Pāñcarātras and Pāśupatas, the Smṛti. Chapter XI refutes doctrines which were fundamentally based on secular reasoning, even though their authors in some cases (the Materialists) denied the metaphysical validity of reason and in others (the Sāṃkhyas and Vaiśeṣikas) paid lip-service to the Veda.

Apart from a few short passages of criticism on individual points, the work of refuting opposing systems closes with the present volume, and the way is left clear for the practical teaching which will occupy the remaining two volumes of the Source-Book, Śaṃkara on Discipleship and Śaṃkara on Enlightenment.

My obligations are the same as in preceding volumes. I was fortunate to obtain the services of Mrs Patsy Clasen for typing the work after the sad decease of my wife. This volume, like its predecessors, is dedicated with the deepest reverence to the late Hari Prasad Shastri, to whom the whole work owes its existence.

A.J. Alston
London, 1988

CONTENTS

TRANSLITERATED SANSKRIT WORDS

The following table gives the most elementary indications of the value of the vowels that are variable in English (but regular in Sanskrit) and of the unfamiliar symbols and groupings of letters found in transliterated Sanskrit words. It is *not* intended as an accurate guide to correct pronunciation, for which see M.Coulson, *Sanskrit*, Teach yourself Books, pp.4-21.

a =	u in but	
$\bar{a}$ =	a in father	
ai =	ê in French crême	
au =	au in audit	
c =	ch in chant	
ch =	ch aspirated (said with extra breath)	
$\d{d}$ =	d in drake	
e =	ay in hay, (better, French é elongated)	
h =	immediately after a consonant aspirates it without altering the value. (bh,ph)	
$\d{h}$ =	strong h	
i =	i in hit	
$\bar{\imath}$ =	ea in eat	

$j\tilde{n}$ =	ja or gya (as big yard)	
$\d{m}$ =	m before b, p, v and y and at the end of a word; elsewhere = n	
$\dot{n}$ =	n in king	
$\d{n}$ =	n in tendril	
$\tilde{n}$ =	n (except in jñ, q.v.)	
o =	o in note	
$\d{r}$ =	ri in rich	
s =	s in such (not as in "as")	
$\acute{s}$ =	sh in shut	
$\d{s}$ =	sh in shut	
$\d{t}$ =	t in try	
u =	u in put	
$\bar{u}$ =	oo in boot	

CHAPTER X

REFUTATION OF INADEQUATE BRAHMINICAL DOCTRINES

1. REFUTATION OF LIBERATION THROUGH ACTION

As will become clear in Volume V Chapter XIII below, Śaṃkara held that no one could attain truth or happiness who did not follow the path of spiritual discipline laid down by the Veda. The texts of the Veda must be accepted as supernatural revelation, and assimilated through obedience to a Teacher who has himself attained enlightenment through adherence to the discipline of a recognized tradition (sampradāya) of Vedic interpretation. From this it follows that all philosophical teaching that promises liberation from ignorance and evil without recourse to traditional Vedic discipline is no better than a snare and an obstacle to the pupil, and Śaṃkara therefore refuted the main non-Upanishadic world-views of his day in texts that we shall be studying in the following chapter. But even amongst those who accepted traditional Vedic discipline, the majority failed to penetrate to the full depths of the Veda's message. This was especially the case with the Brahminical school called the Pūrva Mīmāṃsā, which took its stand on the ritualistic section of the Veda and either explained the metaphysical statements of the Upanishads away as fanciful eulogies of the soul designed to spur the sacrificer on to greater efforts in ritual, or else quite simply dismissed them as the "desert places of the Veda." (1) But later sections of the present chapter will show that even of those who sought salvation through the Upanishadic teaching itself in Śaṃkara's day, most failed, in his eyes, to understand its true meaning. Hence the need for that comprehensive re-interpretation which the texts received in his commentaries.

The present section will not deal with all aspects of Śaṃkara's criticism of the Pūrva Mīmāṃsakas, but only with those parts of it which bear most closely on their theory of liberation. The Pūrva Mīmāṃsakas of the generation preceding Śaṃkara had built up a realist epistemology with which to combat the sceptical and idealist theories of the Buddhists, and had made a variety of pronouncements about the nature of the external world, borrowing a good part of their tenets on this subject from the Vaiśeṣikas. (2) Although Śaṃkara was particular to establish that the Brahma Sūtras formed a block of teaching that could be studied independently of the Mīmāṃsā and without mastering the latter first (see Extract 3 below), he does also refer back to the early commentator "holy Upavarṣa" in terms suggesting that the latter had composed a commentary on both sets of Sūtras in which they had been conceived as forming two separate parts of one single science, Vedic exegesis, where the Pūrva Mīmāmsā Sūtras explained the Vedic ritual and the Brahma Sūtra explained the Upanishadic teaching for knowledge of the Absolute. (3) Hence Śaṃkara accepted the exegetical rules of the old Pūrva Mīmāṃsā Teachers in regard to the handling and interpretation of Vedic texts. But he had to critize the post-Upavarṣa exponents of the tradition, such as Prabhākara and Kumārila, since they strayed beyond their competence to construct a realistic world-theory, parts of which stood in open contradiction with Upanishadic teaching and with the doctrine of the Brahma Sūtras. For instance, in their anxiety to emphasize the authority of the Vedic texts, they treated them as an eternal reality, self-existent and not created or projected by any deity. Indeed, as we shall shortly see, the later Mīmāṃsakas trusted so vehemently in the ritual that they came to place faith in it *alone*, and denied the existence of those very gods whom the ritual had originally been designed to serve. *A fortiori*, the existence of a creator-god of any kind was denied, and it was held that the world was kept in being solely through the merit and demerit flowing from the earlier deeds of living beings. (4) The doctrine of the Brahma Sūtras that the supreme Self created the world "in sport" (5) was explicitly denied, (6) and the monism of the Upanishads and theism of the Epics and Purāṇas rejected in favour of a pluralistic and atheistic world-view.

The later Mīmāṃsakas cut a rather poor figure in Śaṃkara's texts. He dismisses them contemptuously as "prattlers" (7) and leaves the reader in no doubt about the weakness of their claim to be able to explain all the texts of the Upanishads on the basis of principles appropriate to the explanation of the ritualistic section of the Veda alone. Nevertheless, they were powerful and imaginative thinkers, and Śaṃkara adopted a good deal of their epistemology (8) and some of their arguments against the Buddhists. (9) He felt constrained, however, to critize two parts of their doctrine in particular. For one thing, he wanted to refute their belief that a knowledge of the nature of the soul as an eternal reality separate from the body was attainable through empirical means. Frauwallner maintains that this doctrine was already held by the early Vedantin Upavarṣa, (10) and that the later writers of the school merely developed it in the course of their polemic with the Buddhist schools, who denied the existence of an eternal soul and only admitted the empirical means of knowledge called perception and inference as criteria in debate. We shall see at Volume V Chapter XIII section 1 below, however, that Śaṃkara was unwilling to admit that the soul in its true nature could be known through the empirical means of knowledge. Indeed, if the Self were accessible to empirical means of knowledge, this would undermine the authority of the

Upanishadic texts teaching its true nature as one without a second, since one authoritative means of knowledge cannot supplement another in the latter's special field. And the Mīmāṃsakas' arguments about the nature of the Self (ātman), by them equated with the individual soul, were in any case insufficient and self-contradictory.

In the present Chapter, however, we shall be concerned with a different part of Śaṃkara's criticism of the Mīmāṃsakas, namely his statement and refutation of their theory of liberation as occurring through resort to ritualistic action alone. On this point, Śaṃkara's opposition to the Mīmāṃsakas was uncompromising, for reasons that can easily be seen. The Mīmāṃsaka, after all, represented a very different religious ideal from his own, and a much narrower one. As a Brahmin, the Mīmāṃsaka was in theory born to expound the eternal spiritual law (sanātana dharma), but in practice he was apt to be the proud and well-paid servant of the rich ritualist. The goal of his religion was happiness in this world and the next (abhyudaya), a eudaimonism not so very different from the hedonism of the materialist. For him, happiness, both in this world and the next, arose from the correct performance of the Vedic ritual. So far Śaṃkara had no objection. But the later Mīmāṃsakas tended to neglect or explain away the other and deeper side of Vedic revelation, the meditations prescribed in the Āraṇyakas and Upanishads and the metaphysical teaching of the highest Upanishadic passages, leading to conquest of ignorance and liberation in life. The development of a flourishing bourgeoisie, devoted to the comforts of town life, is reflected in the secular literature before and after Śaṃkara's day. His opposition to the Mīmāṃsakas re-enacts the opposition of the forest-sages of the Upanishadic period to the ritualists of the small towns and villages of their own day. In the Muṇḍaka Upanishad, the "great householder" Śaunaka is told that ritualism is an inferior science and that immortality is attained only by those who practise austerity and faith in the forest. (11)

It was not only the monism of the Upanishads and the theism of the Epics and Purāṇas that suffered at the Mīmāṃsakas' hands. The colourful polytheism of the Veda itself was destroyed. The Vedic god was reduced to a "purely hypothetical entity, posited for the sake of the sacrifice." (12) It was expressly denied that the deity was a physical being with power to eat the food that was offered to it, or to be pleased or displeased with a sacrifice, or to reward or punish. All that mattered were the ritualistic acts prescribed in the Yajur Veda and Brāhmaṇas, and the rewards promised for their fulfilment. The mythological conceptions of the Veda were replaced by a quasi-rational world-system, the elements of which were freely borrowed from the Vaiśeṣikas. Respect for the ancient Vedic texts was naturally expressed, yet ways were found to rob them of their original meaning. The traditions of the Purāṇas, too, were viewed with suspicion, and the references they contain to Seers with pretensions to mystical vision were seen as a threat to the teaching that the sole source of human happiness is obedience to the ritualistic injunctions of the Veda. The later Mīmāṃsakas were ritualists in a very narrow sense. They rejected the notion of an omniscient deity, be He called Viṣṇu or Śiva. They rejected both the Gītā ideal of devotion to a personal God (bhakti) and the Upanishadic ideal of renunciation of hearth and home (saṃnyāsa). (13) Their forerunners had already come in for virulent denunciation in a famous text of the Bhagavad Gītā. (14)

Śaṃkara could not stand by and allow this school to claim that the supreme goal of liberation from ignorance and death expounded in the Upanishads could be achieved through the mere selective performance of ritual, without recourse to the traditional Upanishadic texts. Extracts from Śaṃkara's works on this topic provided in the present section are arranged in two Groups. The

(X.1) REFUTATION OF INADEQUATE BRAHMINICAL DOCTRINES

Extracts in Group A explain how Vedanta, conceived as enquiry into the nature of the Absolute, (15) is a separate branch of enquiry from that of the Pūrva Mīmāṃsā, which is confined to enquiry into "dharma", and understood as enquiry into the correct fulfilment of the ritualistic and other injunctions of the Veda. If it can be established that the Vedanta is a separate branch of enquiry, it follows that the Mīmāṃsakas have no right to eliminate or explain away the metaphysical teachings of the Upanishads just because they cannot be brought into harmony with the teachings of their own pluralistic system. The Extracts in Group B state and refute the very artificial theory of the later Mīmāṃsakas that liberation could be achieved through the mere selective performance of the Vedic ritual.

In Group A (Extracts 1 - 7), Śaṃkara is concerned to show that the metaphysical teachings of the Upanishads about the nature of the Absolute (brahman) or the Self (ātman) constitute a separate body of Vedic teaching that cannot be treated as merely subordinate to the main body of ritualistic teaching of the Veda. True, there are texts which at first sight might seem to suggest that knowledge of the Absolute was a reward that arose from obedience to a Vedic injunction. For example, there is the Upanishadic text which has the grammatical form of an injunction to hear about, cogitate over and practise sustained meditation on the Self. (16) We shall see below (Volume V Chapter XII Section 2) that Śaṃkara accepted these texts in a special sense as injunctions to adopt the path of Self-knowledge. But in the Extracts of the present section he is particular to explain that their injunctive form, the fact that they are couched in the imperative mood, cannot be used as an excuse to bring them within the framework of the ritualistic system of the Mīmāṃsakas. The Self or Absolute is not a reward that is brought into being by a ritualistic act performed in obedience to a Vedic injunction. Unlike the rewards promised for the performance of ritualistic acts, it is something that already exists. Unlike them, it does not *come into being as a result of an act.* It is not anything that requires to be brought into being by performance of ritual, but something that already exists and only requires to be fully known. Enquiry into its nature thus constitutes a separate discipline from enquiry into the correct fulfilment of ritual, and this fact is expressed in the actual wording of the opening Brahma Sūtra, which says, "Then, therefore, the desire to know the Absolute." Whenever this desire arises, and from whatever cause, a person turns to the Upanishadic portion of the Veda and receives instruction. But the fact that these instructions include commands to perform actions (such as meditation) helpful towards the knowledge of the Absolute does not mean that the texts of the Upanishads stating the metaphysical truth can be treated by the specialists in ritual as matter subordinate to the ritualistic injunctions, and explained away as mere fanciful eulogies introduced to promote ritualistic activity. Texts from Śaṃkara on the related but different question of whether the initial steps towards enquiry into the Absolute on the path chalked out by the Veda depend on a Vedic injunction will be found in Volume V Chapter XII Section 2.

The Extracts of Group B (Extracts 8 - 12) centre on a theory of liberation evolved by the Mīmāṃsakas in the time of Kumārila and Prabhākara, and the discussions on this topic may require a few words of preliminary explanation. The Mīmāṃsakas, broadly speaking, divided the rituals enjoined in the Veda into two main classes, optional rituals which led to a reward or "fruit", and obligatory rituals which had to be performed by everyone in the three higher castes at specific times, and for which no reward was mentioned other than avoiding sin. Of the latter class, formed chiefly by the daily (nitya) and occasional (naimittika) obligatory ritual, the most important item was the Agnihotra, or daily offering of milk into the sacred household fires. The class called "occasional ritual" (naimittika karma) embraced all ritual prescribed to be performed, without reward and as a duty that it would be sinful to omit, not daily but only on particular occasions.

The Extracts in this Group will show that the later Mīmāṃsakas claimed that liberation could be achieved merely by the selective performance of the ritual. If a man avoided all prohibited actions and all optional ritual, but continued with obligatory ritual, he would create no new demerit or merit such as would result in a new birth, and it must be presumed that through the performance of the obligatory ritual one would avoid incurring further demerit through its omission. In Extract 12 there is an attempt to argue that the function of the obligatory ritual must be to cancel all such merit and demerit as is not exhausted through experience. For no other reward is promised for obedience to the Vedic injunctions to perform the obligatory ritual. And yet the performance of such ritual, since it is prescribed in the Veda, must be presumed to be of *some* utility to man.

Śaṃkara was easily able to dispose of this rather obviously vulnerable theory, but in doing so he drew on one further technical term which may require explanation. He distinguished between the incalculable total mass of merit and demerit that every soul had collected in the course of its repeated births from beginningless time, and that small fraction of this total which was required to initiate and sustain a given life, the latter quantum being known as the "prārabdha karma". The point of introducing the distinction in the present context was to assert that behind the small modicum of merit and demerit from past lives sustaining the present life there lay an infinite untapped reserve of merit and demerit arising from a beginningless series of previous lives, and one could not reasonably maintain that this could all be disposed of by the comparatively insignificant amount of obligatory ritual that could be performed in one life. The Advaita Vedantin's own explanation of this difficulty is of course completely different. If all experience of duality depends on ignorance of the infinite Self, the whole idea that one is an agent, together with all action and its results, can be (metaphorically speaking) "burnt up" once and for all by overcoming the illusion of plurality through knowledge.

TEXTS ON REFUTATION OF LIBERATION THROUGH ACTION: A

1. Attainment of the Self is nothing other than knowledge of the Self: attainment is not here, as in other contexts, attainment of something one does not already possess, because here there is no difference between the attainer and that which he wishes to attain. If the Self wished to attain the not-Self, then the Self would be the attainer and the not-Self the object of its attainment. And that object of its attainment would be something not already possessed, something which yet required for its attainment some form of action, for example of production. It would have to be attained through resort to some definite act brought about by particular instruments of action. Such an object of attainment, not yet possessed, would necessarily be impermanent. It would proceed from action, which in turn proceeds from desire, itself born of wrong knowledge. Its "attainment" would be like the "attainment" of a son born in a dream.

But this Self is the opposite. As it is one's own Self, it does not require any action, such as production, for its attainment. Being eternally attained by nature, the only impediment to its possession is ignorance. One may be perceiving a piece of nacre, and yet not perceive it on account of its appearing through error as a piece of silver. Here the only barrier to the possession of the nacre is wrong knowledge, and right knowledge is the only means for its "attainment", because right knowledge alone has the quality of cancelling wrong knowledge, in this case the only obstacle to the attainment of the nacre. The same is the case with the Self. In non-attainment of the Self, the sole barrier is ignorance. Therefore attainment of the Self can never be anything other than the removal of ignorance of it through right knowledge. That is why we shall be explaining how any other instrument except right knowledge is useless for attainment of the Self. (17)

* * * * *

2. Let us accept, therefore, that the word "then" (at Brahma Sūtra I.i.1) means "following immediately next." Our next task is to state what it is that regularly precedes the desire to know the Absolute, in the way that learning the Veda by heart (svādhyāya) regularly precedes the desire to know the correct exegesis of the ritualistic texts. Learning the Veda by heart cannot be the special condition, as that is a necessary condition for both desires. But could we not say that an understanding of the ritualistic sections of the Veda was the special condition for the rise of the desire to know the Absolute? Not so, for in the case of one who had learnt the Upanishads by heart, desire to know the Absolute might arise before desire to know the correct exegesis of the ritualistic texts. In the case of carving up the heart of the sacrificial animal and other such items of ritual, the regulation about "following next" implies a definite temporal sequence. But there is no such implication here. For, as between desire to know the correct exegesis of the ritualistic texts and desire to know the Absolute, there is no way of establishing that one is a principal and the other a subordinate element in any single activity, or that they are intimately connected in such a way that only he is eligible for either of them who has been made eligible for it by the other.

And there is the further difficulty that the subject about which there is desire for knowledge is quite different in the two cases, as also is the ultimate advantage in view. Knowledge of the correct exegesis of the ritualistic texts results in prosperity (abhyudaya), on condition that the injunctions in those texts are actually carried out. Knowledge of the Absolute results in (something quite different, namely) perfect beatitude (niḥśreyasa), and without the condition that anything further has to be carried out. Furthermore, the future results of one's deeds, about which one desires to know through the correct exegesis of the ritualistic texts, do not yet exist at the time of that knowledge, since their existence depends on future human activity. The Absolute, on the other hand, though one equally desires to know it, stands on a different footing. Being eternal, it is already existent, and its existence does not depend on human activity.

Moreover, the directions (codanā) of the Vedic texts have a different kind of force in the two cases. Directions concerned with ritual only give a person factual information indirectly, in the course of enjoining on him the acts which form their subject-matter. Directions concerned with the Absolute, on the other hand, are designed to give knowledge only. As knowledge cannot be subject to injunction, it is never enjoined on anyone. (It is something that just arises of its own accord when the requisite causes are present), as in the case of the knowledge which arises when the eye and an object stand in (unimpeded) contact... (18)

There are Vedic texts which show that the whole body of Vedic rituals, beginning with the Agnihotra, lead to impermanent results as instruments of welfare. Such a text, for instance, as "Just as the worldly prosperity in this world arising from labour proves transient, so does the high station in the next world arising from ritualistic and meritorious acts prove transient." (19) And one must also take into account other Vedic texts which show that man's supreme goal is achieved through knowledge of the Absolute, such, for instance, as "The knower of the Absolute attains the supreme." (20)

* * * * *

3. It was further contended (by the Mīmāṃsaka opponent) that the cogitation and sustained meditation that are seen to follow on after hearing the holy texts (in the Vedanta discipline) constitute a proof that the Absolute must be being taught as a subordinate element in some injunction to act, and not as anything determinable in its true nature independently. But this view is wrong. For cogitation and sustained meditation are for the purpose of direct intuition, just like hearing itself. If, when there has once been direct intuition of the Absolute, it were then later to become the object of some enjoined action, one could then speak of it as a mere subordinate element in some injunction to act. But such is not in fact the case. For cogitation and sustained meditation are both for the purpose (not of action but) of intuition, just as much as hearing. Therefore, if the Veda is the authoritative means for knowing the Absolute, it cannot be so in the sense that the latter is the mere object of enjoined meditations (which, according to the canons of the Pūrva Mīmāṃsa, might or might not embody truths). Hence it follows that the Veda must be the authoritative means for knowledge of the Absolute in its own right (and without requiring any further action as an auxiliary). And this is evident, the author of the Sūtras says, because one cannot otherwise secure the (total) harmony of (all) the Vedic texts. (21)

And if this is so, it accounts for the opening of a fresh body of teaching with the Absolute for its subject-matter, expressed in the words (of the opening Brahma Sūtra) "Then, therefore, the desire to know the Absolute." For, if the new discipline had been merely concerned with injunctions to perform meditations, no separate body of teaching would have been opened, because the body of teaching entitled "Then, therefore, the enquiry into ritualistic injunction" (22) had already been begun. Or, if a new body of teaching *had* been opened to deal with the injunctions to perform meditation, (23) it would have had the formula "Then, therefore, the enquiry into the subsidiary ritualistic injunctions." (24)

* * * * *

4. If, indeed, (as the Mīmāṃsakas hold) all that was taught in the Upanishads was the existence of the Self as a mere transmigrating soul, as the embodied one, as the agent and experiencer, transcendent only in the sense of being distinct from the body, then the texts asserting that a beneficial result followed from knowledge of the Self might well be mere eulogies in the way that the opponent has described. (25) But, as the author of the Sūtras here remarks, the Self is taught in the Upanishads as being "something more" than the embodied self. It is the Lord, not the mere transmigrant soul. It is void of agency and all the typical qualities of the transmigrant soul. It is the supreme Self, characterizable only through such negative attributes as "free from sin." This is the Self which the Upanishads teach, and they teach it as "that which has to be realized." (26)

Nor does such knowledge have anything to do with inspiring one to perform rituals. (27) On the contrary, the author of the Sūtras will declare later (28) "On the attainment of Knowledge (there is destruction (of the whole world set up by nescience." It follows that the statement of the revered Bādarāyaṇa quoted in an earlier Sūtra "The supreme human goal is achieved through it (through knowledge)" (29) stands true in the form he made it, and cannot be overturned by sophistical reasoning to the effect that texts conveying knowledge are subordinate to texts enjoining action. For there are texts from the Veda itself which show that the Self, as the Lord, is "something more" than the mere embodied individual soul. For example, "He who is omniscient..." (30) and "From fear of Him the wind blows" etc. (31) ... These texts imply that while (in one sense) the true Self is taught as being "something more" than the individual soul, there is in fact complete identity between them. For the true nature of the embodied soul is identity with the supreme Lord and nothing else, its condition as "embodied" being a mere product of illusory adjuncts. This is shown by such texts as "That thou art" (32) and "There is no other Seer but He," (33) and we have already explained it all at length at various places.

It is true that the opponent has claimed (34) that knowledge must be a subordinate element in ritual because there are recorded cases of enlightened men having recourse to ritual. But to this we reply that the conduct of enlightened men in yet other cases tells equally against the idea that knowledge is a subordinate element in ritual. For we have such texts as, "This is what the Kāvaṣeya (35) ṛṣis said, namely, 'For what purpose should we recite texts and for what purpose should we sacrifice?'" (36) and "Knowing this, (37) verily, the enlightened ones of old did not offer the Agnihotra" (38) and "Knowing this Self, the Brāhmaṇas give up desire for a son, for wealth and for a 'world' (39) (i.e. give up the life of a householder engaged in ritual) and wander about living on alms." (40) We see, too, that Yājñavalkya and other knowers of the Absolute (brahma-vid) withdrew from ritualistic action, for we have such Vedic texts as, "'This much, verily, suffices for immortality' said Yājñavalkya, and proceeded away into retirement." (41)

Again, the opponent quoted (42) the text, "I am going to offer a sacrifice, O holy ones." (43) But in this passage there are indications that the general subject-matter of the teaching is meditation on Vaiśvānara. Ritualistic action can very well be an auxiliary to meditation on the Absolute associated with some limiting adjunct (such as the form of Vaiśvānara). But even here, the meditation is not to be regarded as a subordinate element in any ritual, as there is no evidence to this effect from the context or other exegetical criteria..." (44)

* * * * *

5. And it also happens that certain enlightened men, when they have attained direct intuition of the final result of enlightenment, feel, on this basis, that they have no use for the means of attaining further fruits (of ritualistic action) such as sons, wealth and so forth. By the phrase "(some) by preference" the author of the Sūtras refers to the text of the Bṛhadāraṇyaka Upanishad on this topic, "Verily, when they knew this (the supreme Self), the enlightened ones of old did not desire offspring. 'What shall we do with offspring, (they said) 'we, who have obtained possession of this Self, of this world?'" (45) And we have more than once explained previously how the fruit of enlightenment is immediately evident and not something, like the fruit of ritualistic action, that will only accrue in the future. So it is not possible to establish that enlightenment is subordinate to ritualistic activity or to impugn the validity of the texts which speak of the fruit of enlightenment. (46)

Furthermore, there are texts like "But when, indeed, all has become for him the Self, then what should he see and with what?" (47) which speak of the destruction of this world through knowledge – this world which is set up by nescience, which is of the nature of action, its factors and results, and which is the necessary condition for action. But anyone who hoped to couple candidature for ritualistic action with that direct knowledge of the Self which rises from the Upanishadic discipline would find, instead, that his candidature for ritualistic action was itself underminded. So this is a further reason why spiritual knowledge stands above action.

A further point is that the texts of the Veda speak of enlightenment as pertaining to those stages of life which imply strict celibacy. Knowledge cannot be taken as subordinate to ritualistic action here, for in this context ritualistic action cannot take place. (48) Persons in these stages of life do not perform the daily Agnihotra and other Vedic ritual. Nor is it possible to claim (as the Mīmāṃsaka ritualist would like to claim) that celibate stages of life are not mentioned in the Veda, for we find references to them in such Vedic texts as... "It is in search of this world (i.e. of the Self), verily, that the houseless monks wander forth," (49) "He should renounce the world directly from the student state." (50) Both the Veda and the Smṛti admit the principle of adopting the celibate mode of life, whether a person has first become a householder or not, and whether he has paid his three debts or not. (51) So this is a further reason for regarding knowledge as standing above action. (52)

* * * * *

6. *Objection:* Here an objector states his case. How can it be asserted (he asks) that the Veda can serve as a means of the knowledge of the Absolute in face of the counter-assertion that it is concerned solely with action? We find the statement in the Pūrva Mīmāṃsā Sūtra of Jaimini, "Because the Veda is concerned throughout with action, the parts of it that do not contribute to that end are useless." (53) The Upanishads are therefore useless (continues the opponent) as they are not concerned with action. Or else at best they may be reckoned as auxiliaries to the injunctions to act, in that they throw light on the true nature of the active person performing the sacrifice or of the presiding

deities or other factors in it. Or else they could conceivably be taken as enjoining other acts (apart from the physical performance of the ritual), such as meditation on the symbolic significance of the presiding deity and other elements in the sacrifice. It cannot be that they exist to give any information about already existent realities, because determination of the latter belongs to the sphere of perception and the other empirical means of knowledge. Moreover, information about already existent realities is information about what can neither be produced nor removed, and is hence information of no practical value to man. In order, therefore, that Vedic passages (containing mere narrative) like "He wept" (54) might not have to be accounted meaningless, they are taken as designed to influence the sacrificer's conduct through eulogy, according to the principle stated by Jaimini, "Because they occur together in the same passage with injunctions, their purpose is to recommend obedience to the injunctions." (55)

And even the verses in praise of the gods (mantra) are said to be related to the activity of the sacrificer, as passages in them like "Thee for strength (I cut)" (56) refer to the ritual and its factors. We do not find any Vedic text anywhere that is intelligible if not taken in connection with some injunction to act. Nor is it reasonable that we should. But injunctions cannot refer to an already existent reality, as they bear on actions that have to be performed in the future. Hence the Upanishadic texts are but subordinate elements occurring within the system of ritualistic injunctions to act. Their function is to throw light on the true nature of the sacrificer in the context of his sacrifice, and also to give him information about the gods and other matters connected with the sacrifice. Or, if you refuse to accept this on the ground that the Upanishads constitute a separate section of the Veda, different from the section on ritualistic sacrifices, then (we say that) the Upanishads are still concerned with action, for instance, with the carrying out of meditation on the themes for meditation that occur in their texts. Hence we cannot say that the Veda leads us to a comprehension of the Absolute.

Answer: To this opinion (57) we make the following reply. The author of the Sūtras uses the word "but" to show that the refutation of a *prima facie* view is in progress. He says, "But that (i.e. the Absolute) (is what is known from the Upanishads) because of the harmony of the texts." That, the Absolute, omniscient, omnipotent, the cause of the rise, maintenance and dissolution of the universe, is known from the texts of the Upanishads. How? "On account of the harmony." The texts of all the Upanishads co-operate to teach the existence of the Absolute as their ultimate purport. We might instance such texts as, "In the beginning, my dear one, there was Being only... one without a second," (58) and others... Once it has been determined that all words in these texts refer ultimately to the Absolute in its true nature – because their harmonious co-operation towards this end has been noted – it is not then proper to make hypotheses about other meanings, as this will involve contradicting what the Veda teaches and substituting what it does not teach.

Nor can it be claimed that their ultimate purpose is to throw light on the nature of the active person performing the sacrifice, for there are texts such as "What should he then see and with what?" (59) which negate action and its factors (including the agent) and fruits. And while it is true that the Absolute is an "already existent reality", it is not true (as the opponent claimed it was) that its determination belongs to the sphere of perception and the other empirical means of knowledge. For the fact that the Absolute is one's own Self can only be known through the texts of the Veda like "That thou art." (60)

Nor can we accept that our position was in any way undermined by what the opponent said about the existence of the Absolute being of no practical value to man because the Absolute was (an already existent entity and so) not subject to being either produced or removed. For the fact is that the only road to the highest end of man is the knowledge that the Absolute, not subject to production or removal, is one's own Self, as this knowledge (is the only thing that) serves to destroy all suffering.

We can accept as being without any contradiction to our own position the opponent's view that the Upanishads contain passages which expound the nature of the deities and of other elements mentioned in the meditations prescribed in their own texts. But it does not follow from this that knowledge of the Absolute depends on injunctions to perform meditations. For the Absolute is one, and not subject to production or removal, so that knowledge of it must be taken to annul all knowledge of duality, including that of action and its factors. Once the notion of duality has been destroyed by the recognition of unity, it cannot arise again, so that there is no question of supposing that (permanent) knowledge of the Absolute could depend on injunctions to practise meditations.

We accept that outside the Upanishads the texts of the Veda cannot be authoritative except in relation to injunctions (to action which has purpose and brings rewards). But the knowledge of the Self (taught in the Upanishads) carries its own reward (of eternal freedom from suffering) with it, so that one cannot there deny the validity of the Vedic teaching (about a mere matter of fact on the ground that it brings no reward and is purposeless). Nor is the validity of the Veda a mere matter of inference, that it should depend on further evidence (from which to build up a universal law — since its subject-matter lies beyond the range of the empirical means of knowledge, and, in the case of the Self, its validity is open to confirmation through direct experience). So the Veda can and does serve as the means to knowledge of the

Absolute.

Objection: Here some would object as follows (61). We can admit (they would say) that the Veda serves as the means to knowledge of the Absolute. Nevertheless, the Veda can only bear on the Absolute if the latter be taken as the subject-matter of an injunction to know. The sacrificial post and sacrificial fires etc. have supernatural properties that are not accessible to the empirical means of knowledge. Nevertheless, the Veda can only convey authoritative information about them incidentally in the course of giving injunctions. And the same holds true of the Absolute.

How do we know this? Because (continues the objector) the sole purpose of any text of the Veda is to inculcate or prohibit some course of action. For the great authorities on the ultimate significance of the Veda (62) have said: "It is indeed quite visible and evident that the burden of the Veda is instruction in ritual" and "A direction (codanā) is a form of speech inculcating some action" and "It (one's ritualistic and spiritual duty) is known through a revealed injunction" and "Words signifying existent entities are to be taken only in conjunction with verbs denoting action" and "Because the Veda is concerned throughout with action, the parts of it that do not contribute to that end are useless." (63) The Veda, therefore, is significant in so far as it prescribes or prohibits action in some particular regard. All else (that is found within it) is (not significant in itself but) subordinate to that. Because the Upanishads come under the general heading of the Veda, they, too, have significance only under the same general conditions. Seeing that the Veda is concerned with actions throughout, it will be but right to say that knowledge of the Absolute is enjoined for him who desires immortality in just the same way as the Agnihotra and other rituals are enjoined for him who desires a sojourn in heaven.

No doubt you (i.e. the Advaitin) will object

that a distinction has been established between two separate fields of investigation. In the section of the Veda treating of ritual (karma kānda), the subject of investigation is the enquiry into the question of what future actions will lead to what future merit. In the Upanishads, on the other hand, the subject of investigation is the Absolute, ever existent. Acquisition of the fruit of knowledge of what future actions lead to what merit depends (you, the Advaitin, will say) on one's actually performing the action. And you will ask, "Will not the fruit of knowledge of the Absolute be something altogether different in kind, as it is something that is immediately attained by the mere acquisition of knowledge?"

But we (who respect the Mīmāṃsaka tradition) reply (against the Advaitin) that this cannot be so. For the Absolute is only taught in connection with injunctions about actions to be done. Consider, for instance, such injunctions as the following: "The Self, verily, has to be seen" and "That Self beyond all evil – that is what has to be investigated, what has to be enquired into" and "It should be meditated on as the Self alone" and "He should meditate on the Self as his 'world'" and "Whoever knows the Absolute becomes the Absolute." (64) To answer the question, "What is the Self, what is that Absolute implied in these injunctions?" all the texts of the Upanishads have to be drawn in, those, for instance, saying that it is "eternal," "omniscient," "omnipresent," "in perpetual satisfaction and delight," "eternally pure, enlightened and liberated by nature," "knowledge and bliss" and so forth. From (the pious act of) meditating on it (as having these qualities) there will arise a supernatural reward, knowable only through the Vedic revelation, in the form of liberation. If the Upanishadic texts are taken as mere statements of fact without any connection with injunctions for anything to be done, like such statements as "The earth has seven 'continents'" or "That is the king passing," then they would be useless, as nothing could be produced or removed as a result of them.

(XI) REFUTATION OF INADEQUATE BRAHMINICAL DOCTRINES (TEXTS)

Perhaps you (i.e. the Advaitin) will say that we find that some bare statements of fact, like "This is a rope, it is not a snake," do serve a practical purpose in that they remove the fear aroused by erroneous cognition. And you will wish to conclude that, in the present case also, the Upanishadic statement of the true nature of the Self, namely that it is the final principle of reality and not the mere suffering transmigrant, will serve the practical purpose of removing the erroneous belief that one is the transmigrant.

This (the objector) replies against the Advaitin) might be true if the error of believing oneself to be the transmigrant could be brought to an end through the mere hearing of a statement of the true nature of the Absolute. But it does not come to an end, as we see people who have heard the Vedic teaching on the nature of the Absolute and who yet remain afflicted by pleasure and pain and other characteristics of transmigratory life. Furthermore, we find in the text "It should be heard about, cogitated over, subjected to sustained meditation" (65) a definite injunction to practise cogitation and sustained meditation *after* hearing the texts teaching the nature of the Absolute. All this forces us to conclude that the Veda can only serve as a means to the knowledge of the Absolute if the Absolute be regarded as the thing to be known in an injunction prescribing knowledge.

Answer: But our (Advaitin's) reply to all this argumentation is that it is wrong, because the "fruits" of meritorious action and of knowledge of the Absolute respectively are different in kind. Enquiry into what is called "dharma", which means (the nature and results of) action in thought, word and deed as established by the Veda and Smṛti, is what is referred to in the Sūtra, "Now, therefore, the enquiry into dharma." (66) In this science (i.e. the Pūrva Mīmāṃsā Śāstra) one also enquires into the opposite of dharma (adharma), exemplified by causing injury to others and the like, so that one may avoid it. Here the various evil practices are defined by the Vedic prohibitions. The universally experienced fruits of these two forms of action, (67) good and evil respectively, which are defined by the Vedic injunctions and prohibitions, are joy and misery, experienced in the realm of sensation, speech and thought, through the contact of the bodily senses with their objects, familiar to all living beings from the creator-god Brahmā down to the plants of the vegetable kingdom. Moreover, there are passages in the Veda (68) which speak of a hierarchy of different grades of happiness, stretching from the human condition to that of Brahmā. From this we conclude that they must have corresponding degrees of merit to rouse such different degrees of joy. From the existence of different degrees of merit we conclude that sacrificers have been eligible to perform sacrifices of different grades. And it is well known that eligibility for different grades of sacrifice depends on differences of aim and resources. Thus we know that it is only those who offer ritualistic sacrifices who can go by the Northern Path, (69) and this only through the attainment of concentration in their meditation on the symbolic significance of certain factors in the sacrifices as laid down in the revealed texts. (70) On the other hand, the Southern Path (71) is attained through the daily performance of the obligatory ritual plus the mere performance of secular good works (such as using one's wealth to have wells dug by the roadside for public use etc.) and charity (such as gifts of wealth or land to Brahmins etc.) The Veda, too, (72) is evidence of different degrees of joy resulting from different measures when it says, "Having remained in heaven as long as their merit lasts," (thereby implying different lengths of sojourn and different degrees of merit). And in the same way we conclude that whatever insignificant scraps of pleasure may be enjoyed by living beings stretching below man in the scale, and down to the occupants of hell and the world of plants, all have their different degrees of intensity, and result from "dharma" in the form of obedience to the Vedic injunctions. Similarly, we see varying degrees of pain in all embodied beings, whether they be above or below man. From this we conclude that there exist different degrees of the opposite of dharma (adharma), defined by the prohibitions of the Veda, and that those addicted to such practices stand in a hierarchy of higher and lower. Thus the Veda, the Smṛti and reason all confront us with a picture of transmigratory life as that which afflicts all those who are in the grip of nescience and other psychological defects. And this transmigratory life (saṃsāra) is essentially unstable, and is marked throughout by possession of a body derived from merit and demerit of different degrees (arising from the deeds of one's previous lives), which in turn condition the experience of pleasure and pain (in the present life) in varying degrees. Agreeing with the view of transmigration just depicted is the following Vedic text: "Verily there is no remission of pleasant and unpleasant experience for one who still has a body, (whereas the pleasant and the unpleasant do not affect him who has become 'bodiless'.)" (73) This Upanishadic text denies the duty of performing "dharma" as defined by the Vedic injunctions when that bodiless state called liberation (mokṣa) has supervened, as it denies that there is any contact with the pleasant or the unpleasant. For if the Vedic injunctions had to be carried out, it would not have been appropriate to have denied all contact with the pleasant and the unpleasant.

It is not right to say that the "bodiless" state is itself something that has to be brought into being by carrying out the injunctions. For the bodiless state is in fact one's natural state. (On this point we have such Vedic texts as) "The wise man does not grieve. He reflects that the Self is something immense and all-pervading, bodiless amid bodies, stable amidst the unstable" (74).... So it stands established that the bodiless state called liberation is eternal and different from the fruits of deeds which have to to be performed.

Now, the eternal may sometimes be "eternal-but-changing" (pariṇāmi-nitya). This occurs where that in which a modification takes place remains constant and there is nothing to contradict the idea "This is still that." This is the case, for instance, with the physical elements such as the earth in the view of those who hold the world to be eternal. And it is true of the "constituents" (guṇa) as conceived by the Sāṃkhya philosophers. But the eternity with which we are concerned here (i.e. that of the bodiless state) is that form of eternity which is raised above all change (kūṭastha-nitya). (75) It is the eternity of the Self. The latter is real in the highest sense, all-pervasive like the ether, void of all modification, ever fully satisfied, partless and self-luminous by nature. Here merit and demerit and their effects can gain no entry in past, present or future. That is what is meant by the bodiless state called liberation, as is clear from such Vedic passages as, "Beyond merit and demerit, beyond cause and effect, beyond past and future." (76)

It (the "bodiless" state) is therefore itself that very Absolute, enquiry into which is now in progress. If it were only taught as dependent on some act that had to be done, with the act as its necessary pre-condition, then liberation would be non-eternal. We should then have to regard liberation as just one, admittedly outstanding, fruit of ritualistic action among the whole hierarchy of fruits of such action, which we have seen to be ordered in degrees of more and less, and all to be impermanent. But all those philosophers who admit the concept of liberation at all agree that it is eternal. So it could never be right to teach that the Absolute itself was an entity that depended for its existence on some act that had to be done.

Furthermore, the texts which speak of liberation as following immediately on knowledge of the Absolute imply that there can be nothing further that has to be done between the rise of such knowledge and attainment of the Absolute. Such texts include... "What delusion or pain could there be, then, for him who sees all as one?" (77) ... The phrase "Knowing the Absolute and becoming the all" has to be understood on the analogy of "He stands up and sings," where the agent has nothing else he has to do between the standing up and the singing.

Moreover, there are other texts which show that the fruit of knowledge of the Self is nothing more than the cessation of the obstructions which prevent liberation. Under this head we might include... "The holy Sanatkumāra showed him (Nārada) the way beyond darkness (tamas), when his impurities had been removed." (78) We find the same doctrine in a famous Sūtra composed by the Teacher (Gautama) and supported by logical reasoning, *viz.* "Liberation results from the successive elimination of each member of the following series in order after its predecessor – the series, namely, wrong-knowledge, psychological defects, action for external ends, birth, pain." (79) Wrong-knowledge is eliminated by knowing the identity of one's own real Self with the Absolute.

This knowledge of the identity of one's own real Self with the Absolute is not a mere meditation (80) on an assumed identity based on numerical measure (sampat), (81) such as we encounter in the text, "Infinite is the mind, infinite are the Viśvadevas, thereby he wins an infinite world." (82) Nor is it to be identified with symbolic meditation (adhyāsa), as when one meditates on the mind, or on the sun, as the Absolute, according to such texts as "He should meditate on the mind as the Absolute" (83) and "The teaching is that the sun is the Absolute." (84) Nor is it meditation on a hidden identity based on association through a common function, as in the case of the text, "The air, verily, is an absorber, the Vital Energy, verily, is an absorber." (85) Nor is it a mere piece of subordinate ritualistic activity carried out for purposes of purification, like the ritual glance at the ghee. (86)

If knowledge of the identity of one's real Self with the Absolute were taken to be of the type of a mere meditation on fancied identity where no real identity existed, then this would amount to a direct contradiction of the plain grammatical meaning of the texts which proclaim that they are in fact identical – such as "That thou art" and "This Self of mine is the Absolute." (87) Such a conception would moreover conflict with texts like "The knot of the heart is broken, all doubts are destroyed," (88) which state that the fruit of such knowledge is the cessation of nescience. Nor would the idea that the metaphysical statements of the identity of the Self were fanciful meditations accord with the texts proclaiming that they led to the realization of one's identity with the Absolute – texts like "Whoever knows the Absolute becomes the Absolute." (89) Therefore knowledge of the identity of the Self with the Absolute is neither of the nature of meditation on fancied identity based on numerical correspondence nor of any of the other alternatives suggested by the opponent... (90)

Nor is liberation the result of an "improvement" leading to purification, that its rise should be dependent on an active process of any kind. Purification may either proceed through positive improvement or else through removal of blemishes. But liberation certainly cannot be the object of an act of improvement, since it implies identity with the Absolute, on which no improvement could be conceived. Nor could any blemishes be removed from liberation, as it is of the nature of the Absolute, which is eternally pure.

"But," you will perhaps say, "is not liberation a characteristic of one's own true Self that has become hidden? And can it not be made to manifest through self-purification, as the luminous quality of a mirror can be brought to manifestation by active polishing?" But this would be wrong. For the Self cannot be the agent of any act. No act can arise without the agent undergoing some modification. And if the Self were to engage in action and thereby undergo modification this would have the unacceptable result of contradicting such texts as "This Self is said to be unalterable." (91) There can be no activity, therefore, on the part of the Self. Nor can the Self undergo purification through action initiated by another, as it is by nature a non-object.

Perhaps you will reply that the embodied self is seen to undergo purification through actions performed by the body, such as bathing, ceremonial mouth-washing, donning of the sacred thread and the like. But this does not affect our position, as it is only the "self" identified with the body that is so purified, and this "self" is only perceived through nescience. It is evident that bathing and ceremonial mouth-washing pertain to the body. And what is purified by such actions, which pertain to the body, can only be some other principle intimately connected with the body that is taken as the Self through nescience. When, for instance, the humours of the body have been brought back into equilibrium through medical treatment proceeding from one's own bodily action, then the one intimately connected with the body, who has identified himself with it, feels that he has attained his end of regaining health, and has the idea "Now I am well." In the same way, the one who is "purified" by bathing, ceremonial mouth-washing, donning the sacred thread and the like, is simply the one who feels "I am pure and have been purified." And this is (not the true Self but) only the one that is identified with the body. And he is the one by whom all actions are effected, being the one who feels "I" and who is the object of the ego-notion and is the empirical experiencer in general. And he is the one who experiences the fruits of action, as mentioned in the Vedic verse,

"One of these two eats the sweet berries while the other merely looks on," (92) or again in the words "The complex of Self, senses and mind is what the wise call 'the experiencer'." (93) (And the pure Self is not the empirical agent and experiencer, but merely the principle of pure Consciousness to which the latter owes his existence, as is shown by such texts as) "The one divinity, hidden in all beings, all-pervading, the inner Self of all beings, the superintendent of action, dwelling within all creatures, the Witness, the conscious principle, pure, void of all empirical qualities" and "He embraces all. He is luminous, bodiless, unhewn, sinewless, pure and unpenetrated by any evil." (94) The last two texts show that nothing can add any increment to the Absolute and that it is eternally pure. Liberation, however, simply means being the Absolute, so that liberation is no more subject to embellishment or purification than the Absolute is. No one, therefore, can show any way in which action could be brought into relation with liberation. It is knowledge only that is relevant in this context, and action could not be brought to bear on liberation even in a dream. (95)

* * * * *

7. It is true that some (96) claim that there is no section of the Veda that simply expounds the true nature of reality, holding that it consists entirely of injunctions and prohibitions and material subordinate to these. But this view is wrong. For the Spirit (puruṣa) proclaimed in the Upanishads (97) is not subordinate to anything. The Spirit known from the Upanishads is the Absolute. It is not the being that undergoes transmigration, and it is different from substances of the empirical world, which latter are subject to being produced, obtained, transformed or purified. It is taught in sections where it is itself the main topic, and not subordinate to any other topic... Nor can you say "It does not exist" or "It is not known," for we have the text, "This principle that can only be

designated by the words " 'Not thus, not thus' is the Self." (98) which shows that the Spirit taught in the Upanishads is our own Self. And no one can deny the existence of their own Self!

But if the Self is the object of the ego-notion, will it not be wrong to say that it can only be known from the Upanishads? No, for against this it has been called the Witness of the ego-notion. The Spirit (puruṣa) is distinct from the object of the ego-notion, which latter is the agent in activity; for it is the Witness. Present in all beings as one and the same, (99) eternal and raised above all change, it is not knowable from the portion of the Veda that is concerned with ritualistic injunctions, nor is it accessible to rationalistic methods of enquiry. On the other hand, no one can deny its existence or argue that it is brought in as a mere eulogistic tail-piece to encourage people to carry out the ritualistic injunctions, as it is the Self of everyone. It is for the very reason that it is the Self of everyone that it is not subject to removal or production. For while every one of the modifications that arise to make up the world perishes, the Spirit does not perish. It is imperishable, for lack of anything that could cause it to perish. It is eternal and raised high above all change, and for this reason is spoken of as being eternal, pure, enlightened and free by nature. Hence such texts as "There is nothing higher than the Spirit. It is the topmost limit, it is the highest resort" and "But I am asking you about the Spirit proclaimed in the Upanishads"(100) are justified when they imply, by their reference to the Spirit as that which is specially taught in the Upanishads, that the Upanishads exist primarily to proclaim the existence of the Spirit. The statement, therefore, that there is no section of the Veda proclaiming an already existent reality is a mere rash and unfounded assertion.

As for the appeal to the assertion by an

acknowledged expert in Vedic exegesis (Śabara) saying, "Its (the Veda's) purpose is seen to be the explanation of the ritual" (101) and so on, one must realize that such statements refer only to that part of the Veda which deals with injunction and prohibition, as they pertain to the subject of enquiry into the merit arising from religious acts (dharma). And if you took such a statement as, "The Vedic texts are concerned with action because those which are not concerned with it are useless" (102) as holding unconditionally throughout the Veda, this would involve the absurdity of holding that *all* statements in it about existing realities were useless. If your reply to this is that wherever an existent reality is spoken of apart from the injunctions and prohibitions (103) it is only mentioned as something (like life in heaven) that has to come into being in the future, our reply to this is that on that basis there can be no reason why it should not proclaim the existence of an already existent, eternal, changeless reality (as well). An already existent reality is not turned into an action by the mere fact of being taught.

Perhaps you will say that although an already existent entity cannot be an action, still, if it is taught, it must be taught for the sake of an action, inasmuch as existent realities can be the means to action. But we do not accept this as a criticism of our position at all. Even if they are taught for the sake of some action, they are still only taught as existent entities having the power to effect that action. The fact that the existence of a thing is taught for the sake of an action concerns its use. It does not mean that the thing is not taught as an existent reality.

Well, you (Mīmāṃsaka) may reply, suppose it *was* taught as an existent reality. How does it help you (Advaitins) in your argument? We reply that if a substance needed for an action can be taught as an existent reality, then an existent reality can also be revealed by teaching about an as yet imperfectly known Self. With regard to practical significance, (104) it is on a par with teaching about already existent substances as means to action. For the practical purpose envisaged here is the bringing to an end of wrong knowledge (mithyā-jñāna) through right knowledge, wrong knowledge being the (sole) cause of transmigratory existence (and all its attendant pain).

Moreover, there are passages in the Veda, such as "A Brahmin should not be killed," which teach one to withhold from action. Now, withholding from action is not action, nor is it a means to action. If it were really true, as the opponent maintained, that teaching not devoted to action was devoid of all purpose, then this purposelessness would extend to the texts concerned with withholding from action such as "A Brahmin should not be killed." And this the opponent would not be ready to accept. Nor can you make out that the word "not" here implies an injunction to any new (aprāpta) activity, and not an injunction to the mere inactivity resulting from absention from killing. It must be deemed to imply mere abstention from the act of killing, for which latter there is a natural tendency in some persons. And it is the nature of the particle "not" to denote the total non-existence of what it is connected with. The idea of the non-existence of an act promotes indifference to that act, and the act eventually subsides of its own accord, like fire subsiding for lack of fuel.

Hence in prohibitions like "A Brahmin should not be killed" we maintain that the prohibition promotes "indifference" only in the sense of inactivity resulting from the non-performance of an action that one might have performed but for the prohibition. This holds throughout, except in certain cases such as that of the "Vow of Prajāpati." (105) It is therefore only those Vedic texts which bear on past events and are of no significance for the welfare of man – such as some of the mythological stories – which fall into the category of "purposeless." (106)

TEXTS ON REFUTATION OF LIBERATION THROUGH ACTION: B

8. The daily obligatory rites, which are performed to reduce the effects of past sins, (107) together with the optional rites prescribed for those who want specific fruits, have been treated of in the previous section. (108) Now knowledge of the Absolute is extolled, with a view to getting rid of the cause which leads to action. The cause of action is desire, which supplies the prompting force. Those whose desires are all realized do not experience desire. They are established in their own true Self and incapable of being prompted to action. It is only if one's sole desire is for the Self that one can attain all one's desires. For the Self is the Absolute. And the text will say later (109) that he who knows the Absolute attains the supreme state....

Objection: (110) Liberation consists in the mere effortless resting in one's self, through not engaging in any optional rituals or prohibited deeds, because in this way the merit and demerit that occasioned the present life (i.e. the prārabdha karma) are exhausted through experience, while demerit is avoided by carrying out the obligatory ritual. Or else we may say that liberation arises from action in the sense that the unsurpassable joy called heaven arises from action (and this is itself liberation). (111)

Answer: This view is wrong because it fails to take into account the extent and variety of action. The actions in previous births that are responsible for one's experiences in the present birth are not negligible. And the actions in previous births that have no connection with the experiences in the present life are not only likely to be very large in number but also mutually contradictory. (112) The fruits of the latter class of actions (are so wide and various that they) cannot be consumed in one birth, so that there will have to be more rebirth to consume the remainder. Nor are the arguments in favour of this merely negative: there is also proof positive in the form of such texts from the Veda and Smṛti as "Those whose conduct has been good (will quickly find a good womb)" and... "The members of the castes and stages of life engaged in their various duties (experience the fruits of their deeds after death)." (113)

Nor is it right to say that the purpose of the obligatory rituals is to consume both the good and the bad results of the entire stock of deeds that is not responsible for the present birth. For you maintain that there are penalties (in the form of demerit) for not performing them, and the word "penalty" means something undesirable.

If you interpret this to mean that the purpose of performing the obligatory rituals is to avoid the penalty of not performing them, which will arise in the form of future pain, they cannot at the same time also have the sole purpose of consuming the results of all past deeds not connected with the present life. And even granting that there were no self-evident contradiction, they could still only consume the results of impure deeds, not of pure deeds, for they would not be in contradiction with pure deeds. There cannot be any contradiction between the obligatory rituals and rituals carrying good fruit, since both are pure. It is only the impure that can stand in contradiction with the pure.

Moreover, since desire, the cause of action, cannot be brought to an end without enlightenment, there cannot be total annihilation of action and its results without enlightenment either. For desire occurs only to those who do not know the Self, the scope of desire being confined to the not-self. (114) In fact there cannot be desire for the Self, for one is always in possession of it. And, as has already been said, one's own Self is the Absolute, the Supreme.

Moreover, non-performance of the obligatory ritual is (not a positive entity but mere) non-action. (115) Penalties (which are positive entities) cannot arise from it. So "not-performing (i.e. non-performance of) the obligatory ritual" is mentioned as a sign of penalties arising from the massed sins of former lives. That is why the Smṛti text (116) was not wrong to use the positive participal suffix (the "-ing" of "doing") in the phrase "not doing the prescribed ritual" (because the reference was to positive sin requiring to be purged by penance). Otherwise, it would undermine the canons of sound knowledge to admit that a positive entity could arise from a non-entity. (117) So the doctrine that one can remain established in the Self simply through desisting from optional rituals and prohibited deeds is unfounded.

Finally, there was the statement that liberation proceeded from action alone because the unsurpassable joy called heaven was the result of ritualistic action. This is wrong. For liberation is something eternal. What is eternal does not "proceed from" anything. It is accepted as a general maxim that what has a beginning is impermanent. So liberation does not proceed from action. (118)

* * * * *

9. In this connection, we sometimes hear the following view put forward: Man's highest end must be achieved through action alone. For if a man knows the meaning of the whole Veda, this simply fits him to perform its rituals, as is proclaimed by Manu in the text, "The twice-born must know the

whole Veda, together with its secret parts." (119) And this "knowing" includes knowledge of the contents of the Upanishads, such as knowledge of the (nature of the) soul. (120) And everywhere we find action set forth as the prerogative of one who has knowledge, as in such phrases as "(Only) a man of knowledge is to perform sacrifices," "Only a man of knowledge can assist at a sacrifice" and "It is only after he has knowledge that a person can apply himself to the acts." (121)

This is what we are told. For some think that the entire Veda is concerned with action alone, and that if the highest end of man were not attainable through ritualistic action alone the Veda would be useless. But this whole view is wrong. For liberation is to be taken as eternal, and it is generally accepted that the results of any deed are impermanent. If the highest end of man were anything that arose from an act it would be something that was impermanent. Nobody, however, can accept that, especially as it would contradict the text, "As here, on earth, the world that is earned through work perishes (even so there the world which is earned by merit perishes... But for those who depart hence, having found here the Self... for them there is freedom in all the worlds.)" (122)

You will perhaps claim that there may be liberation independent of knowledge if the following conditions are observed: non-performance of the optional rituals or prohibited deeds (which both lead to further experiences), exhaustion of the particular stock of merit and demerit that brought about the present birth by experiencing it, and avoidance of the penalties of non-performance of the obligatory ritual through carrying it out. But this also is wrong. For, as we have already explained, there is likely to be further merit and demerit (not concerned with the present birth) left unconsumed, and this will bring embodiment in a further birth. But between performance of the obligatory ritual on the one hand, and the residue of merit and demerit from previous births which is not concerned with bringing about the present birth on the other, there is no conflict. So the performance of the one will not serve to eradicate the other.

And as for the statement, "If a man knows the meaning of the whole Veda, this simply fits him to perform rituals," it was no better. For enjoined meditations, (even though technically termed "vidyā" or "knowledge") cannot just be dismissed as knowledge of the meaning of the Vedic texts. (123) For it must (on your view) be through that latter kind of knowledge alone that a man acquires fitness to perform rituals, so that meditation would have to be prescribed for another purpose, and that purpose could only be liberation. (124) And it might be claimed that there was positive evidence that they were prescribed for another purpose, too. For after saying that the Self was to be heard about, the text prescribes two further different activities in the words, "It must be cogitated over, it must be made the object of sustained meditation." (125) And it is well known that cogitation and sustained meditation are quite different from mere knowledge derived from hearing (which, according to the opponent, would only suffice to equip a man with the mere knowledge that his soul was an eternal entity, knowledge which he would need in order to qualify for the performance of Vedic ritual." (126)

* * * * *

10. So it is knowledge alone that is the means to the highest beatitude. Against this view, however, some (the Pūrva Mīmāṃsakas) maintain that knowledge without works is not the means. For realization of the transcendent reality is supposed to be eternal, yet (so they say) the non-performance of the obligatory ritual (implicit in spiritual knowledge as the Advaitin is supposed to conceive it) will inevitably occasion demerit and land one in hell

and other (unpleasant phases of transmigratory existence).

They deny that they hold a doctrine that makes liberation impossible, in the sense that there would be no escape from the cycle of action and the experience of the results of that action leading to further action. For they maintain that liberation is the natural and eternal state of the soul. First, (they maintain), one performs one's obligatory ritual, so as not to occasion demerit (by neglecting it). By avoiding (in addition) deeds prohibited in the Veda, one avoids rebirth under undesirable conditions. When the present body dies through the exhaustion of the stock of merit and demerit from previous births that brought it into existence, then there will be nothing left to cause the emergence of a further body. Attachment and other such defects no longer afflict the soul, and it remains in its natural state. This is what constitutes transcendence (kaivalya). Transcendence supervenes naturally in this situation, without any special effort being required to secure it.

If you object against these theorists that there must exist the merit and demerit of many past births, parts of which would have led to such diverse goals as heaven and hell and so could not have co-operated to initiate the present birth, and which must therefore remain over unexperienced and so not exhausted, they are ready with an answer. They say that the trouble involved in the performance of the obligatory ritual may be taken as the experience which exhausts the residual merit and demerit of previous births (i.e. the large portion not concerned with the initiation of the birth in which liberation occurred). Or else, they say, one may take it that the obligatory ritual functions like a penance to destroy (the effects of) previously performed sins...

But all this view is wrong. The Veda says, "Only when one *knows* Him does one go beyond death. There is no other path for transcending it" (127)...

The Mīmāṃsaka theory (which refers only to the exhaustion of the demerit arising from past sins) makes no provision for the exhaustion of merit from previous lives not involved in instituting the present birth. Their theory admits the existence of demerit from previous lives which is not involved in the present birth: but one must also admit the existence of merit by the same token. As the latter cannot be exhausted (on the Mīmāṃsaka theory in question) without taking another body, liberation would be impossible. Moreover, one can never avoid accumulating merit and demerit in one's present body without the eradication of their causes, which are attachment, aversion and infatuation, and the latter can themselves never be eradicated except through knowledge of the Self. They cannot be eradicated by the obligatory ritual, as (despite the artificial theory of the Mīmāṃsakas saying that the obligatory ritual leads to no results) the Veda says that it leads to auspicious worlds. And there is the Smṛti text, "The members of the castes and stages of life engaged in their various duties (experience the fruits of their deeds after death." (128)

We mentioned the view that the obligatory rituals, being troublesome, are the result of past sinful deeds and carry no new results of their own, as the Veda does not mention any, and that they are enjoined merely as an everyday duty. But this view is wrong.(They cannot be the result of all past sinful deeds in all past lives.) For no merit or demerit that was not involved either in the initiation or conduct of the present birth can yield experiences in this birth, so that one cannot say that it gives rise to any particular form of suffering (such as that incurred in the troubles of performing the daily obligatory ritual).

The statement that the total demerit of the sinful actions of all one's past lives was experienced in the trouble arising from the performance of the obligatory ritual was also wrong. For it cannot be right to say that the results of actions which did not begin to initiate new experiences at the time of death could be experienced in a new birth that had been generated by other actions. For if you admit this, you admit the (absurd) possibility that one could experience hell as a result of one's past sinful acts in a birth resulting from one's meritorious acts, such as the performance of the Agnihotra, which ought to have led to heaven. (129)

Nor can the trouble of performing the obligatory ritual correspond to the wide variety of painful demerit amassed in one's previous births. For the number of one's sins could be legion, and of a quality to lead to quite different kinds of pain. If the pain that arose from these could be reduced to the mere trouble arising from the performance of the obligatory ritual, then the (more acute) sufferings (that face everybody) arising from the extremes of pairs of opposites (heat and cold, etc.), and from disease and the like, would have no (karmic) cause at all. In fact it is quite impossible to suppose that the trouble arising from the performance of the obligatory ritual is the only bitter fruit of our past sins, while such miserable circumstances as having to carry heavy stones on the head do not arise from them (since they do not happen to form part of the obligatory ritual).

Furthermore, the assertion that the trouble arising from the performance of the obligatory ritual arises from the demerit of past sins contradicts what is being said in the present context. The subject-matter of the present passage is the demonstration that the portion of the demerit of the sins of past lives that has not initiated the present life cannot be exhausted in this life. And now you come forward and say that the trouble of performing the obligatory ritual constitutes pain arising from demerit that *has* begun to fructify in the present life and not from the demerit from past lives that has not begun to fructify. Or, if you say that all sins of past lives fructify in the present life, then it is wrong to restrict their fruit to the trouble of performing the obligatory ritual. Further, it would render the Vedic injunctions to perform the obligatory ritual unnecessary, (130) as all past sins would produce their bitter fruit inevitably, which would necessarily be exhausted by being experienced. In truth, if the pain incurred by the labour of performing the daily obligatory ritual arises from action – well, the action causing it is the performance of the obligatory action itself, just as the pain arising from any action implying intense physical exertion arises from that action itself, and not from anything else. So it is wrong to assume any external factor.

Nor can the obligatory rituals be the results of previously committed sins any more than expiatory rites can, for the obligatory rituals also are enjoined to be performed on a particular occasion, in their case (morning and evening) for life, with further conditions (such as being a married householder of an upper caste etc.). The expiatory rite that is enjoined to be performed on the occasion of a particular sinful act is not itself the (automatic) result of that act. Or, if the pain of the expiatory act were considered the result of the sin which was its occasion, then the trouble of performing the obligatory ritual would be the result of the occasion of coming alive and fulfilling the conditions of caste and marriage etc. (and not of sins committed in previous lives). For obligatory ritual and expiatory rites are both equally ordained for particular occasions.

Again, both the optional ritual and the obligatory ritual, like the Agnihotra, involve trouble to an approximately equal degree. There is no distinction between the two that would justify the view that the trouble of performing the obligatory ritual arose from the sins of previous lives, whereas the trouble of performing the optional ritual did not. From this it would follow that the trouble in performing the *optional* ritual would be the result of past sins. And this would refute the supposition (of the Mīmāṃsakas) that because no rewards are mentioned in the Veda as resulting from the *obligatory* ritual, the pain involved in its performance can only be the result of past sins. On the contrary, the only way now of explaining the presence of an injunction to perform obligatory ritual would be to assume that this ritual produces *other* results besides the mere trouble of its performance (or otherwise its presence in the Veda would be inexplicable).

The Mīmāṃsaka's doctrine is also self-contradictory. For he says that when one performs the obligatory ritual one does so as the result of other (previous) deeds. But (since the results of previous deeds are limited to the actual performance of the obligatory ritual) the trouble arising from that performance is itself inevitably the result of that performance. So when he says that no results flow from the performance of the obligatory ritual, he contradicts himself.

And there is another point. When the Agnihotra and other such rituals are performed on an optional basis, they are nevertheless performed, and by that token can be said to have been performed on an obligatory basis as well. (131) If the Mīmāṃsaka were right, however, even the results of the Agnihotra when performed on an optional basis for a specific end would not go beyond the trouble of performing it, as the Agnihotra performed for an end is (considered as a mere physical act) nothing different from the obligatory Agnihotra. If you say that the Agnihotra performed for an end has a different result from that of the obligatory Agnihotra, say the attainment of heaven, then it will have to be assumed (on this theory) that the trouble of performing it as an optional ritual must be different from the trouble of performing it as a daily duty. (132) But this is evidently not the case. For the trouble of performing the Agnihotra as a daily obligatory ritual is identical with the trouble of performing it as an optional ritual.

Further, all actions that are neither enjoined nor prohibited in the Veda bring their rewards immediately, whereas actions that are either enjoined or prohibited in the Veda do not. If the performance of the obligatory ritual could have an immediate result (such as spiritual enlightenment), no one would engage in it to obtain remote goals such as heaven, nor would the Veda trouble to mention them. Now, considered as a piece of physical activity, there is no difference between the Agnihotra performed as obligatory duty and the Agnihotra performed for the sake of an end. The parts and details are all the same. It is inconceivable that in the one case the result should be confined to the mere trouble of the performance, whereas in the other they include such great results as a sojourn in heaven, merely on account of the additional presence of the desire for a reward. Hence we must conclude that the daily obligatory rituals invariably bring unseen future rewards.

And from this it follows that (the Mīmāṃsakas' theory of liberation through action alone is discredited and) it is knowledge alone, and not application to the daily obligatory ritual, that brings action, and also merit and demerit, to a complete end, products of nescience as they are. For all action proceeds from nescience and desire, as has been shown. And this further substantiates our view that action is the province of the ignorant man, while devotion to knowledge, associated with the total renunciation of action, is the province of the enlightened man (vidvān). (133)

* * * * *

11. Some argue feebly as follows. The obligatory daily and occasional rituals, they say, are performed that no sin may arise from their omission. Optional ritual is dropped and forbidden acts are renounced in order to avoid heaven and hell respectively. The residue of former deeds that has to be experienced in the present body is elimiminated through its being experienced. In this way one becomes established in one's own true nature (as the individual soul untrammelled by the body and its suffering) on the fall of the present body. There is then no cause that could bring on a further body, although there is no question of liberation (kaivalya) in the form of identity with the Absolute. (134)

This doctrine is wrong, as there is no evidence to support it. For no Vedic text can be found declaring that he who desires liberation should act thus. The whole idea is an invention of their own, based on the notion that because transmigratory life continues on account of deeds committed in previous lives, it will not continue when this cause is removed. But this is a point which can never be established by logical reasoning, for the absence of a cause is difficult to establish in this context. Every living being can have an immense amount of merit and demerit piled up from different births and demanding to be experienced. Not all these mutually contradictory deserts can be experienced at once, so it is only a small number that get their opportunity and bring about this present birth. Others lie waiting for the appropriate place, time and occasion. Since these latter cannot be eradicated by the experiences of the present body, one cannot claim that no causes of future birth remain after death for any one, not even for the one who has acted in the way mentioned above. Texts from the Veda and the

Smṛti also witness to the existence of a residue of merit and demerit after death, as for instance the text, "Those whose conduct here has been good (will quickly obtain a good birth)" and "then through a residue." (135)

You cannot say that this merit can be eliminated by the performance of the obligatory and occasional rituals. For there is no contradiction between merit and demerit on the one hand and the performance of the obligatory rituals on the other. Elimination can only occur when one thing contradicts (and therefore excludes) another. And there is no contradiction between the merits piled up from the good deeds of previous births and the obligatory rituals, both being of the nature of purification. The case with the evil deeds is different. They are contradictory to the obligatory rituals, and we can admit that they might be eliminated by the latter. But this in itself is not enough to prove the absence of any cause for another birth, for the good deeds can still bring their merit, and one could never be sure that *all* the (demerit of the) evil deeds had been eliminated.

Nor is there any evidence that the performance of the obligatory ritual merely eliminates demerit without giving rise to any positive future experience on its own account, as it could (quite logically) do. For the Āpastamba Dharma Sūtra says, "Material benefits arise unsolicited from action performed for duty's sake, just as shade and scent come as by-products from a mango tree planted for the sake of its fruit." (136) Nor can anyone who has not attained right knowledge of the Self guarantee to be able to abstain from optional rituals and forbidden acts for the whole of his life, for even the cleverest persons make a slip here and there. Even if the issue be regarded as doubtful, it is at any rate impossible to be sure that there will be no cause for rebirth. Nor will any one who does not admit that man's true Self is the Absolute, and that this claim is subject to ratification in spiritual experience, desire liberation from the self familiar as empirical agent and experiencer, for the latter cannot abjure its own nature any more than fire can abjure heat.

Very well, you will say, but it is the actuality, not the potentiality, of agency and experiencerhood that is harmful. Liberation is possible even when agency and experiencerhood are potentially present but actually annulled. But this objection is also wrong, for, if a potentiality is present, its ultimate actualization is inevitable. Nor can you aver that a potentiality cannot produce its effect unless stimulated by efficient causes, so that the presence of the mere potentiality (of agency and experiencerhood) alone is harmless. For the constant presence of efficient causes is included in the very notion of a potentiality. (137) Hence there is no hope of liberation as long as agency and experiencerhood continue to appear as the nature of the Self, and identification with the Absolute through spiritual knowledge does not supervene.

The Veda, too, denies the existence of any other path to liberation except knowledge, in the text, "No other path for crossing over (except knowledge) exists." (138) Nor can you object (against our doctrine) that if the individual soul were perfectly identical with the Absolute in its supreme form there could be no empirical experience, inasmuch as perception and the other empirical means of knowledge could not function. For there can very well be empirical experience (before enlightenment), just as there is dream-experience before awakening. (139) And Vedic revelation, too, having first declared that empirical experience in the form of perception and the other means of knowledge obtains in the realm of unenlightenment, in the words beginning, "For where there seems to be a second, there a person who is one sees an object which is another," goes on afterwards to show that such experience does not obtain in the realm of enlightenment, in the words beginning, "But when all has become his Self, what could he see with what?" (140) Hence the one who knows the Absolute in its supreme form cannot have cognisance of any "path to be followed" or the like. Hence it is impossible to justify the notion of "going to" the Absolute in any way whatever (and it is therefore "attained" through knowledge alone and not through action in any form). (141)

* * * * *

12. And there is another point. Suppose that we do have to assume some form of fruit for the obligatory daily rituals laid down in the Veda. Should we assume a fruit (such as liberation) which stands in contradiction with action, which is not a possible effect of either a substance, a quality or a property, and which lies altogether beyond action's range? Or should we not rather assume some fruit which is observed to lie within the range of action and which is not in contradiction with it? You may say that *some* fruit must be assumed to explain how it is that people do in fact observe these rituals. But because presumption in such a case must remain within the confines of what is not in contradiction with action, one cannot here assume that either liberation or the removal of the ignorance blocking one's natural knowledge that one is already liberated could be the fruit. For the fruit cannot be anything (like liberation) contradictory in nature to action, and must be (unlike removal of nescience) something which action has been actually observed to have the power to effect.

Perhaps you will rejoin that the real argument for assuming that liberation is the fruit of the obligatory ritual is the lack of any other alternative. Consider (you may say) all the optional rituals. The fruits mentioned for them comprise all the ritualistic fruits mentioned in the Veda. There is therefore no fruit left over which is not already laid down for some other ritual, and consequently no further fruit free to be assumed to be the fruit of the daily obligatory rituals. The only alternative is to assume that the fruit is liberation, which is a fruit recognized by authorities on Vedic lore. Hence liberation is what we must assume that fruit to be.

But all this argumentation is wrong. For there may be an infinite number of particular results arising from action, so that the rule of "lack of any other alternative" cannot in this case be applied. No one of finite intellect can determine the number of goals envisaged by human desires themselves. The latter being endless in number, their full range cannot be known to man. And if the full range of human means and ends cannot be known in principle, how can one show that liberation must be the fruit of the obligatory daily ritual "for lack of any other alternative"?

Perhaps we shall now hear another argument as follows. Liberation, we shall be told, is that which remains over as the only alternative "result" of the obligatory daily rituals, when all the fruits of action as such have been denied of them. Ends and means may be endless in number, but they must all fall within the class of "fruits of action." But liberation, not being a fruit of action, is left over as "the only alternative." Hence it is right to assume that liberation must be the "result" of the obligatory daily rituals "for lack of any other alternative."

But this argumentation is wrong. For the fact that you admit liberation as a possible alternative "result" of the obligatory rituals shows that, for you, it lies within the class of "fruits of action", and hence cannot be the alternative remaining over when they have been excluded. One should conclude, therefore, that there is no case for applying the criterion of presumption (arthāpatti – the "only-remaining-alternative" form of argument) in the case of the fruit of the obligatory daily rituals. For the fruit can quite well be explained as falling within the usual alternatives for the results of action, namely, production, acquisition, purification and transformation. (142)

You cannot claim that liberation belongs to any of these four kinds of effects of action. It is not subject to production, for it is an eternal state (which can only be recognized, not produced). And it is not subject to transformation, for the same reason. Nor can it be purified (i.e. ritually consecrated), both for the above reason and also because it is not a substance used in a ritual. (143) It is not, for instance, like a sacrificial utensil or the sacrificial butter, which are subject to ritualistic cleansing through the sprinkling of water. Nor is it subject to purification (in the sense of polishing) (144) nor to being brought into existence through carpentry, (145) like the sacrificial post. Is it, then, subject to acquisition, the only alternative (mode of action) remaining? No, for it is of the very nature of the Self and one (without a second).

Perhaps you will contend that, because the obligatory daily rituals are different in kind from all other rituals, their fruit must be different in kind too. But this is wrong, as their fruit will be of the same kind as that of the other rituals, since all rituals belong to the same genus, namely action. Nor can you say that the fruit of the obligatory rituals must be liberation because it is rendered different in kind from the fruit of all other rituals owing to special circumstances. For the presence of special circumstances is not enough to indicate that the fruit must be liberation, as the case of the Kṣāmavatī rite shows. The Kṣāmavatī rite is ordained in the special circumstance of having had one's house burnt down by the sacrificial fire. There are also special oblations enjoined for when a sacrificial utensil is broken or when its contents are spilled. But although these ritualistic acts are performed in special circumstances (and no fruit is mentioned for them), one does not conclude that their fruit must be liberation! And from this it follows that the fruit of the daily obligatory rituals cannot be liberation, because texts such as those proclaiming that they should be done "every day for life" show that they, too, are rituals enjoined in special circumstances, and will not form an exception to this class (as they would do if they had liberation for fruit). (146)

2. REFUTATION OF LIBERATION THROUGH ACTION AND KNOWLEDGE CONJOINED

Of the Extracts dealing with this topic, the first two reject the view that liberation can be attained through ritualistic action supplemented by prescribed meditations on symbolic themes. From Number 3 onwards, the remaining Extracts defend the Advaita doctrine against the counter-claims of those who hold that the mere hearing of the texts cannot yield liberation without being supplemented by ritualistic action and meditation.

Those who taught a combination of ritual with knowledge as the means to liberation naturally did not understand "knowledge" (vidyā) in the sense of the highest knowledge which cancels nescience, as knowledge in this form would have cancelled all plurality and all possibility of action. They conceived knowledge, rather, in the manner mentioned at Īśa Upanishad 9, as meditation practised with a view to attain the world of some deity, and they extended the idea to attainment of immortality and liberation from transmigratory existence.

For Śaṃkara, immediate intuition of the Absolute results from the mere hearing of the supreme texts from the Teacher by the duly schooled and purified pupil. When viewed from the standpoint of the pursuit of liberation, the texts prescribing rituals or symbolic meditations have no other purpose but purification of the mind. When the supreme intuition arises, it dissolves all idea of connection with the instruments of action and all possibility of further action. The texts conveying knowledge of the Absolute (jñāna-kāṇḍa), few in number but all-important in content, are different in kind from those prescribing ritual or symbolic meditations, and supersede them. Even texts like "The Self must be heard about" belong to the Jñāna-Kāṇḍa and are given an injunctive mould only to conform to the ignorant standpoint of the student before he attains knowledge of the Self. When the Self is realized, it is known that it has no connection with action of any kind and never had.

Śaṃkara returns frequently throughout his commentaries to the theme of the incompatibility of liberation with any form of action, and it clearly seemed to him a matter of great practical importance to bring it home to the students of his day. When all the passages are extracted from their setting in his commentaries and juxtaposed, however, they make a rather repetitive and tedious impression, and for this reason a number have here been omitted and others severely curtailed. The same theme will also be found to crop up in other contexts, to be dealt with in later parts of the present work. It pertains, for example, to the two following sections of the present chapter, also to the section on "Injunction" in Volume V Chapter XII and to the whole of the chapter on the enlightened man, Volume VI Chapter XVI. Particular attention should be drawn to the last Extract in section 2, Chapter XIII, Volume V, the section on "The Veda, Smṛti and Reason." Here we find a statement and refutation of Prasaṃkhyāna Vāda, the doctrine that liberation was something that had to be attained *and preserved* through meditation on, and reasoning over, the holy texts, as otherwise knowledge of the Self was always liable to be overpowered by the impressions derived from the previous life of ignorance. As the important text, Brahma Sūtra Commentary

IV.i. 1-2, to be given at Volume VI Chapter XV Section 3 will show, Śaṃkara admitted the need for repeated hearing, cogitation and meditation if the text "That thou art" was to be understood. What he objected to was the idea than an enquirer should go on with this repetition indefinitely, thinking, "I am an agent with a right and duty to perform this act." For this would be to perpetuate a conviction that would prevent him from understanding the true meaning of the text. That is also the underlying theme of the Extracts of the present section.

TEXTS ON REFUTATION OF LIBERATION THROUGH ACTION AND KNOWLEDGE CONJOINED

1. *Objection:* Thus, since liberation cannot arise from action alone, let us say that it arises from ritualistic deeds associated with knowledge (vidyā). For these two operating together can produce a different effect from the effects they produce separately. Compare what happens with poison and curds. Taken alone, their effect on the body is to produce death and a fever respectively. But their effect is quite different if the poison is taken to the accompaniment of a mantram or if the curds are taken with sugar. In the same way, actions can lead to liberation if they are associated with knowledge.

Answer: But this does not escape the criticism already made that whatever is produced is impermanent. And you cannot say that liberation can become permanent, even though it is produced through a revealed text which promises it. For the function of a word is only to convey information. (147) It gives information about the true state of affairs, it does not of its own accord bring into existence what does not already exist. The eternal could not be produced, nor could the produced be rendered indestructible, even by a hundred texts.

Well, let us agree that this is enough to show that knowledge and action together cannot produce liberation. But could it not be that they remove obstructions to (the manifestation of) liberation (while liberation itself is eternal)? Not so, for action is seen to be incompatible with liberation in its results. It results in production, purification, transformation and acquisition. (148) And liberation is contradictory to all this.

You might suggest against this that there were texts showing that liberation could be acquired (through being reached), such as "through the door of the sun" and "going upwards through that" (149) and others. But the truth is that these texts do not imply physical movement. For the state of liberation implies omnipresence and would be non-different (and so not separated) from those supposed to be "going" to it. The Absolute must be omnipresent, as the ether and other great principles arise from it, and conscious souls are all non-different from the Absolute. So liberation is not anything to which one can "go". The place to which any being goes must be something different from the being who is going to it and must occupy a different position in space. Nothing can "go" to that from which it is already non-different. And there are hundreds of texts in the Veda and Smṛti which show that the soul is already in its true nature non-different from the Absolute....

But is there no contradiction here with texts which speak of "going" in connection with liberation or with "attaining" Lordship (aiśvarya)? Arguing thus, one might conclude that to say that liberation was not anything that could be "attained" was to contradict such Vedic texts as, "He, *being* one, (*becomes* threefold...)" and "If he desires the world of the ancestors (the ancestors arise at his mere wish)" and "With women or chariots (such an one moves about... not remembering the appendage of this body)." (150) But this is wrong. For these texts are still concerned (not with liberation but) with the Absolute in its manifest form as the world of effects. Women and the other features (of the experience of the yogī of exalted consciousness referred to by the texts in question) appear in the Absolute in its form as the world of effects, not in its (pure) "causal" form, as should be clear from such texts (describing the latter) as "One only, without a second," "Where one sees nothing else" and "There what should he see with what?" (151)

And another reason why action and spiritual knowledge cannot be combined is that they are mutually contradictory in nature. For spiritual knowledge bears on ultimate reality, in which all distinctions, including those into agent, instrument and the other factors of action, are dissolved; and thus it stands in contradiction to action, which depends on these very factors for its existence. One and the same entity cannot, in the true sense, both have and not have the factors of action (at the same time); one of the two alternatives must be a false appearance. And if one of them is a false appearance, then it must be duality, which belongs to the sphere of natural ignorance....And action is inconceivable without the factors of action such as the recipient (152) and so on. And thousands of Vedic texts show that in liberation perception of difference falls away. Thus knowledge and action are contradictory, and from this it follows that they cannot be combined. So the view voiced above that liberation arose from knowledge and action combined was wrong.

Nor can it be argued that our contention contradicts the Veda on the ground that actions are enjoined in the latter. An objector, for instance, might say that we (Advaitins) have taken the line that knowledge of the unity and sole reality of the Self was enjoined, and that this led to the annihilation of all the distinctions pertaining to the factors of action, such as the agent and the rest, in the manner of the knowledge of the rope leading to the annihilation of the erroneous notion of the snake. And this would be wrong, because it would result in a contradiction with the Veda, through leaving the texts enjoining actions null and void. (153) For the Veda *does* enjoin actions, so that (a view which involves) this contradiction is not right.

But the opponent's whole argument would be wrong, because what the Vedic texts do is to teach (the means to) man's welfare. That part of the Veda which is concerned with teaching knowledge (jñāna-kāṇḍa) is based upon the standpoint that man should be liberated from transmigratory experience, and that, to this end, the cause of tranmigratory experience, namely metaphysical ignorance, should be brought to an end through metaphysical knowledge. It proceeds, accordingly, to affirm the ultimate metaphysical truth. There is no question of contradiction here. (154)

You cannot now argue that this implies a contradiction with the part of the Veda that represents the agent and other factors of action as real. For this part begins by accepting the existence of the factors of action simply as a fact presented to view. On this basis, it enjoins ritualistic actions, to consume the effect of past sins in the case of those desirous of liberation, and as a means to the attainment of specific desirable ends in the case of those who want these. But it makes no claim to establish the existence of the factors of action as an ultimate truth. One who is held back by the obstacle of accumulated sins is not fit for acquisition of spiritual knowledge. But when the sins have been consumed, this knowledge may very well arise, and from this will result the eradication of nescience, and from this, total cessation of transmigratory experience.

And there is another point. Desire has the not-self for its object and can only occur to one who perceives the not-self as real; and only one under the influence of desire engages in ritualistic activity. From ritualistic activity based on desire there results acquisition of a new body and other instruments of experience in order to enjoy the fruits of that ritual – in other words, further transmigration. On the other hand, desire cannot afflict the one who is aware of the unity and sole reality of the Self, as for him no objects exist. And he is in fact liberated, because, since he is aware of his non-difference from the Self, desire is for him impossible, and he just rests in the Self. There is thus a contradiction between action and knowledge. And precisely because of this contradiction, knowledge cannot depend on action for effecting release. (155)

* * * * *

2. There is a view held by some that ritualistic action performed in a disinterested way and associated with "knowledge" (in the form of the merit arising from meditation on the symbolic significance of certain factors in the ritual) can produce an effect (such as liberation) beyond the normal range of action, much as poison, when associated with certain spells, is harmless to the body, or as curds, when taken with sugar, produce (not fever as they are held to do when taken without sugar but) health. But this view is wrong, because liberation is not subject to production. It consists merely in the destruction of bondage, and is not a positive effect. Bondage, as we have already explained, is nescience. And nescience cannot be destroyed by action, since action produces its results only in the field of perceptible objects. Its functions are to produce, acquire, purify and transform, and beyond these it cannot go, as no examples of it doing so are met with. Liberation, however, does not come within

the range of action under any of these headings. For, as we have already explained, it is (not subject to action, but simply) hidden by nescience.

Very well, you will say, we admit that this may be so in the case of action alone. But the case is otherwise when ritual is performed as a duty, and without desire for personal advantages, and in association with the performance of prescribed meditations on its symbolic significance. For it is seen that poison has a different effect from usual when associated with certain spells, and that curds have a different effect when combined with sugar. And in just the same way, ritualistic action has a different effect when combined with meditation on the symbolic significance of certain elements of the ritual.

But this we cannot accept, as it cannot be supported by proof derived from any of the recognized means of knowledge. Neither perception, nor inference nor comparison nor presumption nor revelation (156) will show that action can go beyond the four functions already mentioned (and bear on liberation).

Perhaps you will try to argue that (presumption supplies the proof in that) the presence of injunctions to perform the obligatory rituals is inexplicable on any other basis (except that of their leading to liberation), since no other fruit is mentioned for them. (157) One cannot, in the case of obligatory rituals, apply the rule of the Viśvajit sacrifice, (158) and yet no fruit is mentioned in regard to them by the Veda, although they are prescribed as actions to be done. Hence we have to presume that liberation must be their fruit, there being no other alternative. If there were no fruit at all, people would never perform them.

But this reasoning is baseless. Because you simply *assume* that liberation is the fruit, you are yourself guilty of applying the Viśvajit rule. Your argument, properly analysed, runs as follows: "Men would not act (in the case of a ritual for which no fruit was mentioned) unless some fruit, be it liberation or anything else, be assumed. Hence (i.e. because people do in fact perform the obligatory daily rituals) we must presume (arthāpatti) that the meaning of the texts is that liberation is the fruit, the application of presumption in such a matter being attested in the case of the Viśvajit sacrifice." And, this being so, how can you say in the same breath, "One cannot apply the rule of the Viśvajit sacrifice"? To say "We must assume a fruit" and "The rule of the Viśvajit sacrifice does not apply" is to contradict oneself.

No escape is possible here through the expedient of distinguishing between the mere *words* "result" (kārya) and "fruit" (phala). And to say "Liberation is not a fruit at all" at the same time as saying that it is brought about by the performance of the obligatory daily rituals – and, further, contending that the "result" of the latter is different from their "fruit" – is as contradictory as to assert that fire is cold.....

Can we not, then, assume that there is some occult power in ritualistic actions which can lead to the destruction of ignorance? No. For when destruction of ignorance is attainable through knowledge, it is wrong to assume any occult power. When the husks can be removed from the grains of the rice by threshing, we cannot assume that they are really removed by some occult power latent in the obligatory daily rituals such as the Agnihotra. And the same holds true in the case of that removal of ignorance which results in liberation. We cannot just blandly assume that it is removed by some occult power latent in the obligatory rituals.

As for the view that action associated with "knowledge" (i.e. with the merit deriving from meditation on the symbolic significance of the ritual) can lead to liberation, we have already many times observed that knowledge (in the form that leads to liberation) and action are contradictory. In regard to the form of "knowledge" that is compatible with action (i.e. the prescribed symbolic meditations on elements of the ritual, such as that on the sacrificial horse as Prajāpati at the beginning of the Bṛhadāraṇyaka Upanishad), we have already explained that its function is (not liberation but) attainment of the worlds of the gods, (159) as is stated in the text, "The world of the gods is attained through knowledge." (160)

* * * * *

3. The Self is free from hunger and other infirmities. It is self-existent and self-evident. It is liberation. Verily, thou art He. When the Veda teaches this, how can it at the same time teach the contradictory doctrine, "You should perform hearing, cogitation, and sustained meditation (as an enjoined duty)." (161) Had the texts said, "You *will* achieve (realization of the Absolute)," then hearing, cogitation and sustained meditation would have been enjoined actions. In that case, however, liberation would have been impermanent. And since that would have implied a contradiction, the text should not be twisted to suggest the achievement of a change of state.

Or again, hearing might be conceived as an enjoined action if the hearer were different from what he was to hear about. (162) But that would undermine the doctrine of their identity, which the opponent himself wishes to preserve. On his principles, the text is unintelligible on any assumption whatever. If such a person once knows the Self in the form "I am the self-evident one, liberation itself," then if he ever wishes thereafter to perform action he is deluded and is contravening the authority of the Veda. For that which is self-existent and self-evident has nothing to do. And whoever has something to do is not the self-existent and self-evident one. If one tries to unite both ideas at the same time, one deceives oneself (because they are contradictory).

You might object that the words, "You are the self-existent and self-evident one" merely relate a matter of fact, and that we require to know what it is that prompts the hearer to make efforts to understand them. We reply that empirical experience yields the feeling, "I am an agent and also a sufferer." Later, arise efforts to remove this feeling, based on the idea, "May I rise above agency and the state of suffering." The Veda, it is true, declares that reasoning and other activities have to be performed in order to know the Absolute. (163) But this declaration is made in deliberate conformity with the sense of agency in the ignorant hearer. Its only purpose is to enable him to realize himself to be the ever-existent and self-evident one. But after a person has once come to feel, "I am the non-suffering, actionless, desireless, ever self-existent one, liberation itself," how can he thenceforward accept any idea contrary to that? (164)

* * * * *

4. The eternal reality, it is clear, cannot be produced either by action or by knowledge. But it does not follow from this that bare knowledge is useless. For we find that when the darkness of nescience has been brought to an end through knowledge, attainment of transcendence results, and is the culminating experience of all, as a lamp finally illumines a rope after first removing the obscuring influence of the image of a snake. The result of such an illumination is the manifestation of the bare (real) rope, when the various alternative notions such as "snake" have been made to subside. Such also is the force of knowledge of the Self.

In the case of objects of the empirical world, when, say, cutting fuel (for the ritual fire) or rubbing fire-sticks is in progress, the same agent cannot engage with his organs and instruments in any other act or work for any other goal apart from cutting fuel or producing fire. Similarly, when the actionless "activity" of devotion to knowledge is in progress, (165) the "agent" cannot engage with his organs and instruments in any other activity, which would necessarily have some goal other than that of realization of the Self as transcendent. Hence devotion tc knowledge cannot be combined with action.

Perhaps you will argue that knowledge and action can be combined in the sense that a life devoted to the daily performance of the Agnihotra can be combined with secular activities like eating. But this is not so. For when knowledge of the Self brings its result, namely realization of the transcendent reality, one can no longer feel desire for the results of action. It is as when water floods everywhere, and one feels no need for a well or a reservoir. One feels no desire for realizing any other goal and no desire for any action leading to such realization. One engaged on a course of action leading to the seizure of a whole kingdom does not pause to institute a separate action to secure a single field, nor could he feel the slightest desire for such a trifle. So action forms no part of the (direct) means to the highest beautitude (niḥśreyasa), and neither do action and knowledge combined. Nor does knowledge in any way stand in need of the support of action in order to yield the result of realization of the transcendent Reality, as the very notion of action is contradictory to knowledge's function of bringing nescience to an end. Darkness does not put an end to darkness. So it is knowledge alone that is the means to the highest beatitude. (166)

5. At this point some intervene and say: The state of transcendence (kaivalya) cannot in any way be attained by mere devotion to the path of knowledge, accompanied by the renunciation of all duty. It is (only) attained by knowledge associated with (the performance of) ritualistic duties, such as the daily Agnihotra offering, which are laid down in the Veda and Smṛti. This is the doctrine that emerges as the conclusive teaching of the Gītā as a whole. In support of this view they quote, "If you do not fight this righteous battle" and "Thy concern is with the deed alone" and "Therefore shouldst thou verily perform action" (167), as well as other texts of similar import.

It is quite wrong, these persons argue, to say that Vedic ritual makes for demerit because it involves cruelty. (168) But even the duty of a warrior, which is extremely cruel, because it may involve the slaughter of one's Teacher or brother or son, etc., does not make for demerit when it is pursued as a caste-duty, as is explained in the text, "Thus, if thou abandonest thine own caste-duty, and thy reputation, it will be a sin."(169) All the less, then, could it be a sin to perform rituals involving the slaughter of animals and the like, which one is enjoined to perform for the whole of one's life.

But all this argumentation, we Advaitins reply, is wrong. For the paths of knowledge and ritualistic duty are taught separately and from quite distinct points of view. In the passage beginning, "Thou hast felt pity where pity was not in place" and ending at "Even with regard to thine own caste-duty," (170) we find a description of the Self as the supreme metaphysical principle, which is the teaching called "Sāṃkhya". The standpoint that arises from an understanding of the doctrine taught in this passage, and which consists in thinking that the Self is not an agent because it is void of any of the six states of change beginning with birth,

(171) is called the Sāṃkhya standpoint. And those enlightened souls (jñānin) who are entitled to espouse it are called Sāṃkhyas.

Before the rise of this standpoint, what prevails is "Yoga", or active engagement in the means to liberation, associated with action, partly meritorious and partly base, and depending on the view that the Self is the agent and experiencer, (though recognized as) separate from the body. This attitude is called the "Yoga" standpoint. And those men of action (karmin) who are entitled to espouse it are called Yogins. In this way the Lord Himself has taught the existence of two distinct standpoints in the words, "This, so far, has been the view of the Sāṃkhya standpoint: listen now to the other view of the Yoga standpoint." (172)

And in regard to these two distinct standpoints, He will speak of the Sāṃkhya path separately, as based on the Sāṃkhya standpoint gained through the Yoga of Knowledge (jñāna-yoga), in the passage, "(A twofold path) was taught by Me formerly, when I assumed the form of the Veda." (173) And He will refer separately to the path based on the Yoga standpoint attained through the Yoga of Action (karma-yoga) in the words, "Through the Yoga of Action of the Yogins." (174) It was because the Lord saw the impossibility of one man practising both knowledge and action, based as they are, in the one case, on non-agency and unity and, in the other, on agency and plurality, that He referred to two separate standpoints, those of Sāṃkhya and Yoga, and spoke of separate paths pertaining to them. The Śatapatha Brāhmaṇa (i.e. the Bṛhadāraṇyaka Upanishad which forms part of it) follows the same distinction as is found in the present text when it says, "The Brahmins who renounce the world do so desiring this world (of the Self) alone," and caps that counsel to give up all duties by saying, "What should we do with progeny, we for whom *this* is the Self, *this* our world?" (175) ...

In the same work (176) it is also said that an ordinary person, before taking a wife and after concluding his period of study in which he commits the Veda to heart, desires a son as the means to attain the three worlds (the human world, that of the ancestors and that of the gods). He desires a son, also, as being the means to the twofold wealth, divine and human, where the human wealth is in the merit arising from the ritual leading to attainment of the world of the ancestors, while the divine wealth is knowledge (the merit earned from meditation on the symbolic significance of the ritual), which is the means of attaining to the world of the gods. From these texts it is clear that all the rituals and actions laid down in the Veda and Smṛti are only for him who is afflicted with nescience and desire. Whereas the text, "Giving up those rituals, they wander forth from home" (177) shows that the giving up of rituals is taught only for those who have no desires and who wish for the Self as their "world".

This distinction (between two different paths for two different kinds of people) found in the texts would be inexplicable if they had really meant to teach a path in which the Vedic ritual and knowledge were combined. Nor would Arjuna's question (178) "If You hold that knowledge is superior to action, (why do You direct me to this terrible action?)" have been appropriate (if the Lord had intended both paths to be simultaneously conjoined). If the Lord had not already previously declared that knowledge and action could not be followed by one and the same person (at the same time), then how could Arjuna have falsely imputed to the Lord, in the text just quoted, the teaching that knowledge was better than action (which implies that knowledge and action cannot be combined) when he had heard nothing of that kind?

And there is another point. If it had been taught that in every case knowledge must be combined with action, then this would have included Arjuna's case also. But if he had been taught to follow the path of knowledge and action combined, how could he have asked which of the two he was to follow, as he does when saying, "Tell me conclusively, which is the better of the two?" (179) For when a doctor has told someone to take something sweet and cool to calm down the bile, one does not ask which of the two it is that calms down the bile. And if you think that the reason was that Arjuna had failed to understand the Lord's meaning, then this also is wrong, as the Lord would in that case have given an answer relevant to that situation and would have said, "I said that knowledge and action had to be combined. Why have you made such a silly mistake?" And in that case the answer He actually did give, namely, "Two paths were taught by Me of old..." would not have been at all appropriate, as it would have been irrelevant to the question and not an answer to what had been asked.

Nor would it help to say that the Lord meant conjunction with such action as is prescribed in the Smṛti only, for the Lord's statement that there are two distinct paths contradicts this, to mention only one difficulty. Nor would Arjuna's complaint, "Why do You direct me to perform this terrible action?" have been in place on this view, as he would have known that fighting was his duty as a warrior, laid down in the Smṛti. So it follows that no one can show that even the slightest combination with knowledge of duties laid down in the Veda or Smṛti is taught as the path of liberation in the Gītā.

In this connection we must also consider the case of a man who had first been engaged in action on account of ignorance or of attachment and other such defects. Suppose such a person purified his mind through sacrifices, charity or ascetic practices and acquired knowledge of the highest principle, the One, in the form "All this is the Absolute, which is not an agent." In the case of such a person, action would cease, and so would all need for action. And yet he might engage in vigorous action for the welfare of the world. The action of a person working in this way is not action in the sense of action that could be "combined" with knowledge. (180) The Lord Vāsudeva's performance of the duties of the warrior did not constitute action that could be combined with knowledge for the sake of any human end. And, in the same way, the actions of the enlightened man are void of any purpose of his own, for he has no egoism and no desire for individual fruits. He does not think "I act" and he does not long for the reward of his action.

Or consider the case of one desiring heaven or some such goal, and who is engaged in the Agnihotra sacrifice and other such means to the realization of his desire, and has lit the holy sacrificial fires for this purpose. Suppose that his desire for the goal breaks off while he is in the middle of his sacrifice. In that case, even though he goes on to complete the course of the sacrifice, it does not count as a ritual performed for self-interest.

Hence the Lord says (of the enlightened man), "He is not tainted even though he acts" and (of the Self) "It does not act, it is not tainted," (181) and teaches the same doctrine at other places as well.

As for the texts like, "As the ancients performed action in olden times" and "Janaka and others sought perfection through action alone," ( ) they may be interpreted in either of two alternative ways. The alternatives are as follows. Suppose Janaka and others of old were knowers of truth and yet continued to act for the good of the world, but with the conviction "the constituents (guṇa) revolve among the constituents." (183) Then they would in fact be seeking perfection through knowledge alone (despite the literal meaning of the text "through action alone"). The text would then mean that they did not formally adopt the life of a renunciate even when it would have been appropriate for them to do so, so that they attained perfection even while "acting", that is to say, while abstaining from formal renunciation.

If, on the other hand, Janaka and the rest were not knowers of truth, then the text means that they sought "perfection" by means of action offered to the Lord, where "perfection" means "purification of the mind" or else " acquisition of knowledge (*through* purification of the mind)". The Lord will explain this point, saying, "Yogins perform action... for the purification of their minds." (184) And again at a later point the Lord will say, "By worshipping the Lord through the performance of his duties a man attains perfection (siddhi)," (185) and then says that one who has attained "perfection" (through active purification of the mind) still has to walk the path of knowledge, in the words, "(Hear from Me how) one who has attained perfection attains (*in the end*) to the Absolute." (186)

Hence the conclusive teaching of the Gītā is that liberation is achieved through knowledge alone and not through knowledge combined with action. (187)

Śaṃkara's basic point in the rather obscure Extract to follow is that the earlier Gītā Commentator was wrong in his original statement at the beginning of his Gītā Commentary, when he laid it down that everyone had to carry on with ritual when seeking final knowledge of the Self. The Commentator now (Gītā III.1) finds himself required to explain a question from Arjuna implying that some enquirers give up action altogether. So he now distinguishes between different "stages of life." He starts by saying that it is only householders who may not give up rituals to seek liberation, monks may. Śaṃkara reminds him that he had originally said that no one *could seek liberation without ritual, so that he is still contradicting himself. The Commentator replies that, if he said that the householder could not attain liberation without the ritual laid down in the Veda, it was of course still understood that* everyone, *including monks, had to do that minimum of action laid down in the Smṛti, so that his original point, made at the beginning of his Commentary, that everyone had to do* some *action, still held good. Śaṃkara's reply is that the ritual and other obligations laid down for monks and forest-dwellers in the Smṛti are physically taxing. The Commentator was therefore wrong to say they applied to everyone. For it would be physically impossible for the householder to do these as well as the Vedic ritual. Finally, it is not right to hold that only the householder can acquire liberation because only he can fulfil the full complement of ritual. For there are many texts in the Veda and Smṛti alike which prescribe renunciation of hearth and home for those who desire liberation, and indeed renunciation of action generally. So the Commentator's original claim in his introduction that everyone had to carry on with ritual when seeking final knowledge of the Self was wrong, as he fails to square it with Arjuna's question at Gīta III.1, which implies that some enquirers give up action altogether.*

6. There is a certain person (a previous Commentator on the Gītā) who says in his introduction that the general trend of the Gītā is to teach a combination of knowledge and action for members of *all* the various stages of life (āśrama). He states specifically and categorically (ekāntena) that the the Gītā denies the possibility of attaining liberation by mere knowledge alone, to the abandonment of those ritualistic acts which have been prescribed as life-long duties. When he comes to the present passage (i.e. Gītā III.1), however,

he accepts the distinction between different stages of life (āśrama), and speaks of the abandonment (in some cases) of the rituals specifically prescribed by the Veda as having to be performed for the whole of one's life. But how could the Lord contradict Himself like that in speaking to Arjuna? And how could His hearer accept such a contradiction?

Perhaps it will be replied that (the Gītā's teaching about) the impossibility of attaining liberation through the abandonment of the Vedic rituals conjoined with bare knowledge applies only to householders and not to members of other stages of life. But even this defence would involve self-contradiction. First there would have been the statement that the Gītā taught that members of *all* the stages of life should practise a combination of rituals with knowledge: and now would come the claim that the Lord was saying that for members of some stages of life liberation arose from knowledge alone. And this is a self-contradiction.

Perhaps it will be contended that the statement "Householders cannot attain liberation through mere knowledge associated with Vedic ritual," was made strictly with Vedic ritual in mind. The opponent will maintain that when he said that, in the case of the householder, no liberation was possible through knowledge alone (he did not mean to imply that anyone could acquire liberation without any action at all). The actions laid down by the Smṛti, though accepted as binding on householders (as well as monks) were just not mentioned (being taken as read). But this view also involves self-contradiction. For how could any sensible person accept that it was only the householder who could not attain liberation through knowledge allied to the performance of the religious duties prescribed in the Smṛti, whereas members of other orders could? And if the houseless celibate can obtain release through knowledge allied to performance of the duties prescribed in the Smṛti, so could the householder, without resorting to Vedic ritual.

Perhaps it will be replied that the householder achieves liberation through a combination of knowledge with the performance of the duties laid down both by the Veda and the Smṛti, whereas the houseless celibate achieves it through a combination of knowledge with the performance of the duties laid down in the Smṛti only. On such a view, the earlier Commentator would not be contradicting himself: for members of all stages of life would have to combine knowledge with *some* prescribed activity, but houseless celibates would drop the *Vedic* ritual. This view is also wrong, as it would heap a disproportionate load of troublesome activity on the householder's head. (188)

Perhaps it will be replied that it is on account of this disproportionate load of trouble that the householder only is able to achieve liberation, while members of other orders are not, as they do not perform the obligatory daily ritual. But this view is also wrong. For all the Upanishads, the Epics, the Purāṇas and the technical treatises on Yoga agree that renunciation of all ritual is a pre-condition for spiritual knowledge. Further, the Veda and the Smṛti alike prescribe both a "combination" (of stages of life, in the sense of a progression from student-celibacy to householder, from householder to forest-dweller, from forest-dweller to total renunciation of hearth and home) and also an "option" (for certain spiritually gifted persons of leaping straight out of an *earlier* stage to that of total renunciation).

But will not this mean that a combination of knowledge and action is taught for those in all stages of life? (189) No, for renunciation of all ritualistic activity is prescribed for the one who desires liberation. For we have such texts as,

"When they have risen above desire, they resort to alms" and "Therefore they say emphatically that total renunciation of hearth and home is better than other ascetic enterprises" and "Renunciation, verily, exceeded (all the lesser asceticisms of Brahmā)" and "Just a few have attained immortality: but it has not been through ritual, through progeny or through wealth, but only through renunciation" and "He may wander forth as a houseless monk direct from the stage of celibate student." (190) Consider also (from the Smṛti), "Give up both merit and demerit, as well as truth and falsehood: give up that whereby you have given these two up!" (191) Then there is the teaching of Bṛhaspati to (his son) Kaca, namely, "Perceiving that there is no reality in this hollow worldly life, and wishing to know reality, they renounce the world without marrying (i.e. straight from the state of studenthood), possessed of supreme dispassion." (192) There is also the teaching (of Vyāsa) to Śuka: "All creatures incur bondage through action and acquire liberation through knowledge." (193) And there are texts to this effect in the Gītā itself, such as "Renouncing all actions mentally." (194) Moreover, since liberation is not an effect that can be produced, action on the part of one who desires liberation is superfluous.

Nor is it right to object that the daily obligatory rituals must always be fulfilled to avoid the sin of their omission. For the sin of the omission of the obligatory rituals occurs only in the case of one who is not a renunciate. A renunciate cannot incur sin for not tending the sacrificial fires, which is the duty of celibate students who are not renunciates (in the full sense) and have the duty of performing rituals. Nor can any positive result such as sin be supposed to arise from the mere *absence* of obligatory rituals, as we know from the Vedic text, "How could being arise from non-being?", (195) which denies that anything existent can arise from the non-existent. If the Veda were to declare that demerit followed the non-performance of some prescribed act, even though such a thing is plainly impossible, then people would say that the Veda was inauthoritative and a source of harm. For the performance and the non-performance of the obligatory rituals that it prescribed would then *both* bring nothing but pain. (196) And if a positive result such as demerit arose from the mere non-performance of ritual, this would imply the indefensible assumption that the Veda was itself an agent producing results, and not a mere source of information. (197)

* * * * *

7. "Those who worship Hiraṇyagarbha enter blind darkness." (198) This text, by denying that Hiraṇyagarbha is a proper object of worship, denies the reality of the whole world of effects. For if Hiraṇyagarbha really existed, objection would not have been raised against his worship.

Perhaps it will be contended that the objection against worship of Hiraṇyagarbha is only made in order to enjoin meditation on Hiraṇyagarbha in company with the performance of ritualistic action, as is suggested by the text, "They enter into blind darkness who worship nescience." (199)

It is true that the (exclusive) worship of Hiraṇyagarbha is decried in order to make way for a conjunction of meditation on Hiraṇyagarbha as a deity with ritualistic action, the latter being called (in the Īśa Upanishad) "destruction" (vināśa). The ultimate purpose of ritualistic action called "destruction," however, is to take the practitioner beyond the realm of death, understood as the natural urges to action prompted by nescience. And, in the same way, the conjunction of meditation on deities with ritualistic action is also designed to purify the heart of the meditator and to take him beyond the realm of death, understood as the urge towards action based on attachment to its results. This attachment consists in the longing to accomplish various ends and the consequent longing for the necessary means. (200) Indeed, a purified (saṃskrta) man is precisely one who is free from the impurity of death in the form of this twin longing. Hence that brand of nescience which consists in meditation on deities in conjunction with ritualistic action is for the sake of (purifying the mind and eventually) going beyond death in the sense just explained.

So we must conclude that the one who has gone beyond death, understood as nescience in the form of the twin desire for ends and means, and who is equipped with dispassion and who is intent on studying the Upanishadic teaching, is already on the brink of the achievement of knowledge of the sole reality of the supreme Self. In comparison with his earlier nescience, (201) his present knowledge of the Absolute (brahma-vidyā), which is the means to immortality, is "later". (202) And this knowledge is spoken of as being "conjoined" with nescience in the sense that both relate to one and the same man (though at different times). Worship of Hiraṇyagarbha, therefore, is (in one sense) certainly being decried, because it does not (if pursued for its own sake) lead to the same result as knowledge of the Absolute, which is the means of immortality. Though (if performed as a duty and without desire for personal reward) it is a cause of the removal of impurities, it does not directly lead to liberation in the full sense. (203)

3. REFUTATION OF BHEDĀBHEDA VĀDA

So far, in the present chapter, we have been considering Śaṃkara's refutation of what he considered to be faulty theology. In the first section, we saw how he exposed the errors of interpretation committed by the Pūrva Mīmāmsakas when they strayed beyond their proper confines of explaining the rules and rewards of ritualistic action and constructed an artificial theory of liberation based on selective performance of ritual. In the second section we saw him attack the theories of those who sought liberation in the right place, namely in the revealed teachings of the Upanishads, but who related the latter too closely to the performance of ritual and made them subordinate to injunctions to meditate interpreted in a ritualistic sense. The Extracts of the present section deal with a particular sub-school of those who were attacked in the second section. The doctrine of this school is today usually known under the title of Bhedābheda Vāda or the Doctrine of Difference in Identity. Their teachings call for special treatment because they buttressed their interpretation of the Upanishads with philosophical reasoning supported with examples from ordinary secular experience, which led Śaṃkara to treat their doctrine as, at least in part, a philosophical system, and so to refute it on logical grounds.

The chief name associated with this school in ancient times was that of Bhartṛprapañca, famous for his voluminous commentary on the Bṛhadāraṇyaka Upanishad, now lost, but it has been claimed that Śaṃkara's strictures, in this context, were also aimed at Brahmadatta and Bhartṛmitra as well. (204) Different varieties of the doctrine have been ascribed to the old Teachers Auḍulomi and Āśmarathya (205) (and by Nakamura even to Kāśakṛtsna, (206) supposed usually to have taught a doctrine closer to that of Śaṃkara himself), as well as to the author or final redactor of the Brahma Sūtras. About the ninth century it was revived in modified form by Bhāskara, and again at some time before the fourteenth century, by Nimbarka, who gave the doctrine a Vaiṣṇava theistic twist, but claimed descent from Auḍulomi. Of the two chief Śaiva mediaeval Commentators on the Brahma Sūtras, Śrīkaṇṭha was a Bhedābheda Vādin in practice, while Śrīpati espoused the doctrine openly and by name. (207)

(X.3) REFUTATION OF INADEQUATE BRAHMINICAL DOCTRINES

Bhartṛprapañca (208) distinguished between a supreme and a lower form of the Absolute, both real. They are both identical with and different from each other, which in practice means that they are neither completely different nor completely identical. This doctrine of difference in identity or Bhedābheda Vāda assumed many different forms in classical Indian philosophy, but the conception most typically associated with Bhartṛprapañca is that of a substance (the Absolute in its supreme form) assuming "states" (avasthā) or "modes"(vikāra) to form the "lower Absolute", the manifest universe and the beings enjoying experience in it, as the one ocean undergoes modification and changes of state in the form of waves and bubbles and foam.

From the first and faintest disturbance in the perfect calm of the Absolute in its supreme form arises the Inner Ruler (antaryāmin), from which all else will develop. A more pronounced disturbance results in the emergence of the mode called "Witness" (sākṣin), the conception of "witness" being quite different from what it is in the Advaita tradition. In Bhartṛprapañca, the notion is that of a conscious individual. There are many "witnesses" in the form of the various cosmic powers (deities) and individual souls, though there is some evidence that Bhartṛprapañca may have regarded them all as the various multiple expressions of one cosmic "soul" (jīva). The Inner Ruler, however, receives a grosser "adjunct", distinct from it and yet not absolutely different, called the "Unmanifest", which is the physical universe in "seed" or "causal" or "unmanifest" state. From the Unmanifest springs the "Thread" (sūtra), the special adjunct of Hiraṇyagarbha. From "Sūtra" or the "Thread" springs the gross manifest universe called Virāṭ. From Hiraṇyagarbha spring the "Deities" (devatā), which are the powers which Hiraṇyagarbha possesses on the cosmic plane, analogous to the powers of action and perception that man possesses on the individual plane. The gross manifest universe undergoes specification into "Jāti", meaning types, and "Piṇḍa", meaning individual bodies. Some of these technical terms are already familiar to us from Volume III, Chapter IX, Section 3 above. It will be recalled that the deity Vaiśvānara figured in that context, and we learn from Hiriyanna (209) that Bhartṛpañca was a devotee of Agni Vaiśvānara.

The contrast with Śaṃkara's teaching lies in the fact that for Bhartṛprapañca all the states (avasthā) assumed by the Absolute are modes into which it actually becomes transformed (pariṇāma), real and distinct from the Absolute, and yet at the same time somehow not separate. Their manifestation is not attributed to nescience. For Śaṃkara, as we have already seen, (210) it is "of the essence of being in the realm of nescience" to have a self-contradictory world-view of this kind.

According to another typical Bhedābheda classification, reality can be analyzed into three "categories" (rāśi), corresponding roughly to the traditional "God", "the World" and "the Soul" of Western philosophy. These three categories, too, are real, distinct and yet not separate, just as the different bubbles are distinguishable from each other and from the water of the sea, and yet at the same time not separate from the water of the sea. The soul is actuated by the traces (vāsanā) of its past deeds and experiences. Bhartṛpapañca follows the Sāṃkhya in teaching that these lie embedded in the mind (antaḥkaraṇa), which is a subtle modification of "the world" and hence distinct from the soul. But they are transmitted to the soul, as fragrance (vāsa) (211) is transmitted from flowers into oil when they are distilled into oil from scent. Nescience (avidyā) affects only parts of the Absolute, namely the individual souls, just as parts only of the earth's surface assume the form of a desert. The soul affected by nescience forgets its identity with the Absolute and supposes itself to be an isolated individual. The process whereby the soul emerges as an individual egoity is real enough, and can only be annulled by active steps taken to counteract it. The error promoted by nescience consists only in taking the individuality to be the whole truth of the matter and so neglecting to take the necessary steps to put an end to the painful experience of rebirth.

Perception and the other secular means of knowledge provide us with valid knowledge of a plurality of real objects surrounding us in space. The Veda confirms this by its repeated accounts of creation, while also drawing attention to "the unity underlying it which we commonly miss." (Hiriyanna)

Liberation, according to Bhartṛpapañca, had to be achieved in stages. A preliminary necessity was attainment of identity with Hiraṇyagarbha through the practice of prescribed Vedic meditations. This led to the "intermediate" state of "escape" (apavarga), where the soul is secured against the miseries of re-entry into transmigratory life, but has not yet eliminated nescience and so is unaware of its identity with the Absolute in its supreme form. At this point there has to be further meditation, apparently in order to become aware that both Hiraṇyagarbha and oneself are identical with the Absolute, though on this question Hiriyanna doubts whether we really have enough evidence today to enable us to form a true conception of the final stages of the spiritual discipline as envisaged by Bhartṛprapañca.

While the Extracts to follow are not intended to provide a complete account of everything Śaṃkara said about Bhartṛprapañca, they show him picking out a number of important points in the latter's doctrine and subjecting them to critical scrutiny. We have already encountered a short epitome and criticism of the doctrine at Volume II,

(X.3) REFUTATION OF INADEQUATE BRAHMINICAL DOCTRINES (TEXTS)

Chapter VII, Section 1, Extract 6. A fragment has been omitted from the opening Extract below, because that passage has also been encountered earlier in the present work (see Note 221).

TEXTS ON THE REFUTATION OF BHEDĀBHEDA VĀDA

1. Some (i.e. Bhartṛprapañca) explain this formula (212) as meaning that an infinite effect emanates from an infinite cause. Even during the time of emanation, the emanated effect is infinite and perfectly real and stands over against the cause as a second reality. Then, at the time of world-dissolution, the infinite draws back into itself the infinity of the effect and itself remains over in the form of the cause. In this way, the cause and effect are infinite in the three periods, those, namely, of production, maintenance and dissolution. And this one infinity is taught in the system as undergoing differentiation into cause and effect.

And in the same way, the one Absolute (brahman) is taught as both having and not having a second reality over against it. In this connection, they cite the example of the sea. The sea consists of water, waves, foam, bubbles and the like. And just as the water is real, so also are the waves, foam and bubbles and so on which proceed from it. The latter, it is true, come into manifestation and then pass out of it again, but their essential nature (ātman) is the sea. Similarly, all this world of duality is perfectly real, corresponding as it does to the water and waves, etc., in the illustration, while the Absolute corresponds to the sea.

Another great point in their theory is that, if duality is real, the texts of the ritualistic part of the Veda can stand as authoritative. And they try to maintain that if, on the contrary, the world of duality were only an appearance and false like a mirage, (213) and if only that which is without a second were real in the full sense, then the ritualistic section of the Veda could not be authoritative, for lack of any intelligible subject-matter. There would, moreover, be an inevitable contradiction. The Upanishads, which constitute only one *part* of the Veda, would be authoritative because they proclaim the supreme reality as one-only-without-a-second. The ritualistic portion of the Veda, however, would not be authoritative, as its subject-matter would belong to the domain of the unreal. And it is precisely to avoid this contradiction, they claim, that the Upanishadic formula now under comment occurs. In saying, "That is the infinite, etc.", (214) it affirms the reality both of the cause and the effect, which have to be taken on the analogy of the sea and its waves. And they argue on further in this strain.

All this, however, is wrong. For the argument depends on exceptions and alternatives applying to the Absolute, whereas these in fact apply only within the differentiated realm. The whole conception is untenable. Exceptions apply in the domain of ritualistic activity. When a general rule would have prescribed such and such an action, their force is to rescind part of the general rule. Take, for example, the formula "Not harming any creature except on the path to the altar." Here we have a general law prohibiting injury to any living creature, but with a restriction permitting it in the particular area of the path to the altar on the occasion of a large sacrifice. In the present context, however, no general proposition affirming the existence of the non-dual Absolute can be revoked in any particular area, because the Absolute, being non-dual, cannot have particular areas.

Alternatives, (215) too, are inapplicable in the case of the Absolute for the same reason. For example, the ritualistic section of the Vedas covers the two alternatives "He grasps the ṣoḍaśin cup in the course of the Atirātra Ceremony" and "He does not grasp the ṣoḍaśin cup in the course of the Atirātra Ceremony." It is a conceivable alternative, because grasping or not grasping are merely potential processes, dependent for their actualization on the will of man. But in the case of the affirmation of the existence of the Absolute, there cannot be any such alternative as "either dual or non-dual." For the Self is an existent reality and hence not dependent on the will of man: and it is moreover contradictory to say that one and the same thing can be both dual and non-dual. (216) So this whole theory is untenable.

It also conflicts with the Vedic teaching and with reason. There are Vedic texts of clearly established truth, beyond doubt or suspicion of error, which would all have to be jettisoned as useless on the present theory. We should lose, for example, those which speak of the Absolute as a single mass of Consciousness, homogeneous like a mass of salt, with no gaps or interstices, without any such distinctions as "in front" or "behind" or "outside and inside", also that which speaks of the Spirit (puruṣa) as "including both that which is within and that which is without, unborn," and those which say "Not thus, not thus" and such negative texts as that which speaks of the Absolute as "Not gross, not subtle, not long, not subject to decay, not subject to death, immortal." (217)

Similarly, there would also be contradiction with reason. For that which is many and has parts and activity cannot be eternal and constantly self-identical, whereas the fact of memory, etc., shows that the Self *is* eternal and consequently self-identical, (218) so that contradiction results from a theory that would imply that it was not such. Moreover, the opponent's theory fulfils no intelligible purpose. So far from safeguarding the ritualistic portion of the Veda, it would actually undermine its validity, for it would imply both experience of the fruits of deeds that one had not performed, as well as annihilation of the fruits of deeds one had performed. (219)

Perhaps the opponent will reply that there are perfectly good examples of things such as the sea, that are both dual and non-dual, and ask how, in the face of these, we can say that it is contradictory to claim that one thing can be both dual and non-dual. But this defence is of no avail, as the example they cite is not relevant to the case in hand. It was in regard to the eternal, partless, existent reality that we said that duality-cum-non-duality was contradictory. We do not maintain that it is contradictory in the realm of effects, where everything has parts. Hence this whole theory is to be rejected on the ground that it contradicts the Veda, the Smṛti and reason alike. To abandon the Upanishads altogether would be better than (accepting them with) a theory like this.

And there is another reason why it cannot be the doctrine intended by the Veda. It does not yield any conception of the Absolute that would be fit to meditate on. The Veda never presents either as an object of meditation or of knowledge an Absolute that is variegated in the manner of (such earthly objects as) the sea or a forest, and has hundreds and thousands of distinctions implying birth, death and evil. On the contrary, it expressly speaks of the Absolute as a homogenous mass of consciousness. (220)... It is agreed that one should not do what the Veda condemns, just as it is also agreed that the Veda does not prescribe anything that one should not do. Hence one should not view the Absolute as affected by plurality in any way or as undergoing differentiation of any kind, for all dualistic vision of it is condemned by the Veda. Because duality is condemned by the Veda, it cannot be what the Veda intends to teach. On the other hand, vision of the Absolute as homogeneous is both recommended and eulogized, so this must be what the Veda intends to teach... (221)

Suppose for argument's sake that we granted your case that the doctrine of non-duality would undermine the ritualistic part of the Veda, this would not help you. For the same conflict with Vedic teaching would still rise on the basis of a doctrine of duality-cum-non-duality. For even supposing we admitted that the Absolute could be one yet both dual and non-dual, like the sea, we still would not escape from that conflict with the Veda to which you yourselves have drawn attention. You ask how? Well, there would be the one supreme Absolute, both dual and non-dual in nature. Being beyond grief and delusion and other defects, it would not seek spiritual teaching. Even if there were a Teacher, he would not be other than the Absolute, as the dual-cum-non-dual Absolute would be but one single entity.

Perhaps you will say that the Absolute has a dual aspect which contains plurality, and that there can consequently be teaching within the confines of this aspect, though not in the Absolute as such (brahma-viṣaya). But if you did, you would contradict your own previous statement that the Absolute was one and the same in both its dual and non-dual aspects, and that nothing else apart from it existed. Moreover, such a conception would contradict the example of the sea. For that dual aspect in which there could be the teaching of one being by another being would be one thing, and the non-dual aspect a completely different thing. (222) And if the Absolute be taken as one mass of consciousness as the sea is one mass of water, then it is inconceivable how one being could either receive or impart instruction. One may take the individual, Devadatta, as consisting of duality in non-duality and as constituted by his various organs and limbs. But it is inconceivable that his voice and ears, considered as parts of him, should function respectively as Teacher and receiver of teaching, while he himself was neither Teacher nor taught. Devadatta is but one consciousness, as the sea is but one mass of water. Hence it follows that the opponent's theory involves conflict with the Veda and with reason and fails to establish what it aims to establish. (223)

* * * * *

2. Here some hold as follows. The Inner Ruler, they say, is a condition of light agitation assumed by the Absolute (brahman), the Indestructible (akṣara), which is in itself motionless, comparable to a vast ocean. The violently agitated state of the ocean in the form of the individual souls (kṣetra-jña) (224) does not know the Inner Ruler. They also assume five other "states". (225) And thus they speak of eight "states" of the Absolute. Others say that these are its powers (śakti), and speak of the Indestructible as "possessed of infinite powers." (226) Others, again, say they are modifications (vikāra) of the Indestructible.

Well, we can say straight away that neither "states" nor "powers" are intelligible in the case of the Indestructible. For there is the text saying that it is beyond all worldly characteristics like hunger, etc. (227) And one and the same being cannot both have "states" like hunger and at the same time not have them, being beyond them. And the same thing would apply to its having "powers". And the errors in supposing that it could have modifications and parts have already been pointed out in the fourth section. (228) So all these assumptions are quite false.

Well then, what is the element of distinction amongst all these beings? It is all due to external adjuncts, we say. Neither distinction nor non-distinction pertains to them in themselves, for in their true nature they are massed consciousness (prajñāna-ghana), like a mass of salt...

Hence the Self without adjuncts, being indescribable, void of all distinctions, one and unique, has been taught by saying "Not thus, not thus." When the Self has the adjunct of the complex of bodies and organs making up the psycho-physical personality, individualized through the force of nescience, desire and actions, it is called "the transmigrant" (saṃsārin) and "the individual soul". When the Self has the adjunct of eternal and infinite knowledge and power, it is called "the Inner Ruler" and "the Lord".

That same Self, when void of all adjuncts, solitary, pure, in its own true nature, is called "the Indestructible" (akṣara) and "the Supreme" (para). And then, as qualified by such adjuncts as the bodies and organs of Hiraṇyagarbha, the Unmanifest (avyākṛta), deities (devatā), universal types (jāti), individual bodies (piṇḍa), men, animals, departed spirits (preta) and the like, He assumes their name and form. That is why it has been said, "It moves and it does not move, (it is within all this world and also outside it)." (229) And in this way there is no contradiction with such Vedic texts as, "This is the Self (that is within all living beings" and "He is the inner Self in all beings." (230)... On no other assumption can these texts be explained. Hence the distinction between the Indestructible, the Inner Ruler, and all the (individual) beings is due to external adjuncts and to nothing else. For the conclusion of all the Upanishadic texts when taken as a systematic unity is "One only, without a second." (231)

* * * * *

3. Perhaps you will disagree and argue that the Absolute is pluralistic by nature. Just as a tree has many different branches, you will say, so has the Absolute many different powers. And

there is the example of the sea which is one (if considered collectively) in itself, but many as foam, waves, bubbles and so on. Or there is the example of clay, which is one as clay but many as pots and dishes and the like. Since the Absolute has a unitary aspect, the experience of liberation can very well be explained as arising through knowledge of that. And since it also has a pluralistic aspect, the real worldly activity and obedience to Vedic ordinances implied by the ritualistic teachings of the Veda are explicable as related to that. And this is the right way of explaining the Upanishadic examples of clay (and gold) and so on.

But all this is not right. The text says, "The truth is that it is *only* clay." (232) Thus it specifies, in the example that it offers, that *only* the root-principle is real. And the (nearby) phrase "a mere suggestion of speech" implies that all the modifications are illusory. And there is the further teaching that the embodied soul is himself (already) the Absolute, in the text, "That is the Self. That thou art, O Śvetaketu!" (233)

* * * * *

4. And when the text later, (234) in the example of the trial of the thief by ordeal, speaks of the bondage of the one who lies and the liberation of the one who speaks the truth, it teaches the doctrine of unity. It teaches, that is to say, that unity is the ultimate truth, while plurality is set up by wrong knowledge. If *both* unity *and* plurality had been true, how could the individual who spoke what was true from the standpoint of empirical experience have been branded as a liar? And the Veda confirms our contention by decrying vision of difference in the words, "He goes from death to death who sees an appearance of plurality here." (235) Moreover, the doctrine that *both* plurality *and* unity are real

fails to account for the Upanishadic teaching that liberation arises from knowledge, because it does not admit that the cause of transmigratory experience is wrong knowledge (producing a sense of plurality) such as could be removed by right knowledge. For if *both* plurality *and* unity are real, by what right could one say that knowledge of unity cancelled knowledge of plurality (when it could equally be that knowledge of plurality cancelled knowledge of unity)? (236)

* * * * *

5. An objection to Vedanta (in any of its forms) might be formulated as follows. If this be so (i.e. if the purport of the Upanishads is to teach the student the knowledge "I am the Absolute"), then the supreme Self must be the one subject to transmigration. If the Self be subject to transmigration at all, He must be ever subject to transmigration, a doctrine which is absurd because it would render the Veda useless. And if the Self were not subject to transmigration, the Veda would also be useless, because unnecessary. If the supreme Self, as the innermost Self of all beings, experienced the pains arising in the bodies of all living creatures, He would quite evidently be the one subject to transmigration. If this were the case, the Vedic texts proclaiming that the highest Self is not the one subject to transmigration would stand contradicted, as well as the Smṛti texts on the same topic, not to mention all sound reasoning. If, on the other hand, you conclude from all this that one can and must somehow or other make out that the Self is not connected with the pains arising in the bodies of living creatures, then, because there is now nothing left for the ultimate Self to seek or shun, one cannot avoid the absurdity that the Vedic teaching is useless.

Some (Bhartṛprapañca and his followers) try to fend off this dilemma in the following way. The supreme Self, they say, does not enter the creatures directly in His own form. Rather, He first assumes a modification (vikāra) and becomes the individual soul (vijñāna-ātman). This individual soul is both different from and non-different from the supreme Self. Because it is different, it is related to transmigratory experience. And because it is non-different, it can eventually acquire the conviction, "I am the Absolute." And they think that this covers everything.

On this we (Advaitins) remark that, if the individual soul were a modification of the supreme Self, there would be three possibilities. The supreme Self might be a composite whole made up of many substances, like the earth-substance, in which case the individual soul would be a transformation (pariṇāma) of a part of the supreme Self, as a clay pot is a transformation of a part (a piece of clay) of the earth-substance. Or else the supreme Self might retain its general nature, while a portion of its underwent modification, like hair (growing from parts only of the skin) or a desert (covering part only of the surface of the earth). Or else (thirdly) the supreme Self might undergo transformation (pariṇāma) in its entirety, as milk does when it changes intc curd.

If the supreme Self were regarded as a composite whole of many similar substances, one of which went into modification to become the individual soul, then, because only similarity (and not identity) is predicated of the substances, their unity would only be a figure of speech and not a reality. And this would conflict with the (monistic) principles of the system.

Let us then suppose that the supreme Self is a whole, eternally associated with inseparably connected parts, and that the individual soul undergoing transmigration is part of the supreme Self, thus constituted. But this supposition also produces unacceptable results. For it would imply that, since the whole pervades all the parts, the defects or qualities of every part would apply to the whole, so that the individual soul's defect of being subject to transmigratory experiences would apply also to the supreme Self. As for the view that the supreme Self underwent total transformation, like milk being transformed into curds, that is also to be rejected, as it is clearly repugnant to all the teaching of the Veda and the Smṛti.

Thus it turns out that all these alternatives conflict with the Veda, Smṛti and reason, as evidenced by such texts as, "(I resort to) Him who is partless, actionless, totally at rest" and "That divine and formless Spirit, who exists within and without, unborn" (237) and so forth....

If the individual soul is taken to be a portion of the motionless supreme Self, it will not be possible for it to undergo translation to various different places in accordance with the fruits of its deeds. And we have already shown how the view is wrong in that it makes the supreme Self subject to transmigration.

It might be contended that the individual soul which undergoes transmigration is a "part" of the supreme Self only in the sense that a spark cast off by a fire is a "part" of the fire. But even on this view, the supreme Self will be subject to diminution if parts can break off from it. And if the soul suffers transmigration, it will imply gaps in other parts of the supreme Self, and would contradict the text saying that the Self was "impregnable". (238)

* * * * *

6. There are others, too, who suppose themselves to be great authorities on the Upanishads, who build up the following system. The world of objects, consisting of the formed and the formless, (239) they say, makes one category (rāśi). The supreme

Self forms a second category. And between these two, they claim, there lies a third category, different from either, consisting in the entire mass of an individual's experience, secular and Vedic, his ritualistic works and acquired skills and aptitudes, along with the individual soul himself, who is the agent and experiencer....That which prompts to action is the category of merit and demerit: (240) that which is prompted to act and supplies the means for action is the category of the formed and the formless.

Here they try to reconcile their views with those of the secular philosophers. Having first boldly affirmed that the whole category of merit and demerit resides in the subtle body, they draw back, afraid of falling into the doctrine of the Sāṃkhyas, (241) and say that the whole category of merit and demerit can become displaced from the subtle body and lodged in a particular part of the supreme Self, where it can exist even in the absence of the subtle body, just as the scent of flowers can be extracted from its seat in the flowers and transferred to a cup in a distilled essence (i.e. as scent) and preserved even in the absence of the flowers. This alleged "part" of the supreme Self, though without qualities in itself, receives qualities and powers of action adventitiously from without. This is the individual soul (vijñāna-ātman), the agent and experiencer who is bound and released. Here they follow the thought of the Vaiśeṣikas. (242) The category of merit and demerit accrues to the soul adventitiously from without, as it arises from the category of matter (bhūta-rāśi), whereas the soul is without empirical characteristics in itself, as it is a "part" of the supreme Self. On the other hand they follow the doctrines of Sāṃkhyas when they say that nescience, though a natural and not an adventitious principle, is not to be regarded as a genuine *property* of the Self (as it does not affect the whole of the Self but only that "part" of it that constitutes the individual soul), like a desert (which arises in the earth but does not affect the whole of it).

They look upon all this as splendid because it harmonizes with the views of the secular philosophers, but they do not perceive that it conflicts with the final conclusions of the Upanishads as well as with reason. In what sense? Well, we have already explained the defects of the theory. (243) If parts are attributed to the supreme Self, then it will have to be regarded as the one undergoing transmigration and as "vulnerable". (244) And there are other insuperable difficulties such as that of explaining how there could be transference to various realms after death in accordance with one's deeds (as taught in the Veda). Moreover, the theory takes the individual soul as (in one sense) ever distinct from the supreme Self; and, in that case, how could it (as the theory requires) also be one with it?

Suppose it be contended that the subtle body is figuratively attributed to the supreme Self, as one figuratively attributes to the space-like ether itself the shapes of the pots, jars and pot-holes in which it appears to be enclosed? Even so, this will result in the unacceptable consequence of affirming that the subtle impressions reside in the supreme Self when the subtle body is absent (as in dreamless sleep). And the theory would involve the untenable assumption that nescience could arise of its own accord, like a desert appearing on the surface of the earth.

The notion that an impression could be transferred from its seat to some other receptacle, without there being any intermediary capable of carrying the impressions, is in any case quite inconceivable. Nor is it countenanced by the Vedic texts themselves. The latter (deny that the impressions lie anywhere but in the heart or mind and) say, for instance, "Desire, determination, doubt... are all mind" and "It is through the heart (intellect) that one knows forms" and "It only *seems* to think, it only *seems* to stir" and "Those desires of his which lie in the heart" and "Then (i.e. in dreamless sleep) he has passed beyond all sorrows of the heart." (245) Nor can these texts be interpreted to mean anything different on the ground of contradiction with other Vedic teaching. For the burden of all these texts is to show how the true nature of man is (not the individual soul familiar in empirical experience but) the Absolute, and the ultimate purport of all the Upanishadic texts is just this. All these people who are so skilful at thinking up strange interpretations of the Upanishadic texts are only corrupting the meaning. If they gave the true meaning I would accept it: I have no animus (dveṣa) against them personally.(246)

* * * * *

7. Moreover, the notion (of Bhartṛprapañca and his followers) that sight, hearing, taste, etc., are attributes of the Self, (belonging to it yet distinct in nature), would come into conflict with the Vedic text which proclaims that the Self is a homogeneous mass of Consciousness "like a lump of salt," (247) as also with such texts as "Knowledge, Bliss" and "Reality, Knowledge (and Infinity)" and "The Absolute is Consciousness." (248)

It is also clear from speech usage. There is the common way of parlance, "One knows colours through the eye, one knows sound through the ear, one knows tastes through the tongue," which shows that the word "knowledge" can express all that is expressed by the different words, "seeing", "hearing" and "tasting". And speech-usage is a valid criterion. (249)

Further, our contention can be supported through examples. We have the ordinary worldly example of the crystal. It assumes the hues of various colours such as green, blue and red simply through coming into proximity with them, so that they become "adjuncts". (250) One could not for a moment suppose that the crystal actually gave up its transparent nature or that the green, red and blue colours were its actual properties. Similarly, the Self is massed Consciousness by nature, and self-luminous. On account of its association with various adjuncts such as the eye, etc., it appears to have different powers such as those of sight, hearing, tasting, etc. For massed Consciousness is transparent in nature, like the crystal.

An added reason is that the Self is self-luminous. The light of the sun, though in no way differentiated by the colours that it illumines, becomes associated with them, and *appears* to assume their colour. Similarly, the Self illumines the whole world as well as the organs such as the eye that apprehend the world, and assumes (i.e. appears to assume) their form. And hence it was said in an earlier passage, "He sits by the aid of the Self as his light." (251)

Nor can one attribute plurality to what is partless, for there is no example to support such an idea. It is true that people attribute various different properties to the (partless) ether, such as all-pervasiveness, etc., and suppose, likewise, that primary atoms have various distinct qualities, such as odour or taste. (252) But when the matter is examined closely it turns out that all such distinctions are due to external adjuncts alone. All-pervasiveness, for instance, is not a quality that belongs to the ether *intrinsically*. Our notion of the ether as all-pervading is a relative one arising from the fact that it is everywhere present in its own true form as the common substratum of all external adjuncts. It is not that the ether either pervades or fails to pervade anything intrinsically. For (pervasion involves movement and) movement is defined as that which causes a thing in one place to attain to another place, and it is an action that cannot occur in the case of something that has no internal differentiation. And there are no distinct properties in the ether, for the same reason.

The case is similar with the (supposed partless) primary atoms (of the Vaiśeṣikas) and the like. A primary atom of the earth-element, which latter (according to their theory) is but odour in massed form, would be a minute particle of that mass, and would be *of the very nature* of odour. You could not then conceive it as *having* odour as its quality. Nor would it be possible to claim that an earth-atom included taste and other properties, for these (would not be intrinsic but would) derive from its contact with water and other elements. So it follows that there is no example of a partless thing having a plurality of attributes.

And this argument is also enough to refute the idea of Bhartṛprapañca that the different powers in the Self, such as the power of seeing, etc., underwent further real modification into the sense-organs, such as the eye, and their objects such as colour. (253)

* * * * *

8. But what if the word "knowledge" were here interpreted in a different way to mean the act of knowing? It would then be that, given the fact of the act of knowing, one passed from that to the affirmation of an agent for each act of knowing, in the same sort of sense in which one says, "That which sets the branches of the trees in motion is the wind." (254) The Self would then be a substance possessed of the active power of knowing: it would not be the very essence of Consciousness. Empirical cognitions, however, rise and pass away. Whenever, therefore, an empirical cognition arose, the Self, as agent in the act of knowing, would undergo a modification through the performance of that act.

And whenever an empirical cognition passed away, the Self, would stand undifferentiated as a mere substance. (255) In these circumstances it would be impossible to avoid imputing to the Self a nature subject to modification, resolution into parts, non-eternity, impurity and other defects. (256)

* * * * *

9. Or else, says Bhartṛpapañca, since man alone is qualified to attain the Absolute, the word "Absolute" may here (257) refer to the *individual* who *will become* identical with it. For the topic of mankind has just been introduced in the text "Men think 'We shall become the All,'" (258) and it has been said that the special subject of the passage is the means to man's material and spiritual welfare, and not teaching about the Absolute in its highest form, or even in its lower form as Prajāpati.

Hence he should understand that the term "the Absolute" here refers to the one who *will attain* to the Absolute in its highest form through mystical realization (brahma-vidyā), after he has first attained to identity with the Absolute in its lower form as associated with "duality-cum-unity" through the lower knowledge (attained through prescribed meditations) supported by ritual. This implies an "intermediate stage", where he turns from objects of enjoyment and breaks his ties with desire and action through attaining identity with the All. We see in the world that words are sometimes used to mean something that will only arise in the future, as in "He is cooking the dish of rice." (259) And they are used in a similar way in the sacred traditions, as when it is said, "The houseless monk... (performs a sacrifice) in which the fee he pays is the granting of pardon and protection to all living beings." (260) And some (261) say that the usage here is of this kind, and "the Absolute" here means the man who *will become* the Absolute, the "Brāhmaṇa".

That is wrong, for whatever were to *become* all would have the defect of not being eternal. There is nothing in the world that becomes something new, under conditioning from without, and is at the same time eternal. To say, therefore, that "becoming the All" is a result of knowledge of the Absolute that *will occur*, and also that it will last for ever, is contradictory. It will be an impermanent result, like that of rituals.(262)

If, on the other hand, you hold that the fruit of knowledge of the Absolute is "becoming the All" in the sense that the notion arising from nescience that you are not the All comes to an end, then the whole conception of man's *becoming* the Absolute in the future is beside the point. For even before knowledge of the Absolute all creatures would already be the Absolute and would eternally and truly be the All. The notion that they were not the Absolute and were not the All would be a mere imputation set up by nescience, like the silver erroneously imputed to nacre and colour imputed to the ether of the sky. (263)

* * * * *

10. Here some (i.e. Bhartṛprapañca) propound the following theory. They say that even when the organs and objects of experience and their active source have all disappeared, even then a person is not yet liberated. He remains reduced to little more than a name, cut off from the supreme Self by that nescience which arises from the Self and yet does not cover all of it, in the manner of desert places arising (only) in certain places on the surface of the earth. In this state he remains quite turned away from the world as an object of enjoyment. Pleasure and action are not ends (any longer). He occupies an "intermediate" position. His task is to remove vision of duality once and for all through vision of his identity with the supreme Self. Hence (thinks Bhartṛprapañca) the next stage in the teaching must be the introduction

of the subject of vision of the supreme Self. In this way the thinkers of this school think up an "intermediate" stage called "escape" (apavarga) (conceived as escape from further transmigration without perfect identification with the Absolute), and interpret the next passage of the text in the light of this fancy.

What they do not, however, tell us is how there can be attention to the supreme Self on the part of the bodiless being who has lost all his organs. They tell us that his organs (or vital energies) have dissolved, and only his name is left. And they connect this state with the words "lies dead" which occurred before. (264) They cannot support this idea with even the dream of an argument.

If, to avoid these absurdities, they said that, even while still alive, the enquirer came to the point where he was associated with nescience alone, completely withdrawn from all objects of enjoyment, then they would have to explain how that state arose. If they were to say that it arose through his attaining a sense of identity with the whole universe, then this has already been refuted. Theorizing about the enlightened man, one could either say that he may attain, through meditation on his own identity with the world of duality (in its entirety), supported by ritual, to the state called Hiraṇyagarbha, implying identity with the universe, a goal that would finally be achieved after death, when his organs of knowledge and action had subsided. Or else one could affirm that he could turn away in detachment from objects of enjoyment, and become intent on vision of the supreme Self, while he was still alive and his organs were still active. But no one could attain *both* these goals through one and the same path of discipline. If he followed the discipline for identification with Hiraṇyagarbha, he would not be following the discipline of detachment. And if he was following the discipline of turning away in detachment from all objects of enjoyment, and becoming intent on the enjoyment of the supreme Self, he could not follow the discipline for attaining identity with Hiraṇyagarbha. For a discipline designed to attain something cannot be the same thing as the discipline designed for rejecting it.

And suppose that, for becoming intent on the supreme Self, the qualification was to have died and to have attained identity with Hiraṇyagarbha, with one's organs of knowledge and action in abeyance and only one's name remaining. In that case, the teaching about knowledge of the supreme Self given in the Veda to ordinary people like us would be useless. For knowledge of the Absolute as taught to everyone is a practicable human goal, as is shown by such texts as "Whoever amongst the gods... whoever amongst the divine sages (ṛṣi)... whoever amongst men..." (265) So this whole conception is very unworthy and quite outside the pale of the true tradition. (266)

4. REFUTATION OF PRAPAÑCA VILAYA VĀDA

This was a species of Niyoga Vāda, the doctrine that the Veda is entirely concerned with command. It has been attributed to Brahmadatta. (267) It taught that all other Vedic texts are subordinate to injunctions, and that the ultimate purpose of the injunctions was the elimination of plurality, both in theory and practice. The general injunction, "One should perform ritual sacrifices for the sake of heaven" serves to eliminate the notion that one is identical with the body. (268) For it is not the earthly body which will go to heaven. Moreover, one would not know that one was not the physical body without the help of the ritualistic science deriving its ultimate authority from this text. (269) Nor would one actually do the ritual unless one were going to leave this body and attain another one in heaven.

The effect of the general injunction "he should sacrifice for the sake of heaven" is present in *all* the ritualistic injunctions of the Veda. Since one would not engage in rituals at all but for the general injunction "he who desires heaven should sacrifice," it follows that all ritualistic action has to be treated as subordinate to the general injunction to perform ritual. The purpose of ritual-in-general is the attainment of heaven. But in the course of performing ritual, conditioned in general by the desire for heaven, there may arise additional incidental desires for this or that particular end, and one may perform the special rituals laid down for attaining such ends. But this does not invalidate the general law that ritual is performed for the sake of heaven and leads to the dissolution of the body. For such special ritualistic injunctions have to be understood on the analogy of the text, "One should fetch water in the milk-pail in the case of him who desires cattle." (270) Even subordinate injunctions such as these have dissolution for their function. They dissolve the notion that anyone other than the person qualified for the major ritual in the course of which they occur is qualified to benefit from the actions they enjoin — and they imply that the latter must desire heaven. (271) The prohibitions of the Veda eliminate passions. The texts enjoining obligatory and occasional ritual for which there is no reward eliminate useless actions based on natural instincts. Thus the injunctive texts of the ritualistic section of the Veda prepare the way for final elimination of all distinctions through knowledge of the Self. Of texts in the knowledge-section of the Veda, some attribute form to the Absolute, some do not. The former are indirectly concerned with the elimination of distinctions, the latter directly concerned.

Against this Śaṃkara replies that there are no injunctions in the texts of the knowledge-section of the Veda (jñāna-kāṇḍa) which declare the nature of the Absolute. When such texts have been properly assimilated, the plurality of the world disappears of its own accord, since it was based on ignorance of the Self. If the Absolute has not been known through hearing, cogitating over and meditating on these texts, the world remains real, and no amount of injunctions can dissolve it. And if they could, it would not be dissolved in something greater but annihilated, and the individual soul would be annihilated with it.

There are texts in the meditation-section of the Veda (upāsana-kāṇḍa) which deal with symbolic meditations and speak of the Absolute as "made up of mind." (272) They are associated with their own injunctions, which do not mention dissolution of the world as their goal. Nor is there any initial general injunction that would warrant us to treat all injunctions to meditate on the Absolute, with or without form, as subordinate injunctions designed to co-operate towards the one general end of elimination of the universe, on the analogy of the subordinate injunctions all co-operating towards one end in the Prayāja rituals. And destruction of the universe has no place whatever in the ritualistic section of the Veda (karma-kāṇḍa). "He should sacrifice if he desires ownership of a village" implies the future existence of villages, not their annihilation. The view that rituals have the purpose of destroying the universe is simply untenable. They are performed for the sake of their stated fruits, which fall within the universe. If they also destroyed the universe, there would be no motive to perform them.

If the texts promise possession of villages as the fruit of a ritual, this must be respected. And it will not help to say that rituals lead to the dissolution of the universe indirectly through the attainment of heaven. For if they are for the sake of heaven they are not for the sake of dissolution of the universe. It is futile to introduce false analogies, like those of acts conveying twin results, as, when we convey water through a duct, the water serves both for drinking and washing, or when we bring a light to distinguish the colour of one object, it also incidentally illumines others. For action and the actionless are contradictory. And even if we admit that the prohibitions in the Veda eliminate passions, this cannot be true of the ritualistic injunctions, which do not correct the natural tendency to take the universe of plurality as real.

The truth is that all the rituals produce their stated fruits, but that they also gradually prepare the mind of the performer to desire knowledge of the Absolute and so to become a qualified enquirer into the Absolute. When a person becomes a qualified enquirer into the Absolute, he is then concerned with texts which belong to a different part (kāṇḍa) of the Veda, not the same as the part teaching ritual, and not entirely governed by the same rules. In particular, it makes metaphysical statements which are not dependent for their authority on subordination to injunctions to act.

Other faults in the Prapañca Vilaya theory of Niyoga Vāda are that the Veda would be confined to injunction, which leads to action, while action cannot be directed on the Absolute, the universal, omnipresent Self of all. Hence there could be no liberation, and the texts teaching it would be deprived of authority. Even if, *per impossibile*, liberation could occur, it would be the result of action, and so temporary. The doctrine must have been prominent in Śaṃkara's day, as Maṇḍana notices it, (273) and Sureśvara devotes 51 verses to it in his Sambandha-Vārttika. (274)

Perhaps, as a final point, it is worth drawing attention to Śaṃkara's interesting claim in Extract 1 that the text "The Self should be seen," though cast in imperative form, is not so much an injunction to "see" the Self as a warning to turn away from all else. Further material on this head will appear below, Volume V Chapter XII section 2.

TEXTS ON REFUTATION OF PRAPAÑCA VILAYA VĀDA

1. Some say that even the texts stating that the Absolute has form are really concerned with proclaiming that it is formless and are not concerned with anything else, on the principle that all texts are concerned, directly or indirectly, with the destruction (vilaya, lit. dissolution) of the world (prapañca-vilaya). But their view is not correct. Why not? Well, sometimes an aspect of the world-appearance is attributed to the Absolute even in the course of the exposition of the highest form of metaphysical knowledge (paravidyā), as in such texts as "'His horses (organs) are harnessed to the number of a thousand' – verily, He Himself is the horses, in tens, in thousands, many, infinite in number." (275) Here, say the theorists in question, such aspects of the world (as the organs of living beings) are mentioned for the sake of their destruction, as, (for example in the text just cited) there is the concluding passage, "This Absolute has neither a before nor an after, has nothing inside it and nothing outside it." On the other hand (we Advaitins say that) when aspects of the world-appearance are taught in the course of the exposition of meditation for specific fruits (upāsana), as in such texts as "Consisting of mind, with the Vital Energy for His body, luminous in nature," (276) then they are not mentioned for the sake of being destroyed. For meditations of this kind are connected by context with such injunctions to meditate for specific fruits as "He should have a definite purpose." (277) And since the Vedic passage itself shows that such attributes are mentioned in connection with meditation for the sake of specific fruits, it is not right to interpret them through figurative meaning (lakṣaṇā) (278) as having been mentioned for the sake of being destroyed. And if all the

texts without exception were regarded as being for the sake of the destruction of some aspect of the world-appearance, then there would have been no room for the Sūtra, "The Absolute is in fact without form, as that idea prevails," (279) which mentions a criterion (through which one may know the Absolute is without form, despite the presence of texts of contrary import).

Moreover, the "fruits" mentioned in the passages teaching meditation for a specific fruit are various according to the occasion. Sometimes it is for the remission of the effects of past sinful deeds, sometimes for the attainment of lordly states (aiśvarya), sometimes for liberation at the end of the world-period (krama-mukti). Thus the texts teaching meditation for a specific fruit are distinct even amongst themselves, and should not be interpreted as forming a single topic in common with the texts proclaiming the existence of the (formless) Absolute.

Furthermore, it ought to be explained (by the theorists under discussion) how texts which apparently each teach a different meditation for a different specific fruit can be understood as all forming a single topic (and leading to an identical fruit, *viz.* that of the gradual destruction of the world-appearance). Perhaps you will say that they should be understood as all subordinate to one initial injunction (niyoga), like the texts grouped with the Prayāja rituals of the New and Full Moon sacrifices. But this would be wrong. For in the case of the texts proclaiming the existence of the Absolute there is no initial injunction. It has been explained at length in commenting on Brahma Sūtra I.i.4 (280) how the texts proclaiming the existence of the Absolute are limited to concern with an already existent reality, and do not give out injunctions to act.

And the opponent ought also to explain what the (supposed) injunction in the present context could be about. A man subject to injunction is enjoined to perform some act within his capabilities, with the words "Do (such and such)."

The opponent will perhaps here claim that "Destruction of the World" is an act that can be enjoined. For there is no awakening to the Absolute as a metaphysical reality as long as the apparent world of duality remains undestroyed. So that the apparent world of duality *ought* to be destroyed, as it is a standing obstacle to the awakening to the Absolute as a metaphysical reality. Just as it is taught that the one who wants heaven must offer sacrifices, so is it also taught that the one who wants liberation must (first) destroy the universe. And just as the one who wants to ascertain the presence of a pot or other object that is shrouded in darkness destroys that darkness, since it is an obstacle to his knowledge, so must the one who wants to ascertain the existence of the Absolute as a metaphysical reality destroy the universe, which is an obstacle to such knowledge. For, while the world-appearance is (ultimately) of the nature of the Absolute, the Absolute is not (ultimately) of the nature of the universe. Therefor knowledge of the Absolute as a metaphysical reality proceeds through the destruction of the universe of name and form.

Here we (Advaitins) would ask: Well, but what is this "Destruction of the Universe"? Has the universe to be dissolved in the sense that the solidity of clarified butter becomes dissolved when affected by the heat of the sacrificial fire? Or is it that the world of name and form (is an appearance that) has been set up by nescience and has to be dissolved through knowledge in the same way that the vision of a plurality of moons introduced by chronic squinting has to be dissolved? Let us suppose that we receive the reply that this world, comprehending the whole microcosm, such as the body, and the whole macrocosm, such as the elements like the earth and the rest, is a reality that has to be destroyed (by an act of physical destruction, as one might destroy a pot with a blow of a hammer). In that case the teaching that one must destroy the universe would be a command to perform the impossible, as the whole universe cannot be destroyed by the mere act of a single human being. And even if it could, the elements, such as earth, etc., would all have been destroyed by the first person who ever attained liberation, so that the universe would already now be without the very elements that compose it!

So the opponent will perhaps prefer to say that this universe is an appearance superimposed through nescience on the one Absolute, and has to be dissolved through knowledge. In the latter case, however, (the discipline of meditation based on an injunction is irrelevant); all that is needed is that the Absolute should be known through the negation of the universe that has been superimposed through nescience, through such texts as, "The Absolute is one only, without a second" and "That is the real, that is the Self, that thou art." (281) When the Absolute has once been conveyed (by such texts), knowledge arises of its own accord, and nescience is negated by it. Then this whole world-appearance of name and form, that has been superimposed through nescience, dissolves like the world of dream. Whereas if the knowledge of the Absolute has not been conveyed (by the supreme texts), there will be no such knowledge (arising through meditations). No dissolution of the world -appearance will occur as a result of obedience to the injunction "Practise meditation on the Absolute and dissolve the universe," even though it were to be repeated hundreds of times over.

Perhaps the opponent will reply that when the knowledge of the Absolute has been conveyed (verbally through the supreme texts) there still has to be an injunction either to realize the Absolute in concrete experience or to dissolve the world-appearance. But it is not so. For both goals are already realized when one realizes (through the help of the supreme texts) that the Absolute, void of the world-appearance, is one's own Self. It is through the light of knowledge of the true nature of the rope that one achieves both knowledge of the rope and the destruction of the superimposed appearance of a snake, etc. One does not have to do all over again what has already been done.

And in regard to the individual soul to whom the injunction is supposed to be addressed, we would ask whether he belongs to the sphere of the universe or to that of the Absolute (in its pure form). If to the universe, then through knowledge of the Absolute as void of the universe, the individual would be dissolved himself, just like the earth-element and the rest. And who would then remain to whom the injunction to dissolve the world-appearance could be addressed, or who would then be left to attain liberation through the fulfilment of an injunction? If (on the other hand) the individual soul to whom the injunction is addressed belongs to the sphere of the Absolute, then the real nature of the individual should be the Absolute, to whom an injunction cannot be addressed, and his nature as individual soul would be a mere product of nescience. And in that case, when once the Absolute was known, the one to whom an injunction could have been addressed would have disappeared, so that there would be no injunction.

Texts (cast in the form of a command), such as "The Self should be seen," (282)which are found amongst the texts dealing with the highest knowledge, are fundamentally for turning the attention of the hearer in the direction of the Self, and are not primarily to be regarded as injunctions to have knowledge of the real. Even in the world, when people give such commands as saying "Look here" or "Listen to this," the meaning of such phrases really is "Pay attention" and not "Acquire such and such a piece of knowledge." One whose attention is turned towards a potential object of knowledge sometimes knows it and sometimes does not, so that the most someone who wants him to know some object can do is to point it out to him. When an object has been pointed out, knowledge arises automatically in so far as the nature of that object and the quality of the instruments of knowledge applied warrant it. Nor can a person, even under an injunction, acquire knowledge of anything through a different means of knowledge in a new way, if he already has knowledge of it through another instrument of knowledge in another way. And if anyone, through actions performed under injunction, were to alter the quality of his knowledge of "I", this would not constitute knowledge but only imaginative mental activity. And if the "I" were to manifest in some new way of its own accord, it would just be a plain case of error. Knowledge, however, arises from the application of the certified means of knowledge (perception, inference, listening to the Vedic texts etc.) and has for its object the real in its true nature. It cannot be produced by obedience to a hundred injunctions or effaced by a hundred prohibitions. For it is dependent on reality as it actually is, and not on the will of man. So for this reason also there can be no injunction (in the context of knowledge of the Absolute).

And there is another point. If the Veda were really (as the opponent supposes) limited effectively to (giving) injunctions, then the teaching that the Absolute is the real Self of the individual soul, (which is generally admitted to be true and to involve knowledge and therefore not to be subject to injunction),would be without authority. If the opponent claimed in the face of this that the Absolute *was* the real Self (of the individual soul) — knowledge of which fact is not subject to injunction — and also enjoined man to take cognisance of it, then it would follow that the one science concerned with the Absolute really treated of two subjects (*viz.* injunctions to act and statements affirming the existence and sole reality of the non-dual actionless Self), and two mutually contradictory subjects at that.

Moreover, the view that the Veda is concerned entirely with injunctions is open to certain grave charges, such as those of being in contradiction with what the Veda actually says, of making assumptions that the Vedic texts do not warrant, of making liberation (which is eternal) depend on the results of action, just like rituals, and so making it impermanent, and to other such objections. as well. So the texts proclaiming the Absolute are concerned with conveying information only, and not with injunction.

Now, the opponent has said (283) that the Veda constitutes one single topic, all its texts being subordinate to an initial injunction. But, even supposing that injunction were to be found at all in the texts teaching experience of the Absolute (in its true nature), it would be impossible to show that they formed a single unit in both the teaching about the Absolute as void of the world-appearance and the teaching about the Absolute associated with the world-appearance. For you cannot take your stand on one injunction only, running everywhere, when you yourselves admit that there are distinct injunctions, as evidenced by differences of language used and other criteria.In regard to the texts enjoining the Prayāja rituals and the New and Full Moon sacrifices, unity of topic is defensible, since the portion of the text dealing with the particular qualifications and goals of the sacrificer implies non-difference. But in the present context, as between texts dealing with the Absolute without qualities and texts conveying commands, there is no element in the texts implying the identity of the qualifications and goals of the persons addressed. (284) Qualities like "luminous in form," (which imply a limited form, intelligible to the human mind), do not promise "Destruction of the World." Nor is "Destruction of the World" compatible with the presence of such qualities as "luminous in form," as the two ideas are mutually contradictory. It is not right to attribute to one and the same text both destruction of the world and continued preoccupation with one part of it. Therefore the distinction that we have drawn between texts speaking of the Absolute as associated with some limited form (which are mere injunctions to meditate for some particular goal) (285) and texts teaching the existence of the Absolute bereft of all form (which are statements of the final metaphysical truth) is justifiable. (286)

5. REFUTATION OF SPHOṬA VĀDA

In one isolated but lengthy passage, Śaṃkara considers and attacks a theory of the way in which words conveyed their meanings that had been adopted by the Grammarians. Śaṃkara was not much concerned with the metaphysical implications of the theory, and it seems doubtful if he was acquainted in any detail with the Vākya Padīya of Bhartṛhari, the classical treatise composed about the end of the fourth century A.D., which discusses grammatcal questions in the context of a monistic metaphysical world-view.

At any rate the present Extract, while dropping a hint that metaphysical issues are involved only in a single sentence at the close of the Sphoṭa Vādin's statement of his position, concentrates otherwise on purely linguistic issues, which had been raised by the Grammarians and answered on behalf of orthodox Mīmāṃsā and Vedānta by Upavarṣa and Śabara before Bhartṛhari's day. (287) The Grammarian assumes the existence of an occult entity, the "explosion" or "sphoṭa", which manifests whenever we understand the meaning of a word, and accounts for the fact that the whole word (or sentence) is comprehended simultaneously, even though the separate syllables can only be heard *or remembered* as successive.

Against this Upavarṣa, as restated by Śaṃkara, taught that one had to choose. Either one is really hearing the syllables, in which case one is not hearing any occult entity. Or else one is hearing the manifestation of such an occult entity, in which case one is not hearing the syllables. If the Sphoṭa Vādin were correct in his view that perception of the last syllable plus memory of the previous ones would not suffice for recognition of the word, we could have no knowledge of collective entities like a row of ants or a wood or any army. On the finally accepted view, if we maintain that all that is heard is the syllables, we shall have to assume an element of universality (sāmānya) in the syllables to account for the fact of our recognizing the identity of a syllable each time it is uttered. But Śaṃkara prefers the theory according to which what is heard is the individual vocal utterance (dhvani), and we recognize the identical (universal) syllable under this individual external garb.

It has been suggested that the Mīmāṃsakas had an additional motive for attacking Sphoṭa Vāda besides the mere belief that it was a wrong linguistic theory. (288) For the theory of the Sphoṭa was applied to sentences as well as words, and the sentence, on this theory, would have to constitute a perfect, indestructible unity. But the exegetical technique of the Mīmāṃsaka required that he should be able, on occasion, to detach phrases from the context in which they were originally embedded and show that they had significance in other contexts also.

TEXTS ON REFUTATION OF SPHOṬA VĀDA

1. But how do those who speak of creation as arising from the words of the Veda conceive those words? As Sphoṭa, (289) says our opponent. For

if it be held that the word is nothing more than the syllables of which it is composed (i.e. if the necessity of assuming a "sphoṭa" over and above the syllables were denied), then it would be indefensible to say that the individual gods or individuals of other classes "arose from the eternal words." Moreover, the syllables come into being and pass away (when pronounced) and are perceived as different each time they are spoken.

Let us develop this a little further (continues the opponent). A particular person can be recognized as such from merely hearing his voice and without seeing him, as when we say, "That is Devadatta reciting" or "That is Yajñadatta reciting." And such perceptions, which bear only on the spoken syllables, are not to be dismissed as illusions, as they are not followed by any cancelling cognitions. The meaning of what he (i.e. Devadatta or Yajñadatta as the case might be) says, however, cannot be apprehended from the mere apprehension of the spoken syllables. It cannot be, for instance, that each single syllable conveys a meaning, as there would be many exceptions to such a rule. Nor can the syllables be perceived together as a group, because they follow one another in time. Nor can you claim that it is the last syllable in conjunction with the impressions of the experience of the previous ones that conveys the meaning. For a word can only generate knowledge of its meaning when it is heard in its entirety and when its connection with its meaning is previously known. In this respect it is like an inferential sign. (290) It cannot be said that we have direct perception of the last syllable together with the memory traces which arise from having heard the previous ones, because the impressions are not (as such) subject to perception. Nor can it be said that it is the last syllable in conjunction with the impressions of the previous ones perceived in their effects. (i.e. in the memory images which they produce). For the effects of the impressions, the memory images, will form a temporal series in which each image vanishes with the appearance of the next (just like the series of syllables when they are actually being heard). (291) Hence the word is really the Sphoṭa.

The function of the Sphoṭa (the Grammarian continues) is to burst forth suddenly into manifestation as the object of a single cognition in the hearer, from a "seed" formed by the impressions left during the earlier hearing of the syllables one by one, this "seed" being "ripened" and brought to bursting point by the experience of hearing the last letter. And this "single cognition" is not to be regarded as a mere memory of the syllables of the word, because the syllables, being many, cannot be the object of a single cognition. The word in its true nature as Sphoṭa is eternal, it being something that is simply *recognized* anew each time it is separately pronounced. It is the spoken syllables (and not the word itself, the Sphoṭa) that are heard as different at each hearing.Therefore it is from the "Word" in its eternal form as Sphoṭa and conveyor of meaning that this whole world, consisting of actions, their factors and results, springs forth as the object of meaning.

Against all this, (the earlier Commentator) holy Upavarṣa remarks, "The words consist of the syllables alone." True, it has been declared that the syllables come into being and pass away. But this was wrong. For the syllables are subject to recognition (each time they are spoken, even when it is by a different voice,) as "these same." Nor can it be argued that this is only an apparent recognition arising from the perception of similar but different things wrongly *taken* to be the same, analogous to the way in which we take a person's hair as always the same (although it is in fact continuously growing and changing). For genuine recognition is a stark fact which cannot be refuted by any other means of knowledge. Nor can it be said that recognition applies only to the generic form (ākṛti) of the syllables, (292) for it is the individual syllables themselves that are recognized. If, indeed, it were *different* individual syllables that were heard each time they were pronounced, as we recognize different individual cows as members of the genus "cow", then the recognition would have been of this generic form. But it is the *same* individual syllables that are recognized each time they are pronounced. When, for instance, we have the experience of hearing the word "cow" spoken twice, we do not think we are hearing two different words (on the analogy of perceiving two different cows).

But has it not been said that the syllables, too, are apprehended as different when differently pronounced, in that the difference between Devadatta and Yajñadatta can be apprehended merely through hearing their voices reciting? To this we reply that the syllables themselves are recognized as identical; but they are manifested through air-currents resulting from the opening and closing of the organs of speech. The fact that we experience them as different on the different occasions on which they are heard is due to differences in the medium of manifestation, not to any intrinsic difference in the syllables themselves. (293)

It is noteworthy, too, that even those who believe that the individual instances of the syllables are different each time they are heard have to assume the presence of generic forms (ākṛti) of the syllables to account for their being recognized. Even in the case of those generic forms of syllables, it will have to be admitted that the feeling that the syllable is different each time it is heard is due to an extraneous adjunct. It would therefore be simpler and better to take the notion of difference as arising from an extrinsic adjunct and the recognition as applying to the syllables themselves. (294) Indeed, our recognition of the syllables as identical each time we hear them is itself a cancelling-cognition which exposes the notion that they were different as an error. And how could the one (and recognizably identical) syllable "ga" be different in each case when it happened to be pronounced by several people at exactly the same time in different ways, for example with acute, grave, circumflex, nasalized vowel-sounds? (295)

Or let us rather, to get rid of all difficulties, (296) say that the notion that the same syllable is different each time it is heard arises from the individual tone in which it is pronounced (dhvani), and not from the syllable itself.

But what, then, is this thing called "dhvani"? It is that which enters the ear of one hearer, far away from the speaker, without enabling him to distinguish differences between (the ways in which different) syllables (are pronounced), while enabling another hearer, sitting near the speaker, to distinguish between the various syllables as "shrill" or "soft". The variations in sound expressed in written form by the acute, grave and circumflex signs, which pertain to the tone and pitch of pronunciation, do not pertain to the syllables, as the latter are recognized as the same whenever heard. On this view we can find a basis (and hence an explanation) for the experience of syllables heard in variegated forms, (as expressed through the signs) acute, grave, and circumflex. For the syllables themselves are directly recognized, and hence identical on each occasion heard. If there is no appeal to the principle of individual tone (dhvani), it will have to be assumed that the distinctions of acute and grave and so on pertain to the physical mechanism required for their manifestation. But since this mechanical propulsion is not directly perceived, one cannot with certainty affirm that distinctions pertaining to it apply to the syllables, and so the theory would not account for the fact that individual variations of tone and pitch are heard.

Nor are there any grounds for clinging obstinately to the view that the syllables are recognized as identical and that the notion of their differences arises from differences of tone and pitch. For when a thing is without distinctions, it does not acquire distinctions from distinctions belonging to some completely different thing. It is not maintained, for instance, that distinctions among the individuals of a class introduce distinctions into the class itself.

As for the hypothesis of a Sphoṭa, it is also gratuitious, as the meaning can quite well be perceived from the mere syllables. Here our opponent will perhaps retort, "I do not frame a mere hypothesis about the Sphoṭa. I directly perceive it. For it lights up with an instantaneous flash in the mind when the latter has received the impressions of the syllables, one by one." But this we cannot accept. For the object of this cognition of which our opponent speaks is only the syllables. After the hearing of the component sounds one by one, there arises the one notion "gauḥ" (cow) embracing all the component sounds (i.e. ga + a + u + ḥ = gauḥ), and not embracing anything else (such as the assumed Sphoṭa). You ask how we know this? Because this knowledge embraces the sounds "ga" etc. and not anything else such as "da". If this knowledge embraced a Sphoṭa, which is something quite different from the succession of sounds beginning with "ga", it would exclude those sounds beginning with "ga" just as surely as it would any other sounds beginning with "da". But this is not found to be the case.

It follows, therefore, that this one cognition embracing all the component sounds is a memory. It is true that you said that the component sounds cannot be grasped in one notion since they are many. But against this we reply that groups of things *can* be grasped in a single notion. For we have such examples as the row (of ants etc.), the forest of trees and the army — or numbers such as ten, one hundred or one thousand. And our notion of ga + a + u + ḥ as constituting the one word "gauḥ" is fundamentally of the same nature as our notion of a wood or an army. It is a secondary notion, arising from our own arbitrary act of positing a single overall meaning for the several component sounds.

Here an opponent might perhaps object as follows. If it were the component sounds alone that constituted the word, and these collectively became the content of a single notion, then there ought not to be any distinction between words having the same component sounds (but occurring in a different order), such as jārā(= unfaithful wife) and rājā (= king), or kapi (= monkey) and pika (= cuckoo). To this we reply that though (in listening) all the syllables heard are taken into consideration, it is only those syllables which follow some particular pattern that are taken as forming a particular word, just as it is only those ants found arranged in a particular pattern that are taken as constituting a row. On this basis, the same group of syllables heard on two different occasions in a different order may well be thought to constitute two different words, even though the group of syllables be collectively the same.

It follows, therefore, that those who maintain that the syllables alone constitute the word have the simpler (and therefore better) hypothesis. Their theory is that a person will first hear a particular ordered combination of syllables used by his elders in daily life regularly in connection with some particular thing, and then in his own later experience he finds that these same syllables heard in that order stand out from their environment (as a unity) and regularly apprise him of the same thing. On the other hand, the upholder of the Sphoṭa doctrine is guilty both of contradicting experience and of appealing to what is not experienced. And his theory involves further gratuitous assumptions when he says that the familiar syllables, when heard, manifest a separate unfamiliar entity, the Sphoṭa, and that the Sphoṭa in turn manifests the meaning.

If, on the other hand, we (drop the whole theory that the difference in each hearing is due to the individual tone, dhvani, and) allow that the syllables themselves are different entities each time they are pronounced, then universals (sāmānya) of those syllables will have to be admitted to serve as the identical element making recognition possible. The power of denotation we have so far been attributing to (groups of) particular syllables will then have to be transferred to the universals of the syllables. And on this basis, too, there will be nothing contradictory in saying that individual gods and other such beings proceed from eternal words. (297)

6. REFUTATION OF THE PĀŚUPATAS AND PĀÑCARĀTRAS

In the first two sections of the present chapter, we have seen Śaṃkara refuting faulty theories of liberation offered by those who stood alongside himself on the common ground of Vedic tradition, but who failed to understand its crowning message, the possibility of liberation in life. In the third section we saw him extending the process to include a logical refutation of a world-view that had been designed to give equal value to all the Vedic texts. In the fourth section he disposed of an extreme form of the doctrine that all the texts of the Veda are injunctions or subordinate to injunctions (Niyoga Vāda), which maintained that all texts were injunctive *and at the same time* designed to dissolve, destroy or remove this or that aspect of the universe (Prapañca Vilaya Vāda). In the fifth and immediately preceding section he attacked the Grammarians' peculiar theory of the way in which words convey their meaning, defending the theory of the old Pūrva Mīmāṃsā teachers, but suggesting also that the difficulties could best be solved by appeal to the factor of "dhvani" or the individual tone of the speaker.

In all these sections he was attacking the theories of those who aimed to base their teaching on the Veda, but who for one reason or another gave a false or incomplete account of it. In the next chapter we shall see him at grips with the purely rationalist systems of his day, which either openly derided Vedic revelation in the manner of the Materialists, Buddhists and Jainas, or else paid lip-service to it in the manner of the Sāṃkhyas and Vaiśeṣikas, while in practice developing their own independent views on the basis of perception and inference alone. In the present section we shall study the attitude he adopted towards two groups who occupied a middle ground: they practised piety and devotion and sought unity with God according to traditional beliefs and disciplines sanctioned by the Smṛtis, but they tended to neglect or undervalue the Veda, and their conceptions required refutation where they contradicted the non-dualism of the highest Upanishadic teaching.

The two doctrines of this kind which Śaṃkara attacks in his Brahma Sūtra Commentary are those of the Pāśupatas and Pāñcarātras, representing Shaivism (Śiva-worship and Vaishnavism (Viṣṇu-worship) respectively (298) As far as the Pāśupata faith is concerned, it is believed that it arose on the West coast (Gujarat), was the oldest form of the Shaiva doctrine to take root in the North, and eventually travelled south to Mysore. It appears that their spiritual discipline was not primarily Vedic, but oriented rather towards the worship of Śiva. Their daily routine, which included the smearing of the whole body with ashes three times a day, seems incompatible with normal

Vedic ritual. At Kūrma Purāṇa I.xvi.96 ff. they are represented as nude or nearly nude ascetics, their bodies covered in ashes. The Chinese pilgrim Huian Tsang says he saw many of them in his travels to India, which lasted from 630 to 643 A.D., probably a little over a generation before Śaṃkara. The romance-writer Bāṇa, Huian Tsang's contemporary, represents them as essentially *wandering* ascetics, having some women amongst their number. (299) They have long disappeared as a community, but their Pāśupata Sūtras were found and published at Trivandrum in 1940, with Kauṇḍinya's Commentary. (300)

Śaṃkara's references to the sect in his Commentary on the relevant Sūtras are rather perfunctory, and one cannot but agree with S.K. Belvalkar (301) that his concern is really with the wider task of refuting the "World-Architect" view of God in general, as not doing justice to Upanishadic monism. Hence he includes all theistic adaptations of the Sāṃkhya teaching which reduce God to a mere efficient cause standing over against other souls and the world of Nature, including amongst these the Īśvara-doctrine of the Yoga Sūtras of Patañjali. (302) It is worth recalling, also, that just before Śaṃkara's day two influential writers among the rationalist defenders of the Brahminical faith, Uddyotakara, who wrote a free Commentary (Vārttika) on the Nyāya Sūtras, and Praśastapādya, who performed the same office for the Vaiśeṣika Sūtras, had introduced a "World-Architect" theory of God into their respective atomistic systems, in each case under the influence of the Pāśupatas. Śaṃkara evidently thought, with the authors of the Brahma Sūtras, that all such systems were a threat to the monism of the Upanishads.

In the second Extract we find Śaṃkara attacking those parts of a doctrine he attributes to the "Bhāgavatas" which he regards as incapable of reconciliation with the non-dualism of the

Upanishads. He attributes to the school under attack a doctrine of "Vyūhas" or Serial Manifestations of the Deity which is more specifically associated with the sect of Nārāyaṇa-worshippers called Pāñcarātras in the Mahābhārata. The Sūtras on which Śaṃkara is here commenting have generally been regarded as concerned with this school. Śaṃkara mentions "going to the temple" (abhigamana) and other Pāñcarātra practices. He is clearly concerned with Pāñcarātra teachings in their ancient form, the form in which they are recorded in the Mahābhārata and other early Smṛti literature, and not with the more developed and complicated form of worship with which they appear associated in the later Āgama and Saṃhitā literature.

According to the interpretations of his Commentators Vācaspati and Ānandagiri, Śaṃkara takes the doctrine of the Vyūhas in quite a simple sense to refer to the emanation of the individual soul from the Lord, with the mind emanating from the soul and the ego emanating from the mind, the three manifestations being given names which were originally those of relatives of the historical person, Vasudeva, Kṛṣṇa's father. Śaṃkara's only complaint against the doctrine of the Vyūhas is that it ascribes an origin to the soul, thereby rendering it non-eternal: or alternatively, if, to avoid this, it makes all the Vyūhas so many Vāsudevas, it then ascribes plurality to the Lord. Śaṃkara does not object in general to a doctrine of self-multiplication, as it is instanced at Chāndogya Upanishad VII.xxvi.2. He notes, however, that one of the early doctors of the Pāñcarātra school, Śāṇḍilya, (303) is said originally to have adopted the practices of the Pāñcarātras when he failed to find the highest good in the Veda. That he was still prepared to recommend their discipline of temple worship in the face of this is proof indeed of the high value he assigned to devotion (bhakti) as a preliminary to the path of knowledge (jñāna-niṣṭhā).

TEXT REFUTING THE PĀŚUPATAS

We now proceed to the refutation of the doctrine that makes the Lord the mere efficient cause of the universe. We know that this is the point that the author of the Sūtras has in mind, because he has said earlier, "He is the material cause as well, or the proposition and the example would be contradicted" followed by "And because of the teaching of His will to create." (304) These texts show that the author of the Sūtras has himself already established that the Lord is by nature both the material and the efficient cause of the world. If, therefore, he were here refuting the more general doctrine that the Lord was the cause of the world, he would be guilty of self-contradiction. So the doctrine that is being so emphatically refuted here is that which teaches that the Lord is the mere efficient cause and overseer of the world, and not the material cause. And it is being refuted because it is a doctrine that conflicts with the teaching in the Upanishads affirming the unity of the Absolute.

And this non-Vedic and erroneous conception of the Lord assumes various forms. Some, taking their stand on Sāṃkhya and Yoga doctrines, suppose that the Lord is a mere efficient cause, the overseer of Nature (pradhāna) and the soul (puruṣa), with Nature, soul and Lord all conceived as distinct and different from one another.

But the view of the Māheśvaras (305) is a little different. They speak of five principles, comprising (1) the effect (the various evolved forms of Nature beginning with Mahat), (2) the cause (Nature itself and the Lord governing it), (3) yoga (meditation on OM and practice of the higher forms of abstract meditation), (4) rites (from the three daily "bathings" or smearing of the body with ashes at dawn, noon and dusk, up to the secret rituals of dancing, bellowing like Śiva's bull, simulating sleep, cramp, lameness and amorous dalliance to keep oneself mindful of the defects of the body and mind), and (5) the end of pain (liberation). These five principles have been taught by Lord Paśupati for the destruction of the bondage (pāśa) of the individual souls (paśu). (306) And they speak of the Lord Paśupati as a mere efficient cause. Some others, (307) like the Vaiśeṣikas, also manage to fit the Lord in as a mere efficient cause according to the various tenets of their systems.

To all this the author of the Sūtras replies, "There cannot be a Lord (separate from His subjects) as this leads to impossibilities." That is to say, the cause of the world cannot be a mere overseer in charge of Nature and the soul. Why not? Because of the impossibilities. What impossibilities? Well, a Lord who arranged for high, middling and low station amongst living beings would stand convicted of attachment and aversion (favouring one person rather than another) and would no more be a Lord than people like ourselves (who are also in bondage to attachment and aversion). Perhaps you will say that there is nothing wrong here, as He acts according to the merit and demerit of living beings. But this conception involves mutual dependence, as merit and demerit would both prompt and be dependent on merit and demerit. Nor will it avail to describe this process at beginningless. (308) For we reply that, at any earlier point you like to name, the difficulty of mutual dependence would come in just as it does now, so that the maxim of the endlessly proliferating row of blind men would apply. (309)

A further difficulty in the way of accepting a Lord different from Nature and the soul is the maxim of the Logicians, "The cause of action is a psychological defect." (310) No one is prompted to act, either in his own interest or that of another, except through a psychological defect. And in fact everyone is prompted to act by self-interest, even when they are acting in the interests of another. And if the doctrine (under consideration thus) implies that the Lord pursues self-interest, this is a further impossibility, for the Lord would no longer be a Lord if He were subject to the pulls of self-interest.

That form of the doctrine (i.e. that found in the Yoga school of Patañjali) (311) in which the Lord is said to be a particular soul, and souls are said to be actionless and indifferent, is also faulty (because the Lord cannot be a Lord if He is actionless and indifferent).

And there is yet another difficulty. If the Lord were to be conceived as distinct from Nature and the soul, He could not in fact constitute a Lord over Nature and the soul without being connected to them by some form of relation. That relation cannot be contact, as Nature, the soul and the Lord are all (in terms of the Yoga System) all-pervading and partless. Nor can the relation be intimate inherence, (312) as they are not said to rest in each other like a property in its seat. Nor is one in a position to assume any other causal relation (apart from the above-mentioned ones) from a consideration of the nature of the effect, because the presence of any cause-effect relation (between Nature and the Lord) is just what (on the dualistic terms of the Yoga System) has not yet been proved. (313) If you ask in what way the Upanishadic Absolutists are better placed, we reply that we are able to appeal quite justifiably to an identity-relation. Moreover, the Upanishadic Absolutist expounds the nature of the cause of the world on the authority of revealed doctrine. He is not necessarily forced (as the rationalist operating outside Vedic revelation is) to recognize the law that everything must actually be what it is perceived to be.

Our opponent, on the other hand, who expounds the nature of the cause of the world and other recondite matters on the authority of examples drawn from empirical experience, has to accept everything exactly as it is given in empirical experience. This is a noteworthy point of difference between us.

But is not the opponent also in possession of a revealed science coming from an omniscient being? (314) No, for this claim cannot be made without committing the fallacy of mutual dependence. For the so-called omniscience of the founder of the system depends on our belief that he has received a revelation, and his so-called revelation depends on our belief in his omniscience. Therefore the theory of the nature of the Lord propounded by the Sāṃkhya and Yoga philcsophers is untenable. And all other extra-Vedic conceptions (such as that of the Pāśupatas) must be included in this condemnation through appropriate arguments.

And the author of the Sūtras adds a further reason why the "Lord" advocated by the rationalists is inadmissible. They think up examples like that of the potter and the pot. But Nature and the rest are not malleable in the hands of the Lord in the same way that clay and the rest are malleable in the hands of the potter. Nature (as taught by the Sāṃkhyas) is imperceptible and void of colour or other empirical properties. Being quite unlike substances like clay, it is not malleable in the hands of the Lord.

Perhaps you will suggest that the Lord might be able to manipulate and control Nature in the same way that the soul manipulates the sense of sight and the other senses, even though they are not perceptible and are devoid of empirical properties like colour. But we cannot accept this either, says the author of the Sūtras, for we know about our power to manipulate our senses from our own actual sense-experience of pleasure and pain.

But no experience of pleasure and pain or the like can be actually observed in the case of Nature. And if we assume that the relation of the Lord to Nature is the same as ours to our senses, then this would imply (the absurd position) that the Lord had experience of pleasure and pain just like the denizens of transmigratory life.

Or else the last two Sūtras might be interpreted in a different way. The former may be interpreted, "And also on account of the impossibility of a vehicle." The rationalist's conception of the Lord is shown to be unfounded on this basis also. Kings are found to rule over a kingdom in the world in an embodied state, with a "vehicle" (body), not without any "vehicle". On pain of contradicting (the general law implicit in) this example, whoever wishes to assume the existence of the Lord in some unseen guise must be able to describe His body, the repository of His organs of action and knowledge. But they never will be able to describe it, as all bodies pertain to the time after creation, and are inconceivable before it. And the Lord could not exercise any power of impulsion in the world without a body, as we can understand from what we see in the world.

The second of the two Sūtras would then have to be interpreted to mean, "And if we assume that He *has* organs, that is also wrong: for it would condemn Him to the experience of pleasure and pain (like ordinary mortals)." That is to say, suppose we freely imagine some body as a locus for His senses on the analogy of what we find in the case of causes in the world – not even that will save us. For if the Lord had a body, He would have experience of pleasure and pain, just like a victim of transmigratory life, and this would rob the Lord of His true nature as Lord.

And here is another argument to show that the Lord as imagined by the rationalists is an inadmissible concept. He is assumed by them to be omniscient and infinite. Nature, too, is infinite. And souls are infinite and are assumed to be mutually distinct. Let us ask, then, whether the Lord has any determinate cognition of Nature or of the souls or of Himself as "such and such", or whether He has not. In whichever way the question is answered, the conception breaks down. Suppose you accept cognition. Then Nature, the souls and the Lord must necessarily be finite, as they would be determinable as "such and such." For this is what we find in worldly experience. Any object, like a cloth, which is determinately known as "such and such," is seen to be finite. And following this rule, the triad of Nature, the souls and the Lord would have to be finite, as they would have been determinately known as "such and such." (315) From the point of view of number, too, Nature, souls and the Lord are limited, as they are only three. Their own intrinsic nature must be of limited dimensions, too, as the Lord is able to have determinate knowledge of them. And within the total number of the souls, which (is already finite because they) have been subject to determinate cognition, we find that, in the case of those who have been liberated, transmigratory life has come to an end. Their subjection to transmigratory life was finite. And the transmigration of the others, too, who are due to be liberated in the future, must be finite. Meanwhile Nature, with its evolutionary modifications, is (according to the doctrines under discussion) only presided over by the Lord for the sake of the souls and merely constitutes the field of transmigratory life. When (all transmigratory life, being finite, has ended, with the result that) Nature has disappeared, what would remain for the Lord to exercise His function of Lordship over? On what could He exercise His Lordship and sovereign power? If Nature, souls and the Lord thus have an end, they must also have a beginning. If they have a beginning and an end, you are landed in the doctrine of the Void.

To avoid this predicament, you might accept the other alternative and deny that the Lord has determinate cognition of Nature, souls and Himself. But this would involve you in the other fault of contradicting your own claim that the Lord was omniscient. So there are more reasons why the conception of the Lord as cause adopted by the rationalists is faulty. (316)

TEXT REFUTING THE PĀÑCARĀTRAS

We have already refuted the doctrine of those who hold that the Lord is not the material cause of the world but only the overseer and efficient cause. We now proceed to refute the doctrine of some who hold that the Lord is both the material cause and the efficient cause and controller. It is true that we have already explained how, on the authority of the Veda, the Lord is known to be just this very thing. We did so in the Sūtra, "He is the material cause as well." (317) And a Smṛti text which follows the Veda is accepted as valid. So why do we now wish to refute this very doctrine? The answer is that though *this* part of the doctrine we are considering is the same as our own, and therefore contains nothing to dispute about, other parts of it *are* subject to dispute, and it is for this reason that we embark on a refutation.

The Bhāgavatas (for it is them we are attacking) hold that the Lord, Bhagavān, is the One, Vāsudeva, of the nature of stainless Consciousness. He is the highest principle, the supreme reality. He has divided Himself fourfold into the four "Vyūhas" (serial, ordered, manifestations) known as Vāsudeva, Saṃkarṣaṇa, Pradyumna and Aniruddha. They say that Vāsudeva is the supreme Self, Saṃkarṣarṇa is the individual soul, Pradyumna is mind and Aniruddha is ego. Vāsudeva is the basis and material cause of the others, which are effects proceeding from Him. When a man has worshipped the Lord Bhagavān, thus constituted, with visits to His temple and gifts and oblations and recitals and meditation for a hundred years, his passions disappear and he verily attains to Bhagavān.

There are parts of this doctrine that we do not deny. We do not deny that Nārāyaṇa is the supreme Being, beyond the Unmanifest principle, (318) well known as the supreme Self, the Self of all. Nor do we deny that He has Himself divided Himself into various different Vyūhas. For there are Vedic texts confirming that the supreme Self assumes a manifold form, such as,"He assumes one form, He assumes three forms..." (319) Nor do we see anything wrong if anyone is inclined to worship Bhagavān regularly and one-pointedly by visits to His temple and the rest, for adoration of the Lord is well-known to be prescribed in the Veda and the Smṛti.

But when it is said that Saṃkarṣana emanates from Vāsudeva, Pradyumna from Saṃkarṣaṇa and Aniruddha from Pradyumna, there we have to be demur. For, as the author of the Sūtras puts it, the individual soul under the name of Saṃkarṣaṇa cannot emanate from the supreme Self, Vāsudeva, or it would suffer from transiency and other defects, and in that case its attainment of Bhagavān would not constitute liberation. It would merely be a case of an effect dissolving back into its material cause. And the author of the Sūtras will later deny that the soul is subject to origination of any kind, in the words, "The soul is not subject to birth, because that is not the teaching of the Veda, while it is known from those texts that it is eternal." (320)

And they make another wrong assumption, too. We never find in the world that an instrument, say an axe, springs from an agent, say Devadatta. (321) Yet the Bhāgavatas say that the instrument "mind", technically known as "Pradyumna", springs from the agent, the individual soul, technically known as "Saṃkarṣaṇa". And they add that the ego, technically known as "Aniruddha", springs from that "mind" which is alleged to spring from the agent (i.e. the individual soul). But we cannot accept this when such a thing cannot be corroborated by any worldly example and when we find no Vedic text to support it.

It might, however, be contended that Saṃkarṣaṇa, Pradyumna and Aniruddha are not meant to be interpreted as soul, mind and ego respectively. The idea, rather, is that they are all examples of Lords of the Universe, equipped with the attributes of knowledge, sovereignty, power, strength, heroism and splendour. (322) All are pure Vāsudevas, faultless, standing forth independently in their own right, above criticism of any kind. So it would follow that the difficulty about their being subject to birth does not apply.

To this we reply (in the words of the author of the Sūtras), "The difficulty is not removed." That is to say, the difficulty about their being subject to birth is not removed; it just comes up in another form. Let us suppose that the meaning is that Vāsudeva, Saṃkarṣaṇa, Pradyumna and Aniruddha constitute four separate Lords having the same qualities. Then in that case they cannot have one Self (as the system elsewhere maintains they do). And the assumption of a group of Lords of the Universe is a useless superfluity, since one Lord is quite enough to fulfil that function. And the opponent thereby contradicts his own fundamental position, as he maintains that it is the *one* Vāsudeva who is the supreme principle of reality.

Nor will it help the opponent if he says that the meaning is that these four Vyūhas emanate from the one Bhagavān with mutually identical qualities. For in that case the difficulty about the impossibility of their birth arises again. Saṃkarṣaṇa cannot spring from Vāsudeva, nor Pradyumna from Saṃkarṣaṇa, nor Aniruddha from Pradyumna, because (they are now being assumed to be of like qualities and so) the factor of the pre-eminence of one over another is missing. There must be a factor of pre-eminence in the material cause before there can be cause and effect, as in the case of clay and pot. But the followers of the Pāñcarātra doctrine do not admit any difference of degree in the knowledge and sovereignty, etc., of each or any of their four Vyūhas. They say that all are equally Vāsudeva. Nor can they ever be consistent about the number of "four" for their Vyūhas. For they also claim that all objects from Brahmā to the meanest clump of grass are Vyūhas (self-multiplications) of Bhagavān.

And there are also, as the author of the Sūtras points out, many other contradictions in the system. This appears evident, for instance, in the loose way in which they talk about substance and qualities. Knowledge, sovereignty, power, strength, heroism and splendour are qualities. But we find them also referred to as if they were each a self (ātman) in their own right, and called so many "holy Vāsudevas". There is also contradiction with the Veda. For we find passages decrying the Veda, such as the statement that Śāṇḍilya (323) turned to this tradition when he failed to find the highest good in the four Vedas. And therefore it has been shown that this fanciful doctrine (about the four Vyūhas, which has been conceived without regard to Upanishadic Advaita and which involves the view that the soul undergoes birth) is unfounded. (324)

NOTES TO CHAPTER X

(1) vedoṣarā vedāntāḥ, a view criticized by Kumārila, Tantravārttika p. 156 (2) Frauwallner, G.I.P. Vol. II p.19 (3) B.S.Bh. III.iii.53. The Prapañca Hṛdaya, Upāṅga Prakaraṇa, asserts that Upavarṣa composed a summary of the Kṛtakoṭi Comm. of Bodhāyana on all twenty chapters of the Mīmāṃsā Śāstra. This would indicate that they both regarded the P.M. Sutras and the B.S. as forming one connected work. See Budhakara, p.259, Nakamura, 1983, p.392. Rāmānuja quotes Bodhāyana as actually saying that the two complementary branches of enquiry formed one science, Darśanodaya, p.150. (4) Jha, pp.43-52 (5) B.S. II.i.33 (6) Jha, p.48, quoting Kumārila, Ś.V., Sambandhākṣepaparihāra 56 (7) vāvadūkāḥ, Bṛhad. Bh. I.v.18, trans, Mādhavānanda p.234 (8) Biardeau, Connaissance p.146 (9) Vetter, W.Z.K.S.O. 1968/1969, p.412 f. (10) Frauwallner, G.I.P. Vol.II p.185 and also Note 235 (11) Muṇḍ. I.ii.11 (12) Jha, p.361 (13) Biardeau, Connaissance, p.144 f. (14) Bh.G. II.42-5 (15) brahma-jijñāsā, B.S.I.i.1 (16) E.g. Bṛhad. II.iv.5 (17) Bṛhad. Bh. I.iv.7 (18) A short passage here has been transferred to Vol V Chap. XII Section 4. (19) Chānd. VIII.i.6 (20) Taitt.II.i. The Extract is from B.S. Bh. I.i.1 (21) B.S. I.i.4 (22) Jaimini's P.M. Sūtra I.i.1 (23) I.e. into injunctions indicating the manner of performance of, and benefits flowing from, the prescribed meditations on the symbolic significance of elements in the ritual, as opposed to the general enquiry about ritual that constitutes the subject-matter of the P.M. as a whole.
(24) Jaimini's P.M. Sūtra IV.i.1 runs: 'Then therefore the enquiry into what actions minister to the sacrifice and what actions minister directly to the needs of man.' The Mīmāṃsakas considered it useful to distinguish the enjoined actions which were mere preliminaries to some ritual, which

bore fruit as its reward, from the actions of the fruit-bearing ritual itself. Only those of the ritual itself "ministered directly to the needs of man." Keith, p.87. The Extract is from B.S.Bh. I.i.4 (25) The Mīmāṃsaka opponent's case has been set forth in B.S.Bh. III.iv.2-7. He argues (cp. Kumārila, Ś.V. Sambandhākṣepaparihāra verse 102 f.) that Upanishadic passages teaching knowledge of the Self must always be interpreted as subordinate to some injunction to act. They teach that the Self is distinct from the body, because only one who knows that his "self" is distinct from the body will engage in ritualistic action for benefits that will only accrue after the present life is over. The "self" in question is not transcendent, but is the ordinary individual self with which we are familiar, because it is referred to as "dear" at Bṛhad IV.v.6. Texts such as "free from sin", which describe it in terms implying transcendence, must be regarded as mere eulogies. As the prescribed meditations are, from the standpoint of the Mīmāṃsaka, not themselves complete rituals but mere subordinate elements in some ritual, any statements of "fruit" resulting from them, including knowledge of the "self" in this or that form, must also be regarded (from the P.M. standpoint) as belonging to the domain of eulogy. (26) I.e. not as the object of any action, but as that which remains over as reality when all illusions have been shed. (27) The P.M. opponent argues that the texts about the "self" promote ritualistic action by assuring the potential performer of the existence of an eternal soul, distinct from the body and able to enjoy the results of ritual after the present life. (28) B.S. III.iv.16, on which Śaṃkara comments in the second paragraph of Extract 5 below. (29) B.S. III.iv.1 (30) Muṇḍ. I.i.9 (31) Taitt. II.viii.1 (32) Chānd. VI.viii.11 (34) At B.S.Bh. III.iv.3 (35) The reading is uncertain, some think Kāṇva. (36) Aitareya Āraṇyaka II.vi.6 (37) *Viz.* that the results of all acts are temporary. (38) Kauṣītaki II.5 (39) The doctrine that a sacrificer creates by his sacrifices a "world" in which he is reborn is found at Śatapatha Brāmaṇa VI.ii.ii.27. More detail is found in Mus, pp.145 ff. and 166 ff. In the present work, texts in which Śaṃkara deals with the after-life of those who confine themselves to the performance of the ritual are found in Vol. V, Chapter XII, Section 1; those in which he deals with the ritualist who also practises symbolic meditations in Vol. VI, Chapter XIV. (40) Bṛhad. III.v.1 (41) Bṛhad. IV.v.15. I.e. Yājñavalkya taught that immortality depended on knowledge of the true nature of one's Self and not on action of any kind. (42) At B.S.Bh. III.iv.3 (43) Chānd. V.xi.5 (44) B.S.Bh. III.iv.8 and 9 (45) Bṛhad. IV.iv.22 (46) By denouncing them as mere eulogies. (47) Bṛhad. II.iv.14 (48) The celibate stages of life are all those other than that of householder. Where there is no permanent home there cannot be the permanent fires with which to perform the sacrificial ritual. Many of the rituals, too, imply the physical co-operation of the wife. (49) Bṛhad. IV.iv.22 (50) Jābāla Up.4 (51) To the ṛṣis through brahmacārya, to the gods through ritualistic sacrifices, to the ancestors through progeny. (52) B.S.Bh. III.iv.15-17 (53) Jaimini's P.M. Sūtra I.ii.1 (54) Taittirīya Saṃhitā (i.e. Black Yajur Veda) I.v.i. 1-2. The god Agni wept tears which turned into silver, and the text goes on to claim that this shows that silver should not be offered to the gods on the sacrificial grass. The Mīmāṃsakas take this as an "eulogy" (artha-vāda), in this case merely a fantastic story told to influence the sacrificer's conduct. See Āpa Deva, ed. Abhyankar p.266, trans. Edgerton p.179. (55) P.M. Sūtra I.ii.7 (56) Taittirīya Saṃhitā I.i.i.1, a formula used when cutting a twig to be used in the ritual. (57) Of Kumārila (Govindānanda) (58) Chānd. VI.ii.1 (59) Bṛhad. II.iv.14 (60) Chānd. VI.viii.7 (61) It is the view of an earlier Commentator (Vṛttikāra) which is being attacked, but there is some doubt about his identity. He was evidently later than Upavarṣa, as a little further on Śaṃkara makes him quote Śabara, who himself quotes Upavarṣa. (62) *Viz.* Jaimini and his Commentator Śabara. (63) Śabara on P.M. Sūtra I.i.1: Śabara on P.M. Sūtra I.i.2: Jaimini's P.M. Sūtras I.i.5, I.i.25 and II.i.1. (64) Bṛhad. II.iv.5, Chānd. VIII.vii.1, Bṛhad. I.iv.7, Bṛhad. I.iv.15, Muṇḍ. III.ii.9. The last text is not couched in the imperative, but promises a "fruit" and could therefore be regarded as presupposing an act. (65) Bṛhad. II.iv.5 (66) P.M. Sūtra I.i.1 (67) The *universally* experienced fruits of action are joy and misery. The fruit of knowledge is different, because it is only experienced by the enlightened one, not universally. Ānandagiri. (68) Taitt.II.8 (69) Chānd. V.X.1-2. On the Northern Path, the Path of the Flame, cp. Vol. VI Chap. XIV Section 3 below. (70) Such a meditation is described at Bṛhad. I.i.1 ff. (71) Chānd. V.X.3, cp. Bh.G VIII. 25. On the Southern Path, cp. below Vol.V Chap. XII Section 1, concluding Extracts. (73) Chānd. VIII xii.1. On the conception of being "bodiless", cp. Vol. VI Chap. XVI below. (74) Kaṭha I.ii.22 (75) Both pariṇāmi-nitya and kūṭastha-nitya are technical terms of the Saṃkhya school. The first applies to Prakṛti, which is eternal but undergoes change, the second to Puruṣa, which is eternal and also changeless. (76) Kaṭha I.ii.14 (77) Īśa 7. If there is no delusion on the part of him who sees all as one, then there is no nescience and consequently no action. (78) Chānd. VII.xxvi.2 (79) Nyāya Sūtra I.i.2 of Gautama. Wrong knowledge is not, for Gautama, the source of the appearance of the world of multiplicity. Multiplicity is real. Wrong knowledge is failure to understand the Nyāya system, and the consequent natural conviction that the self is the body. Removal of wrong knowledge permits removal of psychological defects, removal of these permits removal of interested action, removal of this permits removal of rebirth, this means removal of pain and that means liberation. (80) Performed in obedience to a Vedic injunction. (81) More detail on sampat will be found at Silburn, p.61 f. and Oldenberg, Brāhmaṇa Texte p.113, Note 2. (82) Bṛhad III.i.9. Vācaspati's Bhāmatī sub-commentary explains that the affirmation made in this text is not true, but that obedience to the injunction to dwell on it brings great rewards. (83) Chānd. III.xviii.1. Again, the point is that in these prescribed meditations the mind and the sun are *not* in fact the Absolute, but that meditation on them as such, in accordance with Vedic injunctions, brings valuable fruits. (84) Chānd. III.xix.1 (85) Chānd. IV.iii.1-3. If one meditates on the Vital Energy as an absorber (absorbing is its function at the time of death, when it absorbs the sense-functions, see below Vol. V Chap. XII Section 1) valuable fruits follow. (86) The Mīmāṃsaka view here combated maintains that the statements of the identity of the soul with the Absolute found in the Upanishad may be reduced to fanciful meditations observed for the mere purification of the sacrificer, and hence just subordinate elements in the ritual, like the ceremonial glance at the sacrificial ghee performed by the sacrificer's wife to purify that substance. (87) Chānd. VI.viii.7 and Bṛhad. I.iv.10 (88) Muṇḍ. II.ii.9 (89) Muṇḍ III.ii.9 (90) Part of the passage here omitted appears at Vol.I p.128, Extract 3, above. (91) Bh.G.II.25 (92) Muṇḍ. III.i.1 (93) Kaṭha I.iii.4 (94) Śvet.VI.11 and Īśa 8 (95) B.S. Bh. I.i.4 (selected) (96) The sub-commentators refer to Prabhākara and his followers. (97) See Bṛhad. III.ix.26. (98) *Ibid.* (99) Śvet. VI.11 (100) Kaṭha I.iii.11 and Bṛhad. III.ix.26 (101) Śabara on P.M. Sūtra I.i.1 (102) P.M. Sūtra I.ii.1 (103) Reading pravṛtti-nivṛtti-vyatirekeṇa (i.e. omitting vidhi-taccesa). Cp. S.S. Śāstrī and C.K. Raja, Bhāmatī, Catuḥsūtrī p.215. (104) Without which, according to the Mīmāṃsaka, a Vedic text cannot be regarded as an authoritative source of information (105) Here the injunction has the verbal form, "He should not look at the rising sun," but the accepted meaning is that he should positively occupy himself with some deliberate activity that would prevent him seeing the rising sun. Other "special cases" are certain words like "not-friend" (amitra) meaning a positive enemy and"non-meritorious"action (adharma) positive sin. Sac, Sūtra Bhāṣya Tattva Vivecanī, Vol. III p.204, (106) B.S.Bh. I.i.4 (selected) (107) This is Śaṃkara's own view of their function. The Mīmāṃsakas of his day were saying that the obligatory duties brought no reward, though their omission brought demerit. Śaṃkara rejected this view, cp. Bh.G.Bh. XVIII.6. (108) I.e. the Taittirīya Āraṇyaka, of which the Taittirīya Upanishad forms a part. (109) Taitt. II.1 (110) By the P.M. (111) Cp. Jaimini's P.M. Sūtra IV.iii.15, "There is no liberation other than heaven, that is the view of the authoritative interpreters." (112) If the series of births is beginningless, it must be assumed that they contain some very good and some very bad actions. The bad actions would give rise to experiences so different from those produced by the good ones that the two could not conceivably be experienced together in the same life. Since these actions are mutually contradictory in this sense, they cannot all become involved in any given birth. Hence they cannot be exhausted in one life, as the Mīmāṃsaka has just proposed. (113) Chānd. V.x.7 and Gautama's Dharma Sūtra XI.29. Cp. Note 128 below. (114) This is why desire for liberation is not classified as culpable attachment (rāga). Rāga is damaging because it is attachment *for the unreal*. Cp. Maṇḍana, B. Sid. p.3, line 17., Cp. p.56 below. (115) Cp. Bh.G.Bh. III.1 (introduction), trans. Shastri p.87. (116) Manu Smṛti XI.44, "Not doing the required actions , indulging in despicable actions, attached to sense-objects — in this condition a man falls into evil." (117) Śaṃkara proves this point when attacking the Sauntrāntikas, cp. below, p.273 . At present he is appealing to it to refute the Mīmāṃsakas' belief that non-performance of the ritual could *generate* demerit. (118) Taitt. Bh. I.1 (introduction) (119) Manu Smṛti II.165. The "secret parts" means the Upanishads. (120) On this Mīmāṃsaka view, self-knowledge is taught in the Upanishads so that a man will know that his "self" (regarded by the Mīmāṃsaka as the individual soul) is eternal, and so be prepared to carry out ritual which promises results in the unseen future. (121) The sources of these traditions are untraced. Gambhīrānanda suggests Bh.G. XVI.24 for the last. (122) Chānd. VIII.i.6 (123) Enjoined meditations and the merit to which they give rise are both spoken of in the Vedic texts as "knowledge" (vidyā etc.). The Pūrva Mīmāṃsaka with whom Śaṃkara is at present concerned, the Niyoga Vādin of Prabhākara's school, maintains that the only knowledge you derive from Vedic texts is knowledge of what to do. Śaṃkara here points out to him that the texts include references to enjoined meditations that are a form of "knowledge" which will not fit into this category. (124) It has to be admitted that injunctions to meditate on prescribed themes are found in the Veda and are traditionally referred to by the term "knowledge". If the Niyoga Vādin narrows down the meaning of the word knowledge elsewhere in the Veda to knowledge of the meaning of the texts giving commands, then these meditations must fall outside his scheme. As they are present in the Veda, they must be useful for something. And as they are not (according to him) useful for anything else, he must admit that they help towards liberation. (125) Bṛhad. II.iv.5 (126) Taitt. Bh.I.11 (127) Śvet.III.8 (128) Gautama Dharma Sūtra XI.29, quoted by Śaṃkara more fully in his Vivaraṇa on the Adhyātma Paṭala of the Āpastamba Dharma Sūtra. See Bhāgavat, Minor Works p.422, also Leggett, p.33 (129) The Agnihotra is not optional ritual, and no specific fruit is laid down for it. Yet it is taken as emblematic of ritual in general, which leads to heaven. (130) Any theory that can be shown to involve the futility of any part of the Veda is wrong, as nothing in the Veda can be useless. (131) I.e., if they are performed with the idea that they lead to a sojourn in heaven, this performance still counts as a daily obligatory performance, so that one does not incur the sin of omitting it. (132) I.e., the Mīmāṃsaka has put himself in the logically absurd position of saying that the same act causes different degrees of physical strain according to differences in the end for which it is performed. (133) Bh.G.Bh. XVIII.67 (introduction) (134) The Mīmāṃsakas thought of liberation as a kind of euthanasia. The soul was regarded as remaining in its natural state of being an individual, eternally existent and all-pervasive, but without contact with anything external through the medium of a mind or a physical organism, and therefore without consciousness or suffering. (135) Chānd. V.x.7, Āpastamba Dharma Sūtra II.i.ii.3 (136) I.xx.3 (Ed. Chinnasvāmī p. 112) (137) Śaṃkara uses the same argument to make the same point at B.S.Bh. II.iii.40, Gambhīrānanda p.498. (138) Śvet. III.8 (139) Cp. B.S.Bh. II.i.14 (Gambhīrānanda p.330) (140) Bṛhad. II.iv.14 (141) B.S.Bh. IV.iii.14 (142) It will emerge below at Vol V Chapter XII Section 3 that Śaṃkara thinks that the function of the obligatory ritual is the *purification* of the soul. (143) The classification of the four kinds of fruits of action is taken from the Mīmāṃsakas, for whom ritual purification formed a special category among the possible fruits of action (144) Saṃskāra, the polishing of the sacrificial post. (145) I.e to production, one of the four alternative results of acts earlier mentioned. (146) Bṛhad Bh. III.iii.1 (147) This theme is also found at Praśna Bh. VI.2, trans. Gambhīrānanda Vol. II p.490 and at Bṛhad Bh. II.i.20, trans. Mādhavānanda p.301 and *ibid.* III. ix.28.7, trans. p.565 (148) Cp. p.49 above (149) Muṇḍ I.ii.2 and Chānd. VIII.vi.1 (150) Chānd. VII.xxvi.2, VIII.xii.3 (151) Chānd. VI.ii.1, VII.xxiv.1: Bṛhad. II.iv.14 (152) "The person whom one wishes to connect with the object of giving is called the 'sampradāna' or recipient," Pāṇini I.iv.32 (153) For lack of an agent to carry them out (154) Because all the texts of the Veda, both those concerned with the ritual and those concerned with metaphysical knowledge, have the single aim of promoting man's welfare. (155) Taitt. Bh. I.11 (156) This is the only place where Śaṃkara fully enumerates the means of knowledge. The list at Muṇḍ. Bh. I.ii.12 lacks arthāpatti, presumption. Even the present list lacks anupalabdhi (perception of non-existence) amongst the terms usually enumerated by authors of Śaṃkara's school. But Śaṃkara accepted and used the latter term, cp. p.231 below. So exact enumeration of of the various means of knowledge was evidently not a subject to which he attached any importance, a fact which should be remembered when estimating the authenticity of certain elementary Vedanta text-books that have been attributed to his name. (157) The argument is: Every injunction in the Veda must lead to some fruit. No fruit is mentioned in conjunction with the daily rituals like the Agnihotra. Therefore their performance must be assumed to have the fruit of liberation. (158) No fruit is mentioned in the case of the Viśvajit sacrifice, and the rule here is that it must be assumed that heaven is the fruit. But this rule only applies in the case of ritual like the Viśvajit sacrifice, which has the general form of an optional sacrifice performed for a particular end, and where the statement of some particular fruit was consequently *to be expected*. According to the Mīmāṃsaka, the rule does not apply to the obligatory daily rituals, which are not "optional" but have to be performed daily. (159) The "World of Prajāpati" (or Brahma Loka) in the case of the meditation on the horse of the horse-sacrifice taught at Bṛhad. I.i.1 ff. (160) Bṛhad. I.v.16. The Extract is from Bṛhad. Bh. III.iii.1 (introduction). Passages from Kena (Pada) Bh. I.1 and Ait. Bh. I.i.1 are here omitted on the ground that they add little that is new. (161) Bṛhad. II.iv.5 (162) If the hearer were different from what he had to hear about there would be room for a distinction between the subject and the object of the hearing, and so scope for conceiving the hearing as an action, and as such, subject to injunction. R.T. (163) Bṛhad. II.iv.15 (164) U.S. (verse) XVIII.206-214 (165) Reading niṣkriyāyām jñāna-niṣṭhā-kriyāyām, quoted as an alternative in D.V. Gokhale's Ed. of the Bh.G.Bh. (Poona, 1931), p.281 (166) Bh.G.Bh. XVIII.67 (introduction) (167) Bh.G.II.33,II.47,

NOTES TO CHAPTER X

IV.15 (168) The killing of animals in the sacrifice, etc. (169) Bh.G.II.33 (170) Bh.G.II. 11.31 (171) Birth, existence, growth, maturation, decline and destruction. (172) Bh.G.II.39 (173) Bh.G.III.3 (174) *Ibid.* (175) Bṛhad. IV.iv.22 (176) Bṛhad I.iv.17 (177) Bṛhad. IV.iv.22 (178) Bh.G.III.1 (179) Bh.G.V.1 (180) The sub-commentator Ānandagiri explains: According to the implications of Jaimini's P.M. Sūtra I.i.2, only that action which is enjoined as a duty for those of a particular caste or stage of life counts as productive of merit. The knower of the Self ceases to identify himself with any particular body, and therefore with any caste or stage of life. He is therefore unable to qualify for any of the duties laid down in the Veda and Smṛti. His "action" is not the "prescribed action" meant by those who speak of liberation and arising through a combination of (prescribed) action and knowledge. (181) Bh.G. V.7 and XIII.31 (182) Bh.G IV.15 and III.20 (183) Bh.G. III.28 (184) Bh.G. V.11 (185) Bh.G. XVIII.46 (186) Bh.G. XVIII.50. (187) Bh.G.Bh.II.11 (188) He would have to do the heavy ritualistic and other duties of the householder plus the testing forms of asceticism laid down in the Smṛti for the forest life. (189) The previous sentence spoke only vaguely of a "combination", meaning in fact a regular progression from one stage of life to the next. The questioner seizes on the word "combination" and interprets it narrowly to mean a *simultaneous* combination of knowledge and action. (190) Bṛhad. III.v.1, Mahānārayaṇa Up. XXIV.1, XXI.2, X.5, cp. Kaivalya Up. II.3, Jābāla Up. 4. (191) Teaching given twice by Nārada to Śuka, M.Bh. XII.329.40 and XII.331.44, G.P.Ed. Vol. III, p.692 and 694 (192) The passage here quoted is found at Nārada Pārivrājakopanishad III.15, (Rāghorām p.244), but there it is Nārada teaching Śaunaka and other sages. (193) M.Bh. XII.241.7, G.P. Ed. Vol. III p.586 (194) Bh.G. V.13 (195) Chānd. VI.ii.2 (196) On the P.M. theory, to carry them out would be troublesome and would bring no positive reward, while to omit them would produce demerit and consequent suffering in a later life. (197) Demerit, being something positive, can only be generated by some positive force. Non-performance is nothing positive, so the only possible positive source for the generation of demerit is the injunctive text itself. But as certain Extracts in Vol. V Chapter XIII Section 3 will show, Vedic texts are not causal forces. They only exist to give information. The present Extract is from Bh.G.Bh. III.1 (introduction). (198) Īśa 12 (199) Īśa 9 (200) In particular, the longing to attain a higher world, and the longing for sons and wealth as a means to perform the necessary ritual to secure it. (201) That is, with his meditation on deities conjoined with ritualistic action as mentioned above. Sac, M.R.V. p.270 (202) This explains how Īśa 11 can attribute both Avidyā (nescience) and Vidyā (knowledge) to the same person without self-contradiction. It does so through regarding them, from the nescience standpoint of time, space and causation, as successive states. Sac, *ibid.* (203) G.K.Bh. III.25 (204) Darśanodaya p.92 (205) B.S. I.iv.20-21 (206) Nakamura, 1983, p.375 (207) For a detailed account of Bhāskara, see P.N. Srinivasachari *passim* and also Sac V.P.P. pp. 337-393. (Eng. trans. The Method of the Vedanta, pp. 470-545). His relationship to Śaṃkara is dealt with by K.Rüping (see Bibliog. to Vol I). (208) I chiefly follow Hiriyanna's "Bhartṛprapañca: an old Vedantin", reprinted as pp. 79-94 of his "Indian Philosophical Studies", Vol.I. (209) *Loc. cit.* p.91 (210) Above, Vol II, p.164 (211) On vāsanā = fragrance, cp. Vol. III Chapter IX Note 119 (212) "That is Infinite: this is Infinite. From the Infinite there arises the Infinite. When the Infinite is taken away from the Infinite, verily the Infinite remains." (213) The fact that Śaṃkara attributes an attack on illusionistic Vedanta to Bhartṛprapañca is further evidence that illusionistic interpretations of the Upanishads existed and were widely known before his day. (214) See Note 212 above. (215) On alternatives in this context, cp. B.S.Bh. I.i.2, Gambhīrānanda p.16 (216) The logical part of Śaṃkara's refutation of Bhartṛprapañca rests essentially on an appeal to the Law of Contradiction, taken ontologically as a Law of Being, saying that nothing can both have and not have a given characteristic in the same respect at the same time. (217) Bṛhad. IV.v.13, Muṇḍ. II.i.2, Bṛhad. II.iii.6 etc., Bṛhad III.viii.8 and IV.iv.25 (218) Memory implies that the one remembering is the same at two points of time, B.S.Bh. II.iii.25. On awakening from sleep we recognize our identity with the one who went to sleep. This Self is above the vicissitudes of time and change. (219) A theory which implied the non-eternity of the self or soul could not sustain the authority of the ritualistic portion of the Veda, which implies a permanent soul experiencing the fruits of its deeds in past lives and performing ritual for the sake of happiness in lives to come. (220) Bṛhad. IV.iv.13 (221) The bulk of the intervening portion of the text here omitted has already appeared at Vol. I Chapter II Section 4 Extract 5 (222) This would contradict the example of the sea, because the point of the latter was that the sea remained one. Reading "advaitam", not "dvaitam" as printed by Bhāgavat. (223) Bṛhad. Bh. V.i.1 (224) It must be remembered that Bhartṛprapañca sometimes uses the traditional technical terms of Advaita in a different sense from that of Śaṃkara. Here the term kṣetra-jña is used to mean jīva. Śaṃkara criticizes Bhartṛprapañca for distinguishing kṣetra-jña from paramātman, Bṛhad. Bh. III.v.1, trans. Mādhavānanda p.476 (225) Piṇḍa, Jāti, Virāṭ, Sūtra and Daivam. See above p.75f. (226) Conceivably a reference to Bhartṛhari, for whom Brahman, as the Indestructible (akṣara) was endowed with infinite powers (śakti). Cp. Iyer, p.283 (227) Bṛhad. III.v.1 (228) Bṛhad. Bh.II.i.20, see Extract 5 below. (229) Īśa 5 (230) Bṛhad. III.iv.1 and Muṇḍ. II.i.4 (231) Chānd. VI. ii.1. The Extract is from Bṛhad. III.viii.12 (232) Chānd. VI.i.4 (233) Chānd. VI.viii.7. The Extract is from B.S.Bh. II.i.14. (234) Chānd. VI.xvi.1 ff. (235) Bṛhad. IV.iv. 19 (236) B.S.Bh. II.i.14. (237) Śvet. VI.19 and Muṇḍ. II.i.2 (238) Īśa 8. The Extract is from Bṛhad. Bh. II.i.20 (239) Cp. Bṛhad. II.iii.1 ff. (240) That is, the "entire mass" of experience just described, cp. Sureśvara B.B.V. II.iii.114. (241) Who regarded the soul (puruṣa) as actionless pure consciousness, separate from the subtle body. (242) The Sāṃkhyas invoke a "subtle body" and place all psychical activity within it, leaving the soul (puruṣa) as actionless consciousness. The Vaiśeṣikas deny the existence of any subtle body, and make the individual soul itself the agent and enjoyer. (Frauwallner, G.I.P., Vol.II, p.65) Śaṃkara accuses Bhartṛprapañca of a mishmash of the two theories. (243) I.e at Bṛhad. Bh. II.i.20, Extract 5 above. (244) Contradicting Īśa 8 (245) Bṛhad. I.v.3, III.ix.20, IV.iii.7, IV.iv.7, IV.iii.22 (246) Bṛhad. Bh. II.iii.6 (247) Bṛhad. IV.iii.13 (248) Bṛhad. III.ix.28, Taitt. II.i, Ait. III.i.3 (or V.3). (249) The "speech-usage of the elders" was among the criteria accepted by the Mīmāṃsakas for determining the meaning of a word. (250) In the sense defined at Vol. II p.3 above. (251) Bṛhad. IV.iii.6 (252) The (fanciful) view of the Vaiśeṣikas, for whom see below, Chapter XI Section 4. (253) Bṛhad. Bh. IV.iii.30. The argument is directed to showing that because the supreme Self is declared in the Upanishads to be without parts, it follows that it cannot have various sub-species of consciousness, such as sight, tasting and hearing, as its qualities, in the manner claimed by Bhartṛprapañca, who here follows the Vaiśeṣikas. Śaṃkara considers (1) the ether and (2) the primary atom of the Vaiśeṣika theory as examples of partless things to which a variety of different qualities are commonly attributed. And he argues that they supply no example to support Bhartṛprapañca's conception of consciousness, as the attribution is in each case false. In regard to the primary atom of the Vaiśeṣika, Śaṃkara first shows that it cannot have *any* quality, and then afterwards argues *a fortiori* that it cannot have a plurality of qualities, in the way that Bhartṛprapañca attributes a plurality of qualities to the Self. Even if the earth-atom of the Vaiśeṣikas could have any quality at all, that quality could not be anything but odour, as all its other qualities derive from qualities belonging to other elements. More detail on the Vaiśeṣika system is given in the following Chapter, Section 4. (254) Sac in the notes to his ed. of the Kena Bh. sees here a reference to the teachings of Bhartṛprapañca. (255) For the Vaiśeṣika, the soul was *per se* non-conscious. Consciousness only arose in it due to contact with objects through the mind. And change was non-continuous. There would have to be an instant of non-cognition separating the loss of one cognition from the rise of another, though of course too short to be noticed in ordinary experience. (256) Kena (Pada) Bh. II.4 (257) Bhartṛprapañca is querying the meaning of the word "Absolute" in the phrase "Verily all this was the Absolute at the beginning," Bṛhad. I.iv.10. (258) Bṛhad. I.iv.9 (259) Here the words "dish of rice" appear grammatically as the object of the verb "is cooking", but in fact they refer to the rice not *qua* being cooked but to the future product that will emerge from the cooking. As words are sometimes used in this way, it is not altogether absurd to interpret the word "the Absolute" as meaning "He who will eventually *become* the Absolute." (260) Here the sacrificer, by definition a householder, only becomes a monk *after* the ceremony. (261) I.e. Bhartṛprapañca (262) Whereas the reward of knowledge of the Self ought to be better than the results of rituals, or no one would trouble to pursue it. (263) Bṛhad. Bh. I.iv.10 (264) Bṛhad. III.ii.11 (265) Bṛhad. I.iv.10 (266) Bṛhad. III.ii.13 (267) Anantakṛṣṇa Śāstrī, p.26. But this is disputed at S.L. Pandey, pp. 239 ff. (268) Sureśvara, S.V. 378, trans. Mahadevan, p.195 f. (269) Kumārila, Ś.V. Sambandhākṣepa Parihāra 103 (270) Ā.Ś.S. I.xvi.3, cp. Sureśvara, S.V.379 (271) Cp. Maṇḍana, B. Sid. p.27 and Bhāva Śuddhi Comm, for which see Anantakṛṣṇa Śāstrī p.116. (272) Chānd. III.xiv.2 (273) See Note 271 above. (274) S.V. 377-427 (275) Bṛhad. II.v.19 (276) Chānd. III.xiv.2 (277) Chānd. III.xiv.1 (278) Figurative interpretation (lakṣaṇā) plays a capital role in Śaṃkara's teaching, cp. Vol.VI Chapter XV Section 3 below. But although he uses the word several times in his works, it is noteworthy that he does not use it to characterize his own method. (279) B.S.III.ii.14 (280) Cp. above, p.11 (281) Chānd. VI.ii.1, VI.viii.7 (282) Bṛhad. II.iv.5 (283) See above, opening sentence of present Extract. (284) There is no unity of goal. Houseless renunciates qualify for the first class of texts: forest-dwellers practising symbolic meditations for the second: householders with various worldly and next-worldly aims for the third. Their desires, and therefore their "qualifications" for practice, are different. The renunciate wants liberation in life, some forest-dwellers want liberation at the end of the world-period, the remainder of the forest-dwellers, along with the householders, want prosperity (abhyudaya) in various forms in this world and the next. The lesser aims imply an actual contradiction with the highest aim of liberation. It is impossible to bring texts relevant to all these aims under one common injunction. (285) For example, Chānd. III.xiv.2. (286) B S.Bh. III.ii.21 (287) A full treatment of Upavarṣa is promised in the second (forthcoming) volume of Nakamura's History of Early Vedanta Philosophy. (288) Biardeau, Démonstration p.6 (289) Attempts are not usually made to translate this technical term into English. A particular school of the Indian philosophers of Grammar, of whom Bhartṛhari, late fifth century A.D., was the most eminent, evolved a theory that the element of a word or sentence which conveys the meaning cannot be the bare sounded syllables. The difficulty with the syllables is that they have to be pronounced successively in time, so that a polysyllabic word cannot be grasped in perception as a united whole, the earlier syllables having "disappeared" to make way for the last one. We must assume another element, they thought, called the "sphoṭa", over and above the mere heard syllables. It is in fact the most important element in a word or sentence, and the one through which the meaning is "explosively" (sphoṭa = an explosion or the bursting forth of a bud) manifested as an immediately comprehended unity. It is perhaps a little like saying that the fact that we can understand words or sentences at all implies that we are, in this particular area, endowed with some faculty like Spinoza's third kind of knowledge. Various forms of the theory of the sphoṭa are outlined in Kunjunni Raja pp.95-148. Professor J. Brough relates it to modern linguistic theories in the Transactions of the Philological Society for 1951, pp.27-46. On Bhartṛhari, consult K.A.S. Iyer, 1969, and M. Biardeau, 1964. (290) Smoke is a sign from which one infers the presence of fire. But this inference is only possible when (1) smoke is perceived in its totality and (2) its invariable connection with fire is previously known. Similarily, the opponent argues, a word only gives knowledge of its meaning when (1) the word is itself completely heard and (2) there is previous knowledge of its connection with its meaning. The theory that all we hear is the succession of syllables will not satisfy this requirement, as it does not explain how we perceive the word as a unit, seeing that the earlier syllables will have died away before the last is pronounced. The impressions of the syllables heard will at best produce recollection of those syllables in the order they were originally heard: it will not produce that simultaneous perception of them which would be required, according to the theory, if the syllables were to convey a meaning. (291) So that even the last syllable plus the memory-images of the previous ones will not together yield knowledge of the word as a complete entity. (292) On the ākṛti or generic form, see above, Vol. II Chapter VI Notes 177-9. (293) Śaṃkara is here reproducing the old view held by Śabara Svāmin, the chief Mīmāṃsaka Commentator. He held that sound was a property of the ether, and, like the latter, was one, partless and eternal. Though eternal, it is not continually heard because it requires to be manifested. In the case of speech, this manifestation is performed by the speaker. He sets up air-currents which radiate outwards in all directions. If these reach a hearer's ear, they open it in certain ways, and allow him to hear this or that syllable, which, as sound, is always present in the ether in his ear. See Frauwallner on P.M. Sūtra I.i. 6-23, W.Z.K.S.O., 1961, p.115 (294) I.e. even those who take the syllables to be different each time they are heard have to assume a generic form (ākṛti) to account for their being recognized, and have to assume that the notion of difference comes from an extrinsic adjunct over and above the generic form. Since one has to assume the presence of an extrinsic adjunct on both theories, it is simpler to drop the hypothesis of a generic form and maintain that the syllables are intrinsically identical whenever heard, the sense of their difference being due to an extrinsic adjunct. Of any two theories, *ceteris paribus* the simpler (i.e. the one involving fewest assumptions) is to be preferred. (295) An appeal to the Law of Contradiction - nothing can both have and not have a given character at the same time. The terms "acute", "grave" and "circumflex" refer to the pitch of the voice at which vowels were pronounced, which in the early phase of the language affected the meaning. Later, when the ancient texts came to be written down, the pitch could be registered by orthographic marks, conventionally called accents. These of course have nothing to do with the diacritical marks used in modern transliteration from Devanagari (Sanskrit) into Roman script, which are simply there to enlarge the Roman alphabet so that it can register the full range of vowels and consonants expressed by the Devanagari script. (296) It looks as though Śaṃkara, having faithfully expounded the old P.M. theory held in honour by earlier Brahma Sūtra Commentators, is here expounding his own preferred view, in the modest guise of an alternative. (297) B.S.Bh. I.iii.28 (298) Cp. above, Vol I Chapter I Section 3. (299) Cp. Gonda, Religions II p.262 (300) Kauṇḍinya's work is summarized at S.N.Das Gupta, Vol.V pp. 130-149. (301) S.K. Belvalkar, the Brahma Sūtra of Bādarāyaṇa, Part II p.126 (302) Yoga Sūtra I.24, Woods p.49 ff. (303) The Bhakti Sūtras associated with his name are earlier than the Nārada Bhakti Sūtras of the same school, the latter tentatively assigned to the tenth century A.D. Renou and Filliozat, Vol.I p.641 (304) B.S. I.iv.23 and 24 (305) The sub-commentators enumerate various Shaiva schools, but it has been thought that the technical terms used by Śaṃkara suggest that he may have had the Lakulīśa Pāśupatas chiefly in mind. Belvalkar, Brahma Sūtra, Part II p.125 (306) Paśu (= Latin pecus, cp. English impecunious) means literally "cattle", and Paśupati means cowherd. Rudra was the terrible deity called up in Vedic times to "protect" (i.e. not to smite) cattle, and the Pāśupatas took the function in an allegorical sense to mean "pastor of souls". (307) The Naiyāyikas and the followers of Patañjali's Yoga Sūtras. So Govindānanda's Ratnaprabhā Ṭīkā, *ad loc.* (308) In an attempt to take the sting out of the accusation of mutual dependence by denying that either the Lord on the one hand, or merit-and-demerit on the other, could be shown to have been originally dependent on the other. (309) Just as you can go on adding more and more men to your row of blind men grasping eath other's skirts without ever getting any light anywhere as long as the first man in the row is blind, so you can push back the problem of mutual dependence as far as you like into the realms of beginningless causation, without ever solving it. On the maxim, see Jacob, Handfull, Part I p.3. (310) Nyāya Sūtra I.i.18. Thus, even on the theories of the exponents of the World-Architect view of God themselves, God would be saddled with defects. (Bhāmatī) (311) Yoga Sūtra I.24, trans. Woods pp. 49 ff. (312) The distinction between contact and intimate inherence will be explained below, p.221 (313) In the Sāṃkhya system, it is considered legitimate to argue from a perceptible effect, namely the world of perceived objects, to an unperceived causal power called Nature (prakṛti, pradhāna), which is not perceived except indirectly through its effects. Śaṃkara is concerned here to deny that this mode of reasoning can allow the philosophers of the Yoga School to argue from the presence of the world of Nature as an effect to the existence of an invisible Lord as cause, if the latter is regarded, in contradiction with the Upanishadic tradition, as separate from the world of Nature and as a mere World-Architect. (314) The claim of the Sāṃkhyas that their doctrine emanates from an omniscient being (the seer Kapila) is also alluded to at G.K.Bh. I.I.I.17. Cp. p.155 (below) (315) I.e. by the omniscient Lord. (316) B.S.Bh. II.ii.37-41 (317) B.S. I.iv.23

NOTES TO CHAPTER X

(318) There is a reference here to the untraced Purāṇa verse which appears as the opening words of Śaṃkara's Bh.G.Bh. The verse is also quoted by his pupil Sureśvara at B.B.V. III.vii.40. (319) Chānd. VII.xxvi.2 (320) B.S.II.iii.17. Part of Śaṃkara's Commentary on this Sūtra has already appeared above, Vol.III Chapter VIII Section 1 Extract 7. (321) An agent resorts only to an instrument that is already in being. (Ānandagiri) "Devadatta" is of course just a typical name for a man, as we might use "Jones" or "Robinson". (322) These are the six attributes of holiness, which belong to anyone who possesses "bhaga" and is known as "Bhagavān". The present list of qualities is that given at V.P. VI.v.79. Slightly different definitions of the term Bhagavān are given in nearby verses, VI.v.74 and 78. Śaṃkara quotes these latter two at Bh.G.Bh. III.37 *ad init.* (trans. Śāstrī p.114), and he mentions the earlier of the latter two at Chānd. Bh. VII.xxvi.2 (*ad fin*, trans. Jha, Vol. II p.220) (323) The sage with whose name a set of Bhakti Sūtras are connected. Renou ascribes an "Identity-in-Difference" world-view to the Sūtras, for the date of which see Note 303 above. (324) B.S.Bh. II.ii.42-45.

CHAPTER XI

REFUTATION OF NON-VEDIC WORLD-VIEWS

1. DIALECTIC (TARKA): ITS PURPOSE AND RULES

Apart from various specialized uses of the term, dialectic in general, called tarka in Sanskrit, is defined as the art of philosophical argumentation, conceived especially as the effort to discover and eliminate contradictions in thought. According to Śaṃkara, the truth is already possessed in immediate intuition by all, but is obscured by nescience and false convictions. Being infinite, it cannot be encapsulated in any conceptual system. The "means of knowledge" (pramāṇa) relevant to the Infinite is not perception or inference but the authority of the Vedic texts, when the latter are interpreted *with the aid of* reason and *result in* immediate intuitional experience of the Absolute. The final awakening to Truth can only occur through the communication of the supreme Upanishadic texts by a qualified Teacher to a qualified pupil. In Śaṃkara's writing, therefore, the function of dialectic is confined to the removal of obstacles to the pupil's understanding of the true meaning of the supreme Upanishadic texts, particularly the obstacles arising from false convictions derived from the arguments of rival schools.

Indeed, the use of reason on the spiritual path has a remote and an intimate phase. The intimate phase, in Śaṃkara's eyes the more important, concerns the immediate causes of failure to understand the supreme texts, in particular the failure to isolate the texts concerned with the supreme goal from those that concern lesser goals, the failure to interpret them correctly once isolated, and the failure, due to the deeply-ingrained adverse prejudices of nescience, to attain an immediate realization of their truth even when they have been isolated and correctly interpreted. Śaṃkara recognized no distinction between really understanding the meaning of the supreme texts and having immediate apprehension of their truth, since they simply state the true nature of the hearer. The intimate phase of the use of reason, which ministers directly to the understanding of the supreme texts, will be dealt with in Volume V Chapter XIII and Volume VI Chapter XV.

Our concern in the present chapter, however, is with that more remote phase of the use of reason on the spiritual path which we have labelled dialectic (tarka). Here it has the purpose, not of guiding the pupil to an understanding of the texts, but of protecting him from false suggestions coming from outside the pale. Dialectic (tarka) in this sense involves the exposure of the logical fallacies of those who advance world-views based on perception and inference that contradict the highest teachings of the Upanishads. Amongst the Brahminical schools of this kind, who paid lip-service to the Veda, we find the dualistic Sāṃkhyas, whose philosophical tenets were also largely borrowed by the Yoga school, and the Vaiśeṣikas, whose philosophical tenets were largely borrowed by the Naiyāyikas and (to a lesser degree) by the later Mīmāṃsakas. The Materialists, Buddhists and Jainas evolved their teachings in conscious opposition to the Veda.

(XI.1) REFUTATION OF NON-VEDIC WORLD-VIEWS

Śaṃkara's refutation of the thinkers of the above-mentioned schools merely fills out and develops the work of refutation that is already present in nascent form in the Brahma Sūtras. The technique is essentially that of exposing the hidden contradictions latent in the opponent's view that he is himself not aware of. He either fails to remember that what he had said earlier has already sawn away the branch on which he is now trying to sit, or else he fails to see that the hidden implications of what he is saying now land him in contradiction with what is said elsewhere by his own school. The Brahma Sūtras had already charged the schools enumerated above (except the Mīmāṃsakas) with self-contradiction (pratijñā-hāni),(1) the fallacy of infinite regress (anavasthā), (2) and with inability to solve the same problem in one's own system for which the opponent is taken to task (sva-pakṣa-doṣa). (3)

In the course of his own refutations, Śaṃkara mentions a few maxims which help to limit the scope of fantasy in explaining worldly events on the basis of perception and inference. "There can be alternative views in regard to actions but not in regard to facts" (4) and "One cannot make hypotheses that contradict experience" (5) and "No entity is established as real from the mere fact that words are used to refer to it" (6) and "If it were possible to bring inexistent things into existence through the mere power of the imagination, everyone would realize his every desire." (7) These maxims, along with others of similar import, have been extracted from Śaṃkara's writings by Saccidānandendra Svāmin (8) to illustrate how far removed his teachings were from the construction and system-building of some of his later followers, who were prepared often enough to take words for things and to construct hypotheses on a very slender basis of direct experience. For example, Śaṃkara notes that ignorance and error are facts of immediate experience. He therefore feels justified in attributing whatever features of our experience are demonstrably illogical to ignorance and error, labelled nescience. But he does not first reify nescience into a kind of entity, in the manner of his followers, and then attribute to this imaginary entity the reality-grade of "indeterminable as real or unreal" and speculate about what powers it would have to possess it if it were to fulfil a cosmological function. (9) Once engaged in the construction of such theories, his followers became passionately involved in their defence, and the presence of conflicting theories in post-Śaṃkara Advaita is already a symptom of the loss of all reliance on the immediate intuition of the non-dual Self. (10) For Śaṃkara, the fact that Gauḍapāda exhibited in the third book of his Kārikās the conflict between the arguments of the "dualists" and the "nihilists" was an indication that their theories were false because based on enmity and passion (kleśa), and was at the same time an implicit eulogy of the Advaitin's vision-of-non-duality as that which was true because raised above all conflict and passion. (11)

Even in its negative function, dialectic tends to become an all-absorbing end-in-itself, in which the pursuit of the spiritual welfare of the ordinary pupil is forgotten. Consistent preoccupation with leading the average student (muṇḍa-buddhi) to immediate spiritual awareness seems to save Śaṃkara from any of the lapses into formalism and virtuosity which often beset the later dialecticians of his school. Śrī Harṣa (twelfth century), for instance, is prepared to display his ingenuity by examining the basic definitions of the Nyāya school *seriatim* and showing individually that each is circular or otherwise subject to refutation. (12) Śaṃkara is more selective. He tends to fasten onto a key point in the opponent's doctrine and rest largely content with a refutation of that. This is illustrated, for instance, in the special interest he pays, while refuting the Vaiśeṣikas, to their notion of "intimate inherence" (samavāya). For when this is seen to break down, their theory of the relation of a substance to its quality breaks down with it, along with their whole theory of categories. He himself speaks of the "collapse of the entire edifice (of the doctrine)" when "intimate inherence" is shown to involve infinite regress. Similarly, in refuting the various doctrines of the Buddhist schools, he lays considerable stress on establishing the empirical fact that we have experience of recognition, because if this one fact is admitted, the basic Buddhist dogma of the "instantaneity" and "uniqueness" of the real, conceived as the discrete and discontinuous point-instant, becomes hard to maintain.

Likewise in contrast with the formalism of later generations is the spirit of moderation with which he insists that he has no quarrel with any system except where it contradicts the highest teachings of the Veda. He can even quote the maxim, "where the doctrine of another school is not expressly negated, it may be taken as admitted." (13) It is in this spirit, for instance, that he remarks that though the Sāṃkhya must be rejected on its metaphysical side, it must be accepted as authoritative in its account of the play of the "constituents" (guṇa). (14).

One last point remains to be made before appending the short group of Extracts which will conclude the present section. As will become clear below, (15) Śaṃkara regards it as right to refute the opponent who resorts to mere perception, plus inference based on perception, by arguments derived from these sources alone. But one must not forget that he did not believe that mere perception and inference could of themselves lead to the final truth. Hence one must never take the theses he advances while combating an opponent on this basis to constitute his own final view, unless they can be substantiated from the non-polemical parts of his writings. As they stand, they merely represent counter-considerations which are enough to expose the inability of the theory under attack to account for the ordinary facts of experience. If, for instance, he refutes the Materialists's theory of consciousness through appeal to the theory that the facts of experience imply a self as a permanent substance that possesses consciousness and memory as its qualities, (16) it does not follow that he himself maintains this theory of the Vaiśeṣikas as an article of his own belief. Similarly, if he maintains against the Buddhist idealist (Vijñāna-Vādin) that the fact that we experience things as if they were external to consciousness is enough to show that they *are* external to consciousness, this is not to be taken as an assertion that anything external to consciousness actually exists, but only as proof of the failure of the idealist theory of the Vijñāna Vādins to account for the facts of experience. This is already clear from Śaṃkara's own text, to be quoted below, where he says that in refuting the existence of external objects the Buddha said something very close to the final truth, although no one can know the final truth except through the Upanishadic discipline. (17) And we have already had an instance (18) where Śaṃkara has claimed that the secular philosopher is unable to establish that God is the cause of the world for lack of any adequate empirical example to illustrate His causality, whereas the follower of the Upanishads is in a different position, as he has authoritative texts to this effect, and has only to show how they can be harmonized with each other and with experience.

TEXTS ON THE PURPOSE OF DIALECTIC

1. The aim of this school (i.e. Advaita Vedanta) is to explain the exact purport of the texts of the Upanishads, and not, like the school of the Logicians, either to prove or to disprove any

thesis by mere logical arguments. Nevertheless, those who wish to explain the meaning of the texts do have to refute the systems of the Sāṃkhyas and others, since they are potential obstacles to right vision. And so a new section (of the Brahma Sūtras) is opened with that intent. However, the effort to determine the meaning of the Upanishadic texts is undertaken for the sake of right knowledge, and therefore one's own position is established first through determining the meaning of the texts, for that is more important than the mere refutation of other views. (19)

Now, you might very well think that in order to expound right knowledge as the means to liberation for those who earnestly desire it, establishment of one's own position was all that was right or needful, and you might wonder why refutation of other schools was undertaken at all, as serving little purpose except provoking the enmity of members of those schools. There is truth in this. But it also happens that some of the less perceptive students of Advaita, hearing that there are various famous systems claiming to expound true metaphysical knowledge, such as those of the Śāṃkhyas and others, and that they have been championed by great men of past times, conclude that if you want right metaphysical knowledge that is the place to look. And because some deep reasoning appears to have gone into their making and they have had commentaries written on them by seemingly omniscient commentators, such souls begin to believe that they are true. That is why we now begin to demonstrate their hollowness.

Perhaps you will object that the doctrines of the Sāṃkhyas and others have already been refuted at such earlier Sūtras as "Not so: for it is not what Vedic revelation teaches, as we know from the reference to His 'taking thought'" (20) and others.... Why flog a dead horse?

Our reply is that the Sāṃkhyas and other such

rationalistic schools quote Upanishadic texts in support of their own positions and explain the quotations by twisting them round until they support their own theories. All that we have done in our argumentation so far is to show that these "explanations" are not real explanations. Now we are beginning an independent rational refutation of their systems, without any reference to the Upanishadic texts. That is what is new. (21)

* * * * *

2. It is only for the practical elucidation of the Vedic passages dealing with bondage and liberation of the Self that any distinctions are admitted in regard to it, and this only on the understanding that all such distinctions derive from extrinsic defining adjuncts (upādhi), themselves consisting in name and form set up by nescience. This view rests on the assumption that, though the Self is one, it appears in nescience to undergo a distinction according to whether the defining adjuncts of objects, consisting of name and form, are present or not. From the standpoint of ultimate truth, however, one must accept the sole existence of the one principle of Reality, unaffected by extrinsic defining adjuncts. It is to be taken as unborn, beyond danger and fear, beatific (śiva) and unfathomable by the mind of any mere logician. It is not an agent or experiencer, and the distinction between action, its factors and results does not apply to it. For in it all things are one without a second.

The Sāṃkhyas, for their part, at first took agency as well as action with its factors and results to be superimposed through nescience on the soul, the latter being pure consciousness. But, being outside the true Vedic tradition, they evinced at that point a lack of real courage in their own convictions, and proceeded to attribute empirical experience to the soul as the ultimate truth. They also set up a second real principle, Nature (pradhāna, prakṛti), over against the soul. Finally they fell into conflict with the special doctrines of logicians of other schools, and found themselves refuted under their attacks.

Afterwards, the logicians of other schools began to receive counter-refutations at the hands of the Sāṃkhyas, and both sides began thinking up new positions from which to refute the special doctrines of the other, and, as they both began to concentrate one-sidedly on those parts of their own doctrine that stood most in contradiction with the views of the other, they were both gradually drawn further and further away from the ultimate truth, like animals squabbling over a piece of meat.

True seekers of liberation, therefore, should pay no attention to their doctrines, but study rather the doctrine of the unity of all, which is the heart of the Upanishadic teaching. And if, to make this point clear, we say something about these theories now and again to bring out their defects, this does not mean that we take them at their own valuation as offering anything worthy of serious dispute. As someone has said in this connection: "Knowing that the faculty of forming opinions is a source of strife and contradiction, he who knows the true secret of the Veda gladly makes over his own power of forming opinions as a gift to the disputing philosophers and rests calmly without it, happy in the knowledge that it is in their tender care!" (22)

* * * * *

3. Dualists (23) such as the followers of Kapila (Sāṃkhyas), Kaṇāda (Vaiśeṣikas), Buddha and Mahāvīra (Jainas), etc.,each operate within the tenets of their own systems and feel quite sure about the framework of dogma created by them, and

on this basis they become attached to certain views and think that the truth lies there and nowhere else. If they find an opponent with a different view they feel animus against him, and thus come to engage in mutual contradiction and dispute as a means to demonstrate the truth of their own theory, afflicted by attachment and aversion.

Our own doctrine is not contradicted by any of these schools, but they contradict each other. Our doctrine, which derives from the Veda, is that of the unity and sole reality of the one Self, and as it implies that we are non-different from all else, nothing can conflict with it, nothing can refute it, any more than we can ourselves be in conflict with our own hands and feet. The right view, then, is that of the unity and sole reality of the Self, because it is not rooted in psychological defects like love and hate. (24)

* * * * *

4. Daylight is the means whereby all beings apprehend colours. But owls and some other species cannot see colours by its aid. From this we conclude that the eyes of owls and similar species are different from those of other creatures. But this does not permit us to assume that the eyes of owls and similar species are able to perceive the objects normally perceived by other organs, for instance to savour tastes; for the power to savour tastes, along with the remaining powers of sense-perception other than those of the eye, are never actually observed to belong to the eyes of owls. When assuming the presence of any unusual power in an entity (on the grounds that certain phenomena would be "inexplicable otherwise"), one cannot go beyond what one has actually observed in it, though within this limit one may search as far as one likes. (25)

* * * * *

5. If a body of people engaged in a discussion decide to reject what is otherwise universally accepted as true, then no demonstration or refutation that is made within that circle will constitute an intelligible proposition, either for the speaker himself or for the other disputants. One should only advance that of which one can say, "This is verily so." Anyone who speaks of anything else is merely proclaiming his own verbosity. (26)

* * * * *

6. The author of the Sūtras then shows how the characteristic assumptions of the Vaiśeṣikas do not hold, adopting the standpoint and methods of those (the Vaiśeṣikas) who hold them. (27)

2. REFUTATION OF MATERIALISM

Materialism, in India as elsewhere, is of early origin and apt to be associated with statecraft. In the Rāmāyaṇa, (28) a Brahmin priest and ministerial counsellor has to be rebuked by Rāma for trying to lure him back to the throne in contravention of his vow of voluntary exile. The counsellor's arguments are based on the typical doctrines of Indian materialism. He argues that there is no soul, that rituals in general and ceremonial offerings to the dead in particular are a device by the priests to extract an easy living from the gullibility of the people, and that, since there is no after-life and no moral law, the purpose of life is the extraction of the maximum possible sense-pleasure from the body. The setting of the story might suggest to the modern reader that the poet was aiming to edify his hearers rather than to record an actual historical incident, but it testifies to the existence at the time of its composition of court-priests who were ready to give advice to their regal patrons on coldly materialistic lines. The connection between materialism and political counsel is confirmed by the classical text on Political-Economy, the Artha Śāstra attributed to Kauṭilya (perhaps late fourth century B.C.), in which the young prince is recommended to sharpen his wits and prepare himself to rule by studying, among other things, the doctrines of the Materialistis (lokāyata). (29)

No texts of the school have survived, (30) so the teachings have to be reconstructed from the reports of opponents. A fairly lively representation of what one presumes to be the typical sayings of the school is given in the opening chapter of the Sarva Darśana Saṅgraha of Sāyana-Mādhava (fourteenth century). Three quarters of the chapter consists of pungent and often virulent attacks on the Brahmins, partly expressed in what appear to be very ancient verses, some of which are also quoted by the professional Materialist (Cārvāka) who appears in Act II of Kṛṣṇa Miśra's allegorical drama "The Rise of the Moonlight of Enlightenment" (tenth century) or occur in the Viṣṇu Purāṇa. (31) The remaining quarter consists of an arid disquisition on the impossibility of establishing universal laws for inference. It is couched in the dry style of a later epoch, and testifies to the longevity and continuity of the materialist tradition in India.

There are only two passages of any length in which Śaṃkara deals with the Materialists, whom he labels Lokāyatas ("Positivists") and Svabhāva Vādins ("Naturalists"), to say nothing of the well-conceived pun of calling them "Māṃsa-Mīmāṃsakas" or "Flesh-Philosophers" that has come down to us in what is probably an apocryphal work bearing his name. (32) Lokāyatas, Svabhāva Vādins and Nāstikas (negators of the Veda) had originally been separate groups with slightly different aims, but had come to be thought of collectively as constituting one school by about the beginning of the Christian era. (33) They developed a set of aphorisms (sūtra), which were attributed to Bṛhaspati, legendary Counsellor to the gods.

Materialism did not aspire high as a philosophical system in pre-Śaṃkara times, and its adherents were handicapped, in the wave of epistemological enquiry that took place after 500 A.D., by their conviction that perception alone was a legitimate source of knowledge, not inference. (34) Though they were regarded as a danger, not only by the Brahmins for mocking Vedic ritual and the after-life but also by the Buddhists and Jainas for their attack on the doctrine of karma and moral responsibility, they do not seem to have been felt as a very great threat by Śaṃkara, and we can leave him to tell us what he wishes of their doctrines, without filling in any details from other sources.

TEXTS REFUTING THE MATERIALISTS

1. There are some, the Materialists (Lokāyata), who identify the soul with the body and do not believe in the existence of any soul separate from the body. They maintain the thesis that consciousness, though not observed universally in the five elements of the external world either individually or as a whole, nevertheless exists in those elements when they evolve into organic form. And they further hold that consciousness rises up from the elements in the form of intelligence (under certain conditions) like the power of intoxication arising from certain ingredients (which ferment into alcohol when placed together in certain proportions), and that man is his body associated with consciousness. They do not admit the existence of a soul over and above the body that might confer consciousness on the body and attain either to heaven or to liberation (on the demise of the body). On the contrary, they claim that it is the body alone that itself constitutes both consciousness

and the soul. And the reason they give for this is that consciousness is invariably found in a body. For the principle holds that whenever one thing is invariably present in the presence of a certain other thing and invariably absent in that thing's absence, the first thing must be taken to be a property of the second, even as heat and light are properties of fire.

Those philosophers who argue in favour of the existence of a soul, say the Materialists, hold that the Vital Energies, the fiat of the will, consciousness, memory and so on are properties of the soul. But the truth is that these must be properties of the body, for they are only perceived as being inside the body and are never perceived outside it, while the existence of any substance other than the body supporting them has never been demonstrated. Therefore the soul is nothing other than the body.

To this we reply: Your statement that the soul is nothing other than the body is not correct. It *must* be other than the body. For there are cases (such as death) where the body is present but the soul is not. If the Materialist concludes that the properties of the soul (35) are really properties of the body because they are present when the body is present, he ought likewise, by parity of reasoning, to conclude that because they are sometimes *not* present when the body is present (36) they are not properties of the body.

And there is the additional reason that they are quite different in nature from the body. The properties of the body, such as colour and form, etc., last as long as the body does. But the Vital Energies and the fiat of the will (conceived here in the manner of the Vaiśeṣikas as properties of the soul) are not verified after death, whereas the body is. And again, the properties of the body such as colour and form are perceived by others, whereas consciousness, memory and the other properties (regarded by the Vaiśeṣikas as) belonging to the soul are not. Moreover, the existence of these properties can be ascertained as long as the body is present in living condition, but there can be no proof of their non-existence when the body is not so present. When the present body dies, it can very well be supposed that the properties of the soul are transported to another body and come to animate that. This mere possibility is enough to refute our opponent's thesis (that the properties of consciousness, will, etc., that are usually attributed to the soul, must really be properties of the body, for lack of any other conceivable support).

Moreover, the Materialist ought to be asked what is the exact nature of that consciousness which he supposes to be exuded from the elements. For he does not admit the existence of any other principle apart from his four elements. He will perhaps try to define consciousness as consisting in the mere fact that the elements and their products are experienced. But then they would have to be its object, and it could not be a property of them at the same time, for it is contradictory to suppose that anything can act on itself. (37) Fire may be hot, but it cannot burn itself, and not even the cleverest acrobat can climb up on his own shoulders. And, in the same way, the elements and their products cannot form objects of consciousness if consciousness is their property. A colour does not perceive its own colour or the colour of anything else. And yet there is no doubt whatever that the elements and their products *are* perceived by consciousness, both inside and outside the body. Because, therefore, the presence of a consciousness which takes the elements and their products as its objects has to be admitted, it follows that it has likewise to be admitted that consciousness is distinct and separate from them.

As for our own view, (38) we (Advaitins) hold

that the soul (i.e. the Self) is of the very nature of consciousness, (39) and that it is separate from the body for this very reason. Consciousness is eternal and constant, because it is invariably identical, also because we recognize ourselves to have been the same perceiver in quite different times and circumstances, as revealed in the phrase "It was I who saw this", and also because the fact of consciousness being eternal and constant supplies the only possible explanation of memory and similar phenomena.

The view put forward that consciousness was a property of the body because it was "invariably found in a body" should be regarded as having been refuted by the present line of reasoning. Suppose one were to grant that perception only occurred in the presence of external auxiliaries such as lights and to assume for argument that it did not do so in their absence, it would not follow from this that consciousness was a property of the external auxiliaries. In the same way, even if perception was only present when the body was present and was not present when the body was absent, it would not follow from this that consciousness was a property of the body. For the body might very well be regarded as an auxiliary in regard to it, just like the lights and other instruments. Nor is it true that the body is *invariably* an auxiliary to perception. For in dream, when the body is actionless (in the sense that the external senses of perception are inactive) we find various perceptions in evidence. Hence the view that the Self is distinct from the body is unassailable. (40)

* * * * *

2. But when speech has stopped, along with all external supports (to the senses) such as (objects in the form of) odours etc., (41) it might be supposed that all human activity would have to stop

too. What the Upanishad says to meet this is as follows. In the realm of waking-experience, the sense-organs, such as the eye, are directed outwards and receive help from luminaries like the sun. Here a man enjoys vivid experiences. Thus it stands proved that in the waking state the accomplishment of what requires light proceeds from some light that is other than the complex of one's own body, mind and limbs. And from this we regard it as proved that even when, as in dreams or dreamless sleep, or in any condition resembling either of these two that might occur in the waking state, all external lights have ceased, the accomplishment of what requires light still proceeds from some light that is other than the complex of one's mind, body and limbs. And we see, also, that in the case of dreams, accomplishment of what requires light does indeed take place in the form of meeting and parting with relatives and travel to other lands. And (the same is also true of dreamless sleep, for) we wake up from dreamless sleep with the thought, "I slept happily, I was aware of nothing." (42)

But what then is that light which remains after speech has become silent? The text replies, "The Self, verily, is his light." By "the Self" it means that light which is different from the whole complex of the body-mind and the organs and limbs, which illumines them as if it were an external light like the sun, and which is not itself illumined by any other principle. Yet it must still illumine them from within, as this is now the only possibility left. For we have seen that it is other than the complex of the body-mind and its organs. And *external* (physical) light, which is different from the complex of the body-mind and its organs and helps their work, is itself found to be perceived by the eyes and other senses. But that light which remains after the sun and all external lights have disappeared is not thus subject to perception by the senses. However, because the effects of such a light are found, we must conclude that it is verily through the Self (as a transcendent principle beyond the body-mind complex) that one has the inner light wherewith one sits, goes out, does one's work and lives. And from all that it is clear that the light must be an internal one, and that it is different in kind from that of the sun and other external luminaries, and is not physical. And this is the reason why it is not perceptible to the eye and the other senses, as the sun and other external luminaries are.

To this a Materialist might object that the case was otherwise. For the principle has been observed that it is always like that helps like. The notion that one has been able to prove the existence of any internal light different in kind from the physical light emitted by the sun and other bodies is quite mistaken. The complex of the body-mind and its organs is material throughout. And whatever support is given to them is likewise material in kind, and is given to them by the sun and other luminaries, which are material in nature. This is certainly what we ought to infer from what we actually see. Even if there were a separate auxiliary to the body-mind complex and the organs, in the form of some luminary (internal and different from the sun but) illumining them like the sun, we should still have to infer that it must be of like nature with the body-mind complex (i.e. material). For the mere fact that it was an auxiliary to the body-mind complex at all would be enough to show that it was material, just like the sun. As for your (i.e. the Advaitin's) statement that it must be different in kind because it was not subject to perception and functioned from within, that falls to the ground on account of the contradictory example of the eye and the other sense-organs. For the light of the eye and other sense-organs, though immediately evident (43) and functioning from within the body, is material in character. So your view that there exists a non-material light called "the Self" is shown to be a mere fancy.

And again, (if we are to use inference at all) we should infer that the light under discussion must be a property of the body-mind complex. For it only exists in and through that complex. But an inference based on mere analogy (44) has no probative force, as it is always liable to error. And the inference by which you prove the existence of a light other than the mind-body complex, and illumining them like the sun, is precisely of this kind.

Moreover, the (Materialist continues) inference cannot contradict direct awareness. And it is directly evident that it is the complex of mind and body and organs which sees, hears, thinks and knows. Even supposing it did receive help from some other luminary, just as it receives help from the sun, that luminary could not be the real self of the individual receiving such aid, since it would be *another* light, just like the sun and other external luminaries. But only that which can be directly perceived to do the work of seeing, etc., is the real self of the individual. And that is the body-mind complex and nothing else. For a mere inference has no probative force if it contradicts direct awareness.

Perhaps you (i.e. the Advaitin) will ask how it could be that the Self, if it is just the complex of body, mind and organs, could, since it is admitted to be the agent in all cognitive activity such as seeing, etc., sometimes exercise this agency and sometimes (as in dreamless sleep) not. But there is nothing wrong in our position here. For it is seen to be so. And what is actually seen is above criticism. In the case of a fire-fly, for example, we do not have to affirm any external cause when we actually perceive it to be both luminous and not-luminous. And if we had to infer an external cause on the basis of mere analogy, anything could be inferred as the basis of anything, an unacceptable principle. Nor is it right to say that the objects do not have intrinsic properties of their own. (45) The heat of fire is not introduced into it from any other cause from without, nor is the cooolness of water. (46) Nor can you say that all changes in the world depend, not on the nature of the objects which change, but on (such extraneous factors as) the merits and demerits of living beings. For that merit and demerit would have to depend on another cause, namely the natural properties (svabhāva) of things. And this would lead to infinite regress (in that merit and demerit would be conditioned by natural properties and natural properties by merit and demerit), and that is unacceptable.

But we Advaitins reply that all this argumentation is contradicted by the fact that in dream and memory one sees only what has been seen before. The Materialist's (svabhāva-vādin) doctrine that seeing and the other forms of perception pertain to the body alone and not to any separate principle is wrong. If the activity of seeing, etc., belonged to the body alone, then, (since the body of waking experience is absent in dream,) sight in dream would not be confined to what had been seen before (because it would be a novel creation). But even a blind man seeing a dream sees only what he has seen before, and not scenes in (outlandish realms like) Śāka Dvīpa. And from this we draw the following conclusion. He only (i.e. the dreamer, separate from the body,) who sees the previously-seen object in dream is the one who saw it in the first place, when in possession of his eyes. It cannot have been the body that did so. If it had been the body which first saw it, then, when a person had lost the organ of sight whereby he first saw it, he could not again see that previously-seen object in a dream. And yet even those people in the world who have lost their eyes do have such experiences as, "Today I saw in a dream that Himalayan peak that I saw of old." (47) And from this we conclude that, even when sight has not been lost, in that case, too, the one who sees the dream must be the one who saw (the objects previously). And he is not the body.

Similarly, in the case of memory, the seer and the rememberer are the same, so that it is only the one who saw that remembers, and no one else. From this it follows that even one whose eyes are closed sees whatever he remembers just as he saw it before. But what is "closed" cannot be the seer. We conclude that that which sees a form in memory when the eyes are closed must be the same as that which saw it when the eyes were open (and therefore other than the eye).

Moreover, when the body is dead it has no cognitive action like seeing of forms, etc., even though intact in all its parts. If the body were really the seer, it would continue with seeing and other cognitive activities even when dead. It follows that that only is the agent in seeing and other cognitive activities in whose presence in the body they occur, and in whose absence there they do not occur. And this principle cannot itself be the body.

You cannot say that it is the various senses that are themselves the agents in seeing, etc. For if the agent in the activities of the different senses were different in each case, the memory expressed in "I am now touching what I formerly saw" would be inexplicable. Nor can the mind be the agent in the act of knowing, since it is itself an object of knowledge, and therefore could no more take on the role of the subject than any other object, such as a patch of colour. Therefore the inner light under which cognitive and other activities take place is different from the body, mind and organs, just like the external luminaries such as the sun.

What was said about the internal light having to be inferred to be of like kind with the complex of the body-mind and senses, because luminaries like the sun, which aid the sense-organs, etc., are like them (i.e. physical) – that was wrong. For there is no universal rule to say that that which receives aid and its auxiliary must be of like nature or of different nature. Grass and straws, etc., all products of the element earth, are seen to co-operate as fuel in the production of fire. But this would not justify us in inferring that auxiliaries for producing fire were always of the same species (i.e. that they were always products of the earth-element). For it is seen that fire, both in lightning and in the digestive processes of the stomach, is aided by the different element water. So that there is no rule that the auxiliary and what it aids should either be of like nature or of different nature. Sometimes men are aided by their own kind in the form of other human beings, sometimes by beings of a different kind, such as material objects or animals. So the argument, "Because the complex of the body and its organs is aided only by things of like kind (i.e. physical things) like the sun, etc., (it cannot be illumined by any non-material inner light)" is no argument at all.

And then there was another point you made. We had argued for the presence within of an inner light, different in kind from the body-mind complex and its organs, because such a light was evident but not perceived by the eye or the senses, as external luminaries like the sun were. This you denied, on the ground that the eyes, etc., possessed their own subtle light that was material in character yet not subject to perception. But this argument is useless. For all we have to do is to emend our own statement by the inclusion of the words "other than the eyes and other organs." Your statement that the light was but a property of the body-mind complex was wrong, for it is contradicted by inference. We have already put the inference, "The light is different from the body-mind complex from the mere fact of being light, just like the light from the external luminaries such as the sun."(48)

Your view that the light is present whenever the body-mind complex is present rests on a false premise, for the light is not present when the body is present but dead. And if, as you tried to claim, analogical reasoning has no probative force, then all worldly activities, beginning with eating and drinking, would be at an end, and that is unacceptable. For if it were true we ought not to find people resorting to food and drink to appease their hunger and thirst on the mere ground that it had done something similar before. But the fact is that people who have once taken food and drink are seen to reason analogically later that their present hunger and thirst will be appeased by food and drink and to act accordingly.

As for the view that it is the body alone that is the agent in cognitive activities like seeing, etc., this has already been refuted by our demonstration that the seer in the case of dream and memory must be different from the body, which has likewise refuted the contention that the inner light (of dream) could be other than the Self. Your attempt to point to the firefly as something alternately luminous and non-luminous by its very nature was also unfounded. For its apparent alternations of luminosity and non-luminosity are caused by external factors, the contraction and expansion of its wings and other limbs. (49) Nor have you any right to say that, if merit and demerit necessarily bring results, "natural properties" (svabhāva) have to be admitted. For merit and demerit find no place in your system. And this also refutes your charge of infinite regress on this head. Hence we conclude that there exists an inner light different from the body-mind complex, and that it is the Self. (50)

3. REFUTATION OF THE SĀṂKHYAS

The remaining sections of the present chapter are taken up with Extracts covering fairly comprehensively the statements and logical refutations given by Śaṃkara of the doctrines of the Sāṃkhyas, Vaiśeṣikas, Buddhist schools and Jainas. The order follows that of the "Tarka Pāda" of the Brahma Sūtras, the second Quarter (Pāda) of the second Book (Adhyāya), in which the Sūtras pass over from defending the Upanishadic texts against the wrong interpretations of the Sāṃkhyas to a refutation of the above-named systems as such. The Extracts will include almost all the material from Śaṃkara's Commentary on this philosophically important section of the Sūtras, with the addition of a few further relevant passages from the Upanishad and Gītā Commentaries and the Upadeśa Sāhasrī. One cannot burden the present book with a rounded account of each of the systems Śaṃkara is attacking, for which the reader must turn to the standard surveys of Indian philosophy. But the Extracts in each section will be provided with a few pages of introductory material designed to give some glimpse into the circumstances in which the doctrines Śaṃkara is attacking arose.

The Sāṃkhya system as we know it stands expressed in the 72 Kārikās (verses designed to be memorized) of Īśvara Kṛṣṇa, of which the last three are generally regarded as later additions. According to a recent estimate there are grounds for thinking that this work may have been already regarded as a standard authority as early as 300 A.D., (51) though it has also been claimed that it was not in existence at the time Nāgārjuna composed his Mādhyamaka Kārikās, at a date estimated by Frauwallner as about 200 A.D. (52) Several Commentaries on the Sāṃkhya Kārikās have survived, of which the Tattva Kaumudī of Vācaspati is the most famous, while the anonymous Yukti Dīpikā (mid-sixth century) is regarded as the most informative. By the time of these commentaries, however, the creative work of the system had been done, and they merely elucidate the doctrine as it lay in the Kārikās, defending it here and there against the views of rival systems. A rather earlier figure of some importance is Vindhyavāsī, active *circa* 425 A.D. Apart from certain modifications that he introduced into the doctrine as it stood in the Kārikās of Īśvara Kṛṣṇa, modifications designed to help defend the Sāṃkhya teaching against the attacks of the Vaiśeṣikas and Buddhist schools, Vindhyavāsī either influenced the commentator on the Yoga Sūtras called Vyāsa, or else, according to some, actually *was* that commentator under a different name. (53) We shall be noting passages in his attack on the Sāṃkhyas in which Śaṃkara refers directly to Vindhyavāsī's views. Vindhyavāsī defeated Vasubandu's Teacher Buddhamitra in a debate held at Ayodhyā *circa* 425 A.D., but with the defeat of the later Sāṃkhya Teacher Mādhava by the Buddhist Teacher Guṇamati (*circa* 500 A.D.) the Sāṃkhya tradition appears to have passed into eclipse until it was revived many centuries after Śaṃkara's death in the so-called Sāṃkhya Sūtras, a work that is unknown to, and therefore presumed to be later than, the author of the fourteenth century Sarva Darśana Saṅgraha. The main Commentator of the new school was Vijñāna Bhikṣu (*circa* 1450), who took over a good deal from the Vedanta in its theistic form.

Unlike the Vaiśeṣikas, Buddhists and Jainas, therefore, the Sāṃkhyas were a spent force by the time Śaṃkara came to attack them. There was no one like the Naiyāyika Jayanta Bhaṭṭa or the Mīmāṃsaka Śālikanātha to come back after Śaṃkara's time and defend the Sāṃkhya standpoint against all comers. The great creative work of the Sāṃkhyas belonged to an altogether earlier epoch. The works of the two main Teachers who evolved and expounded it, Pañcaśikha and Vṛṣagaṇa, have been lost, and the Kārikās of Īśvara Kṛṣṇa are probably to be regarded as no more than a systemization and brief summary of their views. Frauwallner has referred to the desperation with which the Sāṃkhya Teachers after Vṛṣagaṇa tried to combat their opponents with twists and turns and concessions, (54) suggesting that it was a symptom of the decadence into which the system had already fallen. We shall see that the fact that the various Sāṃkhya Teachers offered conflicting solutions to the same problems was one of the charges levelled against them by Śaṃkara himself. (55)

But this decline may be regarded as no more than a natural regress from the wonderful success enjoyed by the system in earlier times. It was too deeply rooted in ancient ways of thinking to be able to make a credible adaptation to the more exacting critical standards attained by the Vaiśeṣika and Buddhist logicians in the sixth century A.D. When we look back over the earlier period of Indian spiritual teaching and tradition, we see that for long the Sāṃkhya was the dominant Brahminical system, so much so that a large part of the Law-Books, Epics and Purāṇas, including the Bhagavad Gītā, had to be given in the terminology which it had evolved. Neither Vaishnavism nor Shaivism, nor even the Upanishads of the so-called "Middle Period", escaped. What with all these foreign adaptations of Sāṃkhya teaching, it is clear that we have to reckon both with a variety of loose religious forms of the doctrine, and also with a stricter philosophic form, which itself underwent development and bifurcation into sects, but which eventually emerged encapsuled in the Sāṃkhya Kārikās as what is conventionally referred to as the "classical" form of the Sāṃkhya system.

Professor Frauwallner believes that it is possible to trace some kind of a thread leading straight on from the teachings of Yājñavalkya in the early Upanishadic period right through till the final summary of the Sāṃkhya teaching in the Kārikās of Īśvara Kṛṣṇa. An important stage is marked by a certain group of texts in the Śānti

Parvan of the Mahābhārata, not quite the earliest, where the deeper implications of Yājñavalkya's insistence on the transcendence of the Self are realized, and the Self (ātman) is relieved of all its active functions. The world and its objects are traced to the play of the five Great Elements. Within every body, within every mind, stands the one Self as the actionless Witness. Those mental modifications which bring joy are called the "state of goodness" (sattva), those associated with sorrow are traced to "passion" (rajas), those which are dull or obscure are taken as "darkness" (tamas). The Self cannot know its own true nature as long as it looks outwards through the mind and senses. But when the mind withdraws the senses from their activity, the Self stands revealed like a flame. (56) These texts express the implications of Yājñavalkya's doctrine of the transcendence of the Self more rigorously than those of the Bṛhadāraṇyaka Upanishad itself, as they derive the senses and the mind alike from the play of the external elements and not directly from the Self. The goal of the teaching is direct apprehension of the Self, for all other experiences bring pain.

But Professor Frauwallner thinks it is possible to trace another stage in the development of the Sāṃkhya system, which he associates, "as a working hypothesis", with the name of Pañcaśikha, though G. Oberhammer has suggested that the texts attributed to Pañcaśikha may in fact have come from Vṛṣagaṇa. (57) Here the implications of Yājñavalkya's teaching about the transcendence of the Self are again taken seriously, but because the reality of the world is accepted, the source of the evolution of the latter is found in a totally distinct entity. The world is made to unfold from and in Nature, much in the same way as it had in the Upanishad been made to unfold from and in the Absolute, while the Self is seen as the actionless spectator. Uddālaka had spoken, in the Chāndogya Upanishad, (58) of three elements or divinities from the intermixture of which all objects of the three worlds proceed, and these three basic elements now re-appear under the name of "guṇas" or "constituents". Later the three constituent elements in Nature came to be somewhat differently conceived. They were named "sattva", "rajas" and "tamas" because their interplay evoked in the mind of the experiencer the three feeling-states already associated with these three names. (59)

A doctrine of an eternal cycle of evolutions and involutions of the world out from and back into the Absolute had been taught in early Mahābhārata texts. When the Absolute "awoke" to project forth the world once more, the first evolute was the principle called "the Great One" or "Mahat"; from this principle proceeded "Mind", from which in turn proceeded the elements from which the world was ultimately composed. (60) In the form of the Sāṃkhya doctrine that is tentatively associated with the name of Vṛṣagaṇa, "Knowledge" or "Intellect" (buddhi) proceeded as the first evolute from Nature in much the same way as "Mind" had formerly been considered to proceed from the Absolute at the beginning of the world-period. But if Nature can have a cosmic Intellect it can equally well have a cosmic Ego (ahaṃkāra), and this is the next principle in the Sāṃkhya system, from which the elements on the one hand, and the senses that apprehend them on the other, both proceed. That two such different series as the elements, the source of the known objects, and the senses, the "powers" through which they are known, should both be able to proceed from the same principle, the Ahaṃkāra, is made possible by the theory of the constituents, according to which the elements proceed from the "tāmasika" aspect of Ahaṃkāra, and the senses from the "sāttvika" aspect, while the organs of action are supplied by the "rājasika" element. It was at this stage of the development of the system that the term "Puruṣa" or "man" was substituted for "Ātman" or "Self", (61) the world-process being conceived as the outcome of the union of a male with a productive female principle (prakṛti).

It is clear that a Sāṃkhya doctrine of the kind must have gained prevalence well before the time of the Śvetāśvatara Upanishad, which has been tentatively assigned above to the region of 300 B.C., (62) and the name of Pañcaśikha is connected in several Mahābhārata texts with that of Janaka, (63) which would take him back to the time of Yājñavalkya himself, who may have lived about the eighth century B.C. No real credence, however, can be placed on the texts connecting Pañcaśikha with Janaka, as the name of Pañcaśikha is frequently associated with other legendary or half-legendary figures, while the tradition preserved in Aśvaghoṣa's Buddha Carita connects the Buddha (*obiit circa* 478 B.C.) with a Sāṃkhya Teacher who expounded the system in a form which did not yet recognize the doctrine of the "constituents". (64) Perhaps, therefore, the form of the Sāṃkhya that we are now associating with the name of Pañcaśikha took shape somewhere about 400 B.C., though this is, of course, a mere guess. At all events, it seems certain that Sāṃkhya Teachers holding a dualistic form of the doctrine were claiming the right to interpret the Upanishadic texts according to their own system. They eliminated the Absolute as a conscious principle in favour of their own conception, non-conscious Nature, the material cause both of the world and its objects and also of minds and their modifications. It was chiefly to restore the Upanishadic monistic doctrine at the expense of the dualistic interpretations of the Sāṃkhya philosophers that the Brahma Sūtras were composed. And, as we have seen, (65) the original core of the Brahma Sūtras could well have come into existence before the Christian era.

A yet later stage of the Sāṃkhya doctrine is that associated with the Ṣaṣṭi Tantra of Vṛṣagaṇa, of which the Sāṃkhya Kārikās of Īśvara

Kṛṣṇa are said to be a summary. Even this form of the doctrine appears to have arisen fairly early, as it is referred to by Aśvaghoṣa in his Buddha Carita, composed about 75 A.D. (66) One change that took place in the doctrine at this stage is of particular importance for us, as it helped to make the Sāṃkhya more remote from Upanishadic conceptions. The general trend in the Upanishads was to conceive the individual soul as a "spark" or "ray" of some greater principle that stood beyond and above man as an individual. (67) And in the earlier form of the Sāṃkhya system, the "Puruṣa" in all individual organisms was conceived as a supra-individual principle and as one. This conception was finally given up, however, possibly through a failure to answer the attacks of the pluralistic Vaiśeṣikas. (68) And the Sāṃkhyas were left with the unlikely conception of an infinite number of distinct individual souls, each all-pervading, each of the identical consistency of "pure consciousness". This is one of the developments of the doctrine associated with the name of Vṛṣagaṇa.

With this short preliminary survey, we can allow Śaṃkara to take over the statement and refutation of the Sāṃkhya system, so far at it suited him to do so. A large part of the first Book of the Brahma Sūtras is occupied with refuting the "atheistic" interpretation of the Upanishads offered by the Sāṃkhya system, which shows that the doctors of the Sāṃkhya school had set themselves up as exegetes of the Upanishadic texts, eliminating the Absolute (brahman) in favour of their non-conscious principle, Nature. It is known that the Sāṃkhyas opposed the performance of Vedic ritual and the accompanying donations to the priests. (69) What had begun as legitimate creative extension of Upanishadic speculation degenerated into an obviously vulnerable rationalistic system, while claiming descent from the Vedic sage Kapila and consequent orthodoxy. As the Mahāyāna Buddhists retreated from preoccupation with mystical experience to preoccupation with the epistemology of empirical experience, (70) so the Sāṃkhyas, while retaining their concern with liberation, retreated from the intuitional vision of the earlier post-Upanishadic period to the view, expressed by the school of Vṛṣagaṇa, that liberation arose through discrimination in the form of *logical* thinking and the formation of cosmological hypotheses. (71) Śaṃkara wanted to sweep away these ideas once and for all to make sure they could never again become an obstacle to the traditional discipline of the Vedanta. So in the Commentary on the second Book of the Brahma Sūtras he states the core of their doctrine and refutes it on purely rational grounds.

TEXTS REFUTING THE SĀṂKHYAS

1. In this connection the Sāṃkhyas hold the following views. We find in the world a variety of clay objects such as pots and dishes which all have the nature of clay and are associated with the one universal principle clay. And we must likewise accept that all the various objects of the world, both physical and mental, have the nature of pleasure-pain-delusion, (72) and are regularly associated with the one universal principle "pleasure-pain-delusion." That universal principle of pleasure-pain-delusion is Nature (pradhāna), consisting in the three "constituents"(guṇa). Non-conscious like clay, it undergoes transformation (vivartate) (73) into variegated modifications to serve the ends of the conscious soul. The existence of Nature has to be inferred from such signs as the presence of transformation (from which we deduce the presence of a hidden substance undergoing transformation).

To this we answer that if the reasoning here be by analogy from example of what we see in the world, then no example is found in the world of any non-conscious entity producing modifications to serve the various ends of the soul, except when it is under the influence of some conscious being. Objects which promote joy or dispel pain, such as houses, palaces, beds, seats, pleasure-gardens and the like, are invariably observed in the world to be the work of intelligent craftsmen, each on a particular occasion. But the case is quite different with this whole external universe that we perceive, consisting of all the objects of the five elements that are needed from the enjoyment of the fruits of all deeds, as also of this whole universe of persons with bodies, senses and minds, distributed according to various castes, and each equipped with a highly organized physical vehicle (body) to serve as the locus of the experience of the fruits of manifold previous deeds. Nothing so highly organized as this could be so much as conceived by the most potent intelligent craftsmen imaginable. How then could a non-conscious principle like Nature not merely conceive it but actually bring it into being? We do not see such feats performed by clods of earth or stones. Inanimate substances like clay, too are only found to assume special forms under the control of some intelligent craftsman, such as the potter: which suggests that Nature, too, is controlled by some conscious being different from itself. Nor is there anything to show that the root cause of the world must be conceived solely in agreement with the inherent properties of insentient material causes in the world, such as clay, to the exclusion of the qualities (such as intelligence) of external efficient causes like the potter. Nor would any contradictions result from assuming that a conscious being was at work. On the contrary, such reasoning would support the Veda, as it would make provision for a conscious cause.

Hence the Sūtra (74) says, "And because such a cause could not compass the formation of the universe." For this reason, that is, one should not infer a non-conscious cause of the universe (such as the Nature of the Sāṃkhyas). The word "and" in the Sūtra hints, further, at a fault in another part of the Sāṃkhya's reasoning, his reference, namely to "regular association with the one universal principle of pleasure-pain-delusion." (75) For the various objects of the physical and mental world cannot all be regularly associated with the one universal principle of pleasure-pain-delusion, for pleasure, pain and delusion are apprehended as belonging to the mental world, while the objects of the external world are perceived as being of a different nature from pleasure, pain and delusion and as being the causes that bring the latter into being. That pleasure, pain and delusion are one thing and the external world quite another is also clear from the fact that when a single state of the external world is the common environment of several observers, there can be differences of pleasure, pain and delusion amongst those various observers on account of differences of mental attitude.

A further point is that if from observation of the fact that all limited effects involve a composite cause (saṃsarga), as in the case of the seed and the sprout, (76) one infers that the cause of the whole world and of external objects and mental phenomena (i.e. Nature and all its evolutes) must also be composite (composed of the three constituents, sattva, rajas and tamas), because it is also limited, then it would follow that the constituents sattva, rajas and tamas themselves must also have a composite cause, since they, too, are limited.

And again, since the relation of cause and effect is seen to subsist in the case of things like beds and seats which have been made through intelligent foresight, one cannot conceive the entirety of the objects of the external and mental worlds as proceeding from any non-conscious principle, as they, too, belong to the domain of cause and effect.

But let the question of compassing the formation of the world pass. Activity is needed to bring it about, and this already implies the fall of sattva, rajas and tamas from their primeval state of equilibrium to a state of imparity tending towards action in pursuit of particular ends. But no such thing is intelligible if Nature is taken as both spontaneous in its activity and non-conscious. We do not see change or motion in non-conscious objects like clay or chariots, in the absence of any influence of some conscious being (to form them into pots or draw them along the ground respectively). Non-conscious as they are, clay and chariots are not seen to engage in action for particular ends except under the influence of some conscious being like the potter or the horse. And in cases (such as the nature of the world-cause) where we cannot see, we have to reason by analogy with what we do see. Hence it is wrong to infer a non-conscious cause of the world, because such a cause could not act.

Perhaps you will say that we do not see action on the part of a being that is pure consciousness either. This is perfectly true. Nevertheless we do see action on the part of chariots and the like when they are linked to a conscious being, while we admittedly do not find activity in the conscious being thus linked to the non-conscious, if the conscious being is considered strictly in its nature as consciousness. How is this to be interpreted? Should we say that the activity belongs to that which is seen or to that which has to be linked to the thing seen as the necessary pre-condition of the movement?

Perhaps you will say that activity must belong to that in which it is seen, as both the activity and that in which it is seen are, after all, objects of direct perception, whereas the conscious entity as such is not directly observed as the abode of the activity in the way that chariots and the like are. The conscious entity, you will perhaps say, is only known to be present as linked with a body, etc., while the latter is the abode of the activity. For the existence of a separate conscious entity (puruṣa) is only inferred by us (Sāṃkhya philosophers) as connected with a body and organs specifically engaged in action, since a living organism of this kind is perceived to be different from non-conscious things like chariots. (The existence of a conscious entity separate from the body is thus only established by us by inference.) That is why the Materialists (who do not accept the validity of inferences claiming to establish the existence of things that are never perceived) are able to argue that, since what is seen exists and what is not seen does not exist, it follows that consciousness must be a property of the body alone, since that is all we directly perceive. So we should conclude that activity belongs (where it is seen, namely) to the non-conscious object.

To this we reply as follows. We do not say that activity does not belong to the non-conscious object in which it is seen. Let it do so. But what we insist on is that it proceeds from consciousness. For when consciousness is present there is activity, and when it is not present there is no activity. It is like the case of a piece of burning wood. The piece of wood is observed to undergo modification in the form of throwing off light, etc. But since this only occurs when it is burning, it proceeds from the burning, being found when the burning is found and not otherwise. Our view that consciousness is the source of activity is not even contradicted by the doctrine of the Materialists, when they maintain that it is the body *as consciousness* that prompts activity in non-conscious objects like the chariot.

Here you will perhaps object that the Self as we (Advaitins) conceive it, though linked to the body and senses, cannot itself indulge in activity, as it is nothing but (77) pure Consciousness, and hence that it cannot be the source of activity in others either. But this is not right. For magnets, and colours, etc., can be the source of activity even when themselves without activity. The magnet promotes activity in the iron filings without itself acting. And objects like colours, even though themselves non-active, can elicit activity from sense-organs such as the eye. In just the same way the Lord, the Self of all, Omnipotent, Omniscient, Omnipresent, can be the source of all activity without acting Himself.

Nor will it do to suggest that, since He alone exists, He cannot promote activity in others, on the ground that nothing else exists apart from Himself in whom it could be promoted. For we have repeatedly exposed the fallacy of such an idea, by explaining how He is associated with an illusory display (māyā) of name and form set up by nescience. Thus activity is explicable if the cause of the world be the omniscient Lord, but not if it is the non-conscious Nature of the Sāṃkhyas.

But why should not non-conscious Nature act spontaneously to serve the ends of the soul, just as milk, though non-conscious, flows spontaneously to serve the nurture of the calf, (78) or as non-conscious water flows spontaneously in rivers for the good of the people? This will not do either. For we infer that even the milk and the water have to come under the influence of some conscious being before they can act. Both of us, the opponent must acknowledge, agree that original activity is not found in non-conscious objects like the chariot. The Veda also teaches that all motion in the world proceeds under the influence of the Lord, in such texts as "He who, dwelling within water, controls it from within" and "At the command of this Imperishable One (akṣara), O Gārgī, some rivers flow to the east." (79) So it was a mistake, says the Sūtra, to bring up the examples of milk and water, as they tell equally in favour of our own thesis, In the case of the milk, it is perfectly intelligible that the cow, a conscious being, should impart flow to the milk through its own tender desires, especially as the milk is already under attraction from the sucking of the calf. Even the water is not absolutely independent in its flow, as it needs a declining slope and other favourable factors. But dependence on a conscious being is a constant feature (of all activity), as we have already shown.

Of course, it is quite true that an earlier Sūtra (80) ran, "If you say that the Vedic Absolute (brahman) cannot be the cause of the world because (in the case of a conscious efficient cause) we regularly find resort (to instruments, whereas it is not admitted that the Absolute resorts to instruments), we reply that you are wrong, for the process is conceivable on the analogy of (the flow of) milk (from the udders of a cow)." But this was only advanced from the standpoint of secular reasoning to show that an effect can take place of its own accord without the need for external compulsion. From the standpoint of Vedic revelation, however, all things depend on the Lord, and this doctrine we in no way abandon.

The "Nature" of the Sāṃkhyas is the three "constituents" (initially) in a state of equilibrium. Nothing external to them exists, either to promote activity in Nature or to help bring it to an end. The soul stands indifferent, neither prompting activity nor causing cessation from activity, so that Nature is independent in regard to taking up or leaving off action. But, if Nature is independent in this regard, it cannot be right to affirm that Nature sometimes undergoes transformation (pariṇāma) into the Cosmic Intellect (mahat) and other evolutionary forms of Nature, and sometimes does not. But taking up activity and desisting from it can occur without contradiction in the case of the Lord, since He is Omniscient and Omnipotent and possessed of the great power of Māyā.

Well, say our opponents, we can let that pass, but what about the following. Grass, foliage and water, etc., transform themselves (in the stomach of the female ruminant) into milk, and this quite spontaneously and without the help of any external cause. Why, then, should not Nature transform itself into the Cosmic Intellect and other forms in the same way? We know that the grass and the rest require no external cause to help them, as nothing of the kind is actually observed. If we knew of one, we could combine it with the grass and the rest and manufacture as much milk as we liked, but actually we are not able to do any such thing. So it follows that the transformation of grass and the rest into milk is spontaneous, and Nature may undergo transformation in a similar way.

To this we reply as follows. We might allow that Nature could undergo spontaneous transformation in the manner of grass and the rest if it could be shown that grass and the rest really underwent spontaneous transformation! But in reality they do not, for we have knowledge of an external cause. We possess this knowledge indirectly. It arises (as the Sūtra puts it) "Because they do not transform themselves into milk elsewhere." That is to say, they become milk only when actually eaten by a cow, not when refused by a cow or eaten by a bull, etc. If the transformation were purely spontaneous it would not only take place in the body of a cow, but in other places as well.

Nor is the fact that it cannot be manufactured by men a sufficient reason to prove that it arises spontaneously. Some activities arise from men, some from cosmic forces (daiva). And in any case men *can* produce milk from grass and the rest along with the appropriate means. For if they want extra milk they simply give the cow extra grass, and it is seen that they actually get it. So that it follows that Nature cannot be said to undergo spontaneous transformation in the manner of grass and the rest.

We have now established that the activity of Nature is not spontaneous. Let us now, for the sake of argument, suppose, according to your belief, that it was. But even then further defects appear in your theory. Why? The Sūtra replies, "For lack of any purpose." If you say that the activity of Nature is spontaneous and requires no external cause, it is as much as to say not only that it requires no auxiliaries but also that it requires no final cause either, and this amounts to a contradiction of your own dogma that Nature acts to fulfil the ends of the soul.

The Sāṃkhya philosopher will perhaps reply that Nature can dispense with auxiliaries but not with final causes. In that case the final cause that prompts Nature to act will have to be specified as either the enjoyment of the soul, or the release of the soul, or both. But what could it mean to speak of the "enjoyment" of the soul when the latter is conceived as unable to receive any alteration from without? (81) And if Nature acted for the enjoyment of the soul (to the exclusion of other ends) the soul could never be released. And if Nature worked solely for the release of the soul, then, because release would already be realized before the activity of Nature began, all its activity would be useless. Moreover, if this view were true we ought never to perceive any world of objects. And even if it be taken that Nature works for *both* the enjoyment *and* the release of the soul, the case is no better. For one thing, since the number of things produced by Nature to be enjoyed is infinite, there would be no release (as enjoyment would be never-ending). Nor could Nature suddenly decide spontaneously to liberate the soul in the way that people act spontaneously to relieve their desires, (82) for a non-conscious entity like the Nature of the Sāṃkhya philosophers could not conceive desires — and neither could the soul on their theory, as it is partless and stainless consciousness. If the Sāṃkhya philosopher were to say that we have to assume that activity originates in Nature somehow, as otherwise the power of vision in the soul and the power of self-projection in Nature would be useless, we reply that if such powers really existed in the soul and in Nature in the way the Sāṃkhya supposes them to, then the power of self-projection would be as ineradicable in Nature as the power of vision would be in the soul, and there would be no possibility of liberation. So it is not correct to say that Nature acts for the sake of the soul.

Very well, the Sāṃkhya may say, but listen. It is possible with the help of further examples to rehabilitate the view that the soul causes Nature to act. It does so as a lame crippled man, who yet possesses the power of vision, can prompt to action a blind man who is physically active, (83) or as a magnet, while itself remaining motionless, can provoke activity in the iron filings.

We reply that even this provides no escape from the charge of faulty reasoning, the fault consisting in contradicting your own system. For you maintain that activity arises spontaneously in Nature and that the soul does not prompt anything to activity. And how, indeed, could the soul prompt to act when it is represented as "indifferent" (udāsīna)? (84) The lame person prompts the blind person with words and the like.

But the soul cannot (on your view) indulge in any such prompting activity, because it is actionless and without any qualities. Nor does it prompt to activity through its mere presence, like the magnet. For if it did, activity in Nature would be constant and eternal, (85) since the soul is ever-present in Nature. The magnet, on the other hand, is not in constant proximity with the iron, so that the fact that it sometimes comes into proximity with it depends on our activity, not to mention the need for rubbing and exact adjustments of position. Hence the Sūtra says that there is no argument for the prompting activity of the soul on Nature to be extracted from the examples of the lame man or the magnet.

Thus Nature is non-conscious, the soul is indifferent, there is no third thing to connect them, and so they cannot come into relation. And, if they were related by nature, they would always be related, and there would be no release. And we have to understand that here, as before, the absence of any intelligible purpose in the activity of Nature, either to promote the enjoyment or the liberation of the soul, or both, is also part of the argument suggested by the Sūtra. But in the case of the supreme Self of the Upanishadic doctrine, there is an extra factor. The Self is indifferent (actionless) in its own true nature, but prompts to activity as associated with the power of Māyā.

And there is yet another reason why Nature (as conceived by the Sāṃkhyas) cannot enter on activity. Nature properly so called (pradhāna) consists in that state of the three constituents (guṇa), sattva, rajas and tamas, in which they have lost their state of imparity and rest in equilibrium in their natural state. In that state, they each have their independent nature; and they cannot be supposed to enter any state implying dominance or subservience among themselves, on pain of forfeiting that independent nature.

Hence, on account of the absence (in addition) of any external instigator, the Cosmic Intellect and other transformations (taught by the school) could never arise, for their rise depends on a state of imparity arising from the constituents.

The Sāmkhya will perhaps now say that he can formulate his inference a little differently and in such a way as to avoid the last objection. We do not, he will say, conceive the constituents (guṇa) as being of an independent nature, changeless and imperishable (kūṭastha), as there is nothing to prove that they are so. We conceive their nature according to their effects. We build up our view of them according to the effects we see arise from them. And the view at which we arrive is that they are changeful. And from this we conclude that, even in their state of equilibrium, the constituents remain capable of a shift to imparity.

But even on this assumption the defects mentioned earlier, such as the inability of Nature to compass the formation of the world in the absence of any intelligent power, still remain. And if you argue from this to the presence of an intelligent power, you abdicate from your position as our opponent (and set yourself up as a new adherent of our own view). For the view that one conscious principle (the Absolute) is the source of the manifold universe is the doctrine of the Upanishadic Absolutism (brahma-vāda). Besides, even if the constituents were in principle capable of a shift to imparity from the state of equilibrium, they still could not enter into imparity in actual fact, for lack of an efficient cause. Or if they did, they would always be in a state of imparity (which would render impossible the very thing the Sāṃkhya sets out to teach, namely release from transmigration and pain). So it follows that our last objection (that the Cosmic Intellect and other transformations could not intelligibly arise) holds after all.

And the assumptions of the Sāṃkhya are mutually contradictory. Sometimes they speak of the "senses" (indriya) as seven, sometimes as eleven. (86) Sometimes they teach that the subtle elements proceed direct from the Cosmic Intellect (mahat), (87) sometimes direct from the (subordinate principle the) Cosmic Ego (ahaṃkāra). (88) And in the same way, they sometimes speak of three "inner organs" for the human individual, (89) sometimes of only one. (90) As for the contradiction that their doctrine presents with the Veda and Smṛti, both of which speak of God as the cause of the world, it is too notorious to need any special stress here. So these are some further reasons for rejecting the doctrines of the Sāṃkhyas.

Here our opponents interpose (91) and say that if the truth be told the doctrine of the Vedāntins has to be rejected too, because it fails to recognize that the one who undergoes suffering and the one who causes suffering cannot be the same. Those who affirm the one Absolute (brahman), the Self of all, as the cause of the whole appearance of plurality, cannot accept that the one Self contains two distinct principles, the one undergoing suffering and the one causing suffering respectively. Or, if it did possess them, it could never be liberated from them, and the revealed Vedic teaching how suffering can be brought to an end through right knowledge would be useless. A lamp, which has heat and light for its properties, cannot be freed from them, as they constitute its very nature. The Vedanta makes a great deal of the illustration of water and its ripples and foam. But the waves and other distinctions in the one substance are eternal inasmuch as they come in and out of manifestation. The water can never be freed from them. (92)

Moreover, the fact that the one undergoing suffering and the one who causes suffering constitute two distinct principles is recognized (says the Sāṃkhya) in ordinary worldly dealings.

For instance, the seeker and his desired end are taken as mutually distinct. If the desired end were not by nature different from the seeker, whatever end were sought by any seeker would be eternally in his possession, and he would not be a seeker in relation to it, just as a lamp, which is of the nature of light, is eternally in possession of the end called "light", and cannot be a seeker of it. A seeker can only seek what he has not got.

Similarly, the desired end could not be an end unless it were different from the seeker. And if it were an end without being different from the seeker, it would be its own end. For the words "seeker" and "desired end" stand for the terms of a relation, and a relation can only subsist between two terms, not one. Therefore, the seeker and his end must be different. So also must the evil and the one who seeks to avoid it. That which is favourable to a seeker constitutes his desired end: what is unfavourable to him constitutes evil. He himself remains one, and comes into contact with both these two alternately. As realized desirable ends are few and evils many, the two are spoken of collectively as an evil. And this evil is that which gives suffering, while the soul (puruṣa) is the one who undergoes suffering. If it be taken that the latter, remaining one and the same, comes into contact with the favourable and the unfavourable alternately, then if both he and they, as sufferer and pain-giving principle respectively, are manifestations of the same Self, he can never be liberated from them. But if (as on our Sāṃkhya system) he and they form separate categories, then if one could inhibit the cause of their coming together in contact, the soul might be liberated.

But all this, we reply, is wrong. There cannot (on our Advaita doctrine) be two separate entities, one undergoing suffering and the other causing it, since on our view both would be one. The fault you mention might have attached to our doctrine if we had claimed that there was a suffering entity and a separate pain-giving entity, of the form of subject and object respectively, when the Self of both of them was one and the same. But this is just what is not possible, from the very fact of their fundamental unity. Fire has the separate properties of heat and light, and is capable of undergoing transformation (pariṇāma), yet it cannot burn itself or illuminate itself, from the mere fact of being one with itself. How then could the Absolute (brahman) possibly assume the form of a suffering principle and a pain-giving principle, when it is (not even capable of undergoing transformation but) immutable?

Well then, the Sāṃkhya will ask, where lies this suffering and pain-giving which we all expe-ience? We reply, "Are you not perfectly aware of this living body as the sufferer and as the object of the scorching activity of the sun?" Perhaps the Sāṃkhya will reply and say, "Being scorched is pain, and that pertains, not to the non-conscious body, but to the conscious principle which animates it. If suffering pertained only to the body, it would cease of its own accord with the cessation of the body, and no one would need to look for ways of bringing it to an end." To this we reply, "(If this is an argument to show that pain must belong to the conscious principle animating the body, since it is not possible to attribute pain to the body without making the Veda superfluous, it fails. For) no pain is found in pure consciousness as such, in the absence of the body. (93) Nor do you yourselves attribute any such modification as "pain" to the animating principle, consciousness, in its pure and isolated nature, while you cannot maintain that conscious-ness and the body undergo real amalgamation, as this would involve the pure consciousness of the soul in impurity and other defects. Finally, you do not admit that pain accrues to pain, so how can you yourselves explain the suffering and pain-giving?"

It will not do for the Sāṃkhya to say that the constituent called "sattva" is the sufferer, while "rajas" is the pain-giving principle. For consciousness cannot enter into any real composition with "sattva" and "rajas". (94) Nor will it help to say that consciousness becomes identified with "sattva" (95) and "suffers as it were." For to say "suffers *as it were*" means that in reality it does not suffer. To say that consciousness "suffers as it were" is not to attribute any evil to consciousness. One does not attribute poison to a harmless grass-snake merely by saying it is *like* a venomous snake, nor does one attribute harmlessness to a venomous snake by saying it is *like* (i.e. looks like) a grass-snake. So the conclusion is that we must accept that suffering and pain-giving are set up by nescience and do not exist at all from the standpoint of ultimate reality. This being so, there is nothing whatever wrong in our own position. But if the opponent continues to maintain that consciousness is a sufferer in the true sense, then his doctrine will involve the loss of all possibility of liberation, especially as he holds to the eternity of the pain-giving principle. (96)

The Sāṃkhya might here interpose anew. The suffering entity and the pain-giving entity, he might say, are both eternal as potentialities (śakti). But *actual* suffering depends on their being brought together by some particular cause. That cause is nescience. When this (nescience) is brought to an end, all contact between the suffering entity and the pain-giving entity ceases absolutely, and on this basis the absolute liberation of the soul is perfectly intelligible. But this argument is not right. For the Sāṃkhya makes of "nescience", or the constituent "tamas", an eternal principle. And he further maintains that the dominance and subservience of the various constituents among themselves never assumes any final static form. Thus, on his doctrine, the withdrawal of ("tamas" as) the cause of contact between the suffering entity and the pain-giving entity could never be final. Hence the separation of the suffering entity and the pain-giving entity can never be final and eternal either. And hence the Sāṃkhya philosopher is unable to escape from the consequence that his doctrine implies the impossibility of liberation.

The Advaitin, on the other hand, preaches the unity and sole reality of the Self. What is one and the same cannot possibly assume the form of object and subject at the same time. And the Veda itself has declared that a modification is (never a reality but) only a result of speech. (97) The charge that his doctrine implies the impossibility of liberation could not be laid against him even in a dream. As for empirical experience, there the presence of a suffering entity and a separate pain-giving entity must be accepted as and where perceived. (98) So the question of being attacked or defended on that score does not arise. (99)

* * * * *

2. Here the Sāṃkhya philosopher objects: Is it not true that the soul (ātman) is non-active, and that it is Nature that is really the agent? Nature adopts as its own the ends of the soul (puruṣa), and with these ends in view undergoes transformation into the Cosmic Intellect (mahat) and other forms. From this it follows that there is no justification for attributing agency and the power of spontaneous "thinking" (i.e. of projecting and creating the world)to the soul (puruṣa). (100) For an agent for the act of creating the world can be shown to exist either in the form of Nature with its three constituents (guṇa) initially in equilibrium, or else in the form of primary atoms obedient to the will of God. (101) Moreover, the Self (of the Vedantins) being one without a second, it will have no instrument (according to the Sāṃkhya) wherewith to perform its activity, not

to mention the absurdity of the implication (latent in the Vedantin's doctrine) that the Self (in creating the world) would work its own injury. No conscious intelligent agent deliberately works mischief on himself. So the Vedic teaching beginning "He took thought" will have to be interpreted as a metaphorical expression applied to non-conscious Nature as if it were a conscious being, because it (Nature) acts according to fixed laws for the good of the soul *as if* it were "thinking". It is like when we speak metaphorically and say of the actions of the king's responsible minister that they were done by the king.

But this is wrong. For if the Self can be an experiencer (and the Sāṃkhya declares that the puruṣa or soul *is* an experiencer), He can just as well be an agent. If the Sāṃkhya can make the Self (puruṣa) an experiencer even though it is (even on his own theory) just bare consciousness and not subject to transformation, the follower of the Veda can very well make the Self an agent in the act of creation with the power to think, etc., especially as he has the authority of the Vedic texts themselves.

Perhaps the Sāṃkhya will reply and claim that it is only the transformation of the soul into something of a different nature that could cause its impermanence, impurity or plurality, (102) not modifications assumed by bare consciousness as such. So the modifications of consciousness, he will continue, that take place strictly within the individual soul (puruṣa) as experiencer do not imply any defect in it. But on the view of the Vedantins, he would say, the Self is the agent in creating the world. This involves the Self in becoming transformed into something different from what it was before, and all the attendant defects such as impermanence, etc., follow.

But this is wrong also. For although the Self is one and the same, we accept a distinction according to whether or not it is beset with limiting adjuncts of name and form pertaining to the realm of nescience. (103). . .

Perhaps the Sāṃkhya will contend that he has already explained how the soul is bare consciousness and undergoes modifications in the course of experience without altering its essential nature and without becoming transformed into anything different. But Nature, he will say, becomes transformed through real change into new forms, and that is why it has such characteristics as being impure, non-conscious and many. The soul (puruṣa), however, is the opposite of all that. (104)

But (according to us Advaitins) that is not a real distinction, only a verbal one. If before the rise of experience in the soul it were just bare consciousness, and if it underwent a distinction at this time and became an experiencer, and if, on the conclusion of its experience, it lost that distinction and reverted to the state of bare consciousness – well then, when Nature becomes transformed into the Cosmic Intellect and other principles and then emerges from them again to remain standing in its original form, where lies its contrast with the soul? On this conception, there would be no difference between the behaviour of the soul and that of Nature. The distinction between the two would be one of words alone, not of reality.

Nor can the Sāṃkhya claim that the soul remains as bare consciousness at the time of experience just as it was before, without undergoing any change. For this would mean that the soul did not really undergo any experience. (105) If he turns round and says that bare consciousness *does* undergo a real modification (vikāra) and have experience in this way, his case is no better. For Nature, too, is admitted to undergo modification at the time of the experience of the soul, so that it ought, logically, to be an experiencer too. (106) If he says that modification assumes the form of being an experiencer in the case of consciousness and not in any other case, then it will be difficult to show that anything anywhere that has special qualities will not be an experiencer – like fire, for instance, with its special qualities of heat, etc. (107)

It will not help to suggest that both Nature and the soul are experiencers at the same time. For it will not then be possible to explain how Nature can serve the purposes of another. (108) There can be no relation of superiority and inferiority in quality between two experiencers, any more than two lights can illumine one another.

Perhaps the Sāṃkhya will say that the soul undergoes no modification, but that its "being an experiencer" consists in the rise of its reflection in the mind, which has the constituent "sattva" predominating and is hence apt for experience. But this will not do either. For if no difference is held to result to the soul from this circumstance, it will be meaningless to suppose that it can become an experiencer. Moreover, if the soul never undergoes any differentiation and consequently suffers no evil in the course of experience, then what would there be that needed to be removed, that the Sāṃkhya should found a traditional science purporting to lead to liberation? If he says that the purpose of his science is to remove evil that has been falsely attributed to the soul through nescience, then it would follow that the basic theories of the Sāṃkhyas, which are foreign to the true Vedic tradition, would stand exposed as useless and without foundation and not worthy of notice to those who seek liberation. For if evil were attributed to the soul solely through nescience it would no longer be possible to claim that the soul was in the last analysis an experiencer but not an agent, and that Nature was an agent but not an experiencer, while being a perfectly real principle standing over against the soul, different from it in all respects.

The Sāṃkhya may well reply that if everything that exists is one (as the Advaitin maintains), founding a traditional science for liberation will be just as useless as it has been claimed to have been on the Sāṃkhya view. But this objection would be wrong, because where all is one there is no traditional science! The question of whether the foundation of a particular science is or is not useless can only occur where the founders of sciences and persons desirous of profiting from them actually exist. When all is one as the Self, then there are neither authors of sciences, nor sciences, nor students of them, and all is the undifferentiated Self. In the absence of authors, sciences and students, one cannot raise the question of whether founding any particular science serves a purpose or not.

Moreover, if you admit the unity and sole existence of the Absolute, you must admit the utility of the authority that establishes it. That very authority, the Veda, itself declares that if the unity and sole existence of the Absolute be admitted, the question of the utility of founding a traditional science cannot arise. For it says, "But when all this has become the Self, then what could he see and with what?" (109) Here (i.e. in the Atharva Veda to which the Praśna Upanishad belongs) the two realms of enlightenment (vidyā) and of nescience (avidyā) have been distinguished as "the higher knowledge" (parā vidyā) and "the lower knowledge" (aparā-vidyā) respectively. (110) So the realm of the unity and sole existence of the Absolute is one into which the troops of the sophistical arguments of the dualists cannot penetrate, guarded as it is by the strong arm of the regal authority of the Upanishads.

And this should be taken as sufficient to refute the charge (111) that the Absolute of the Upanishads has no wherewithal with which to engage in such acts as the creation of the universe. For it is associated with numerous distinctions in the form of powers and instruments which accrue to it through the adjuncts of name and form set up by nescience. Such charges as the absurdity of the Self working injury on itself (112) also stand refuted on similar grounds.

Finally, that example which the opponent put forward, claiming that we speak metaphorically about the responsible minister of a king saying that his official acts are "done by the king" – that example is out of place in the present context. For it would contradict the plain meaning of the authoritative text that it was invoked to explain, namely "He took thought." (113) One can only assume that a statement has a metaphorical meaning when its primary meaning is impossible. In the present context it is quite unreasonable to suppose that non-conscious Nature could engage in strictly regulated activity to serve the various ends of the soul in the matter of bondage and liberation, observing all the required distinctions between released and bound souls and all the elaborate laws of subject, object, space, time and causation. But if the omniscient Lord is taken as the agent (through instruments set up by nescience) in the way we have described, then all this becomes explicable. (114)

* * * * *

3. The doctrine of the Sāṃkhyas, that (at the beginning of a new world-period after dissolution) the constituents (guṇa) fall from their state of equilibrium, cannot be established on the principles of the system. For nescience and the rest are then dissolved, (115) and no other cause is admitted. (116) If the constituents prompted

activity amongst themselves they would either always do so or never do so: (117) There could be no definite laws about the activity either of the constituents or of the Self.

Nor can the Sāṃkhya establish the distinction between bound and liberated souls, if Nature be supposed to serve their interests. In fact, on the principles of his system, no relation can logically be established between an interest and an entity having an interest. The soul, as pure consciousness, can have no interest, and neither can non-conscious Nature.

Nature cannot serve the interests of the soul if the latter is not subject to modification of any kind. And it cannot be subject to modification on the principles of the Sāṃkhya system. And Nature (being non-conscious) could not serve the interests of the soul even if the latter were capable of modification. Moreover, there can be no relation between the soul and Nature (118) and this is a further reason why Nature cannot serve the ends of the soul. If action were supposed to arise in the soul, the soul would be subject to (change and therefore to) destruction. But if the soul were pure consciousness and so actionless, the difficulties already mentioned would arise again. And yet if there were no external cause (in the form of the soul) acting on Nature, (Nature would never be prompted to act and so) the soul could never attain release. (119)

* * * * *

4. The Sāṃkhya doctrine of transformation (pariṇāma) agrees with the Vaiśeṣika doctrine (120) in point of admitting that a new characteristic can first come into existence and later suffer destruction. (121) Even on the theory that the effect (exists eternally and

merely) enters into and withdraws from manifestation (122) there is the same contradiction with the principles of right knowledge. This will soon be clear when it is asked whether the manifestation and withdrawal themselves existed before their own occurrence, (an enquiry which will show that *they* at least came into being and that this contradicts the theory). (123)

* * * * *

5. But those who hold to a plurality of souls, all of which are all-pervading, have a theory which lands them in this very confusion. (124) Some of them (the Sāṃkhyas) say, for instance, that there are many all-pervading souls, of the nature of pure consciousness, free from worldly attributes and perfect in every way. One common force, called Nature, exists for their benefit, and through this they are able to attain their two ends of empirical experience followed by liberation. . . .

As far as the Sāṃkhyas are concerned, our reply is that, on their view, when one (all-pervading) soul became affected by pleasure or pain, all would be, as all are of the nature of pure consciousness and there is nothing to distinguish any of them from the others by limiting it to proximity with one particular mind. (125)

The Sāṃkhya might concede this, but say in reply that Nature's processes went on in order to arrange for the soul (puruṣa) to attain liberation. Otherwise we could find no reason for the self-unfoldment of Nature apart from the mere desire to show off its riches, and if this latter were the case, no liberation would be possible. (126) But such a reply would be wrong. For we cannot just blandly assume that some arrangement must exist because it would happen to serve our purposes. Some proof of the existenc of such an arrangement must be offered. As no proof is forthcoming, we shall have to drop all hope of the soul's being able to attain liberation (in terms of the Sāṃkhya system). What, however, would quite certainly result from the absence of any arrangement would be, precisely, "confusion." (127). . . (128)

* * * * *

6. Gauḍapāda's Kārikā runs: "Just as the dust and smoke present in the ether (or space) enclosed in one pot has no connection with the ether in other pots, so the pleasure and other individual experiences of one soul have no connection with those of another."

This is said by way of contradicting those dualists (the Sāṃkhyas) who maintain that if there were only one soul present in all bodies the birth, death and psychological experiences such as happiness of one soul would pertain to all souls, (129) and this would undermine the law according to which every action brings its peculiar fruit to the agent.

Well, but do we not ourselves claim that only one Self exists? We do. We have just said that there is only *one* Self pervading all organisms, like the one ether pervading all pots. The Sāṃkhya objects that the notion that there is only one Self leads to absurdities. For whenever it was either happy or unhappy in one mind it would have to be happy or unhappy as the case might be in all the other minds at the same time. But on his own principles the Sāṃkhya has no right to make this objection. For he does not admit that the soul experiences happiness or unhappiness *at all* !! He maintains that happiness and unhappiness are inherent qualities of the mind (buddhi).

As for his notion that the souls, as pure consciousness, form a plurality, such a notion cannot be supported by any of the criteria of knowledge (pramāṇa). It cannot, for instance, be argued that there must be a plurality of souls on the ground that the fact that Nature serves the various interests of others cannot be explained on any other hypothesis. For the "interests" that Nature is supposed to serve cannot be connected with the soul on the principles of the system. If the bondage and liberation effected by Nature really did pertain to the souls severally, according to the tenets of the school, they would then quite correctly argue that Nature's serving the various interests of others could not be explained by the hypothesis that there was only one soul, so that souls must be many. But the fact is that the Sāṃkhya does not admit that such ends as bondage and liberation do actually pertain to the soul. (130) And they maintain that the souls are of the nature of pure consciousness, void of all distinctions. Hence their proof that Nature serves the interests of another can only be grounded on the existence of the soul (puruṣa) as a principle separate from Nature, not on the presence of mutual distinctions between a plurality of differentiated individual souls.

Thus the notion that Nature serves the interests of others is not a ground for arguing that there must be a distinction amongst souls. And the Sāṃkhyas produce no other proof of it either. What their doctrine really amounts to is that something other than Nature exists, and that Nature binds itself and releases itself as conditioned by that. And that other entity induces activity in Nature by its mere existence as pure consciousness, not by any distinctions it assumes. Hence the assumption of a plurality of souls and abandonment of Vedic teaching on the point proceeds from mere delusion. (131)

7. And the *prima facie* view might be further supported by the claim that it was not only the view of reason but also supported by traditional texts of certain Vedic schools, for the Kaṭha Upanishad I.iii.11 says, "The Unmanifest Principle lies beyond the cosmic Intellect (mahat) and the Spirit (puruṣa) lies beyond the Unmanifest Principle." The argument here would be that in the series of terms "Cosmic Intellect – Unmanifest Principle – Spirit" we recognize the technical terms of the Smṛti. The term Unmanifest Principle is familiar from the Smṛti. The term can be explained etymologically as meaning that which is not perceived because it is without sound and the other perceptible elements, so that it can mean nothing other than the "Pradhāna" of the school in question. (132) Since (it has been shown above that) there is Vedic authority for this, it will not do to object that there is not. And this Pradhāna is known from the Veda, the Smṛti, reason and common knowledge to be the cause of the world.

But we cannot accept this statement. For the passage of the Kaṭha Upanishad in question is not concerned with affirming the existence of the Unmanifest Principle and the cosmic Intellect in their form familiar from Smṛti works specifically of the Sāṃkhya school. For we do not find in the Kaṭha Upanishad any mention of the Pradhāna in the manner in which the latter is presented by the (strict philosophical form of the) Sāṃkhya as an independent causal principle composed of the three "constituents" (guṇa). All we have is the mere word "unmanifest". And this could be explained etymologically as applicable to other subtle principles, as it merely means "not manifest", so that there is no need to appeal to any special or technical meanings whatever.

As for the special technical terms of the Sāṃkhyas, they are technical terms belonging to their own system only, and cannot be used to throw light on the meaning of the Vedic texts. Nor will the mere identity of two series of terms guarantee identity of subject-matter in two passages, unless the forms to which the two sets of terms refer are recognized as being the same. Only a lunatic would think that a cow was a horse simply because he saw it in a horse's stable.(133)

* * * * *

8. "In the evaluation of the constituents (guṇa)" means "in the philosophy of the school of Kapila (i.e. the Sāṃkhya school)." This science of the evaluation of the constituents (i.e. the Sāṃkhya school) is the special authority on questions connected with the nature of the constituents and of the one who experiences them (i.e. the soul or puruṣa). Although the Sāṃkhya doctrine stands contradicted by the Veda on the subject of the funadamental identity of all in the Absolute (brahman), nevertheless it is accepted that these followers of Kapila have a special competence in the description of the play of the constituents and their effects. Therefore there is nothing contradictory if we find the Lord calling in even their tradition to help eulogize the doctrine He is about to teach. (134)

4. REFUTATION OF THE VAIŚEṢIKAS

If the Vaiśeṣika tradition is not quite as ancient as the Sāṃkhya tradition, it nevertheless goes back well before the Christian era (135) and its origins are lost in the mists of antiquity. Only two pre-Śaṃkara works of the school survive, apart from the somewhat oracular Sūtras attributed to the legendary figure Kaṇāda. These are the Daśapadārtha Śāstra of Candramati, *circa* 500 A.D., preserved in a Chinese version which has been translated into English by the Japanese scholar, H. Ui, and the "Bhāṣya" of Praśastapāda, a free elaboration of the Sūtras dating from the second half of the sixth century, preserved in its Sanskrit form and available in the English translation of Ganganatha Jha with the sub-commentary of Sri Dhara, dated by the author 991 A.D. The "Bhāṣya" was apparently known to Śaṃkara, and later became the standard authority for the doctrines of the school. But the system itself was in evidence long before the date of the two pre-Śaṃkara works that have survived, and the fact that Śaṃkara states and attacks an atheistic form of the doctrine has, with other considerations,(136) led to the supposition that he was familiar with the lost Rāvaṇa Bhāṣya on the Sūtras, dating from an earlier period. God is certainly a notable absentee from the cosmological theory of the Vaiśeṣikas as sketched by Śaṃkara at the beginning of the first two Extracts to follow, where evolution of the world from its dissolved state at the beginning of the world-period is traced to the impact of past action on the atoms, without any appeal to the guiding hand of the Lord.

Already in the time of Nāgārjuna's pupil Āryadeva (*circa* 200 A.D.) the Vaiśeṣika stood along with the Sāṃkhya as the leading philosophical school of the Hindus. Yet, despite its antiquity, the Vaiśeṣika, unlike the Sāṃkhya, was still a living system in Śaṃkara's day. And as it was adopted by the "Logicians" or Naiyāyikas to give body to their system, it was still being subjected to creative adaptations, and defended in debate, far into the late Middle Ages. On the other hand the Sāṃkhya system, as we have seen, was already by Śaṃkara's day being summarized as a standard but now defunct system of the past.

The Vaiśeṣika, however, had for long been a dogmatic system, relying on ingenuity of argument rather than genuine enquiry. Though the impulse behind the original formulation of their doctrine had been the desire to give an account of the physical world, it lapsed gradually into a kind of scholasticism, as the defence of traditional theories by an ever more complicated system of hypotheses supplanted that practice which alone can give a naturalistic system true vigour, namely observation of nature.

Although the Vaiśeṣika system had not originally been an atomistic doctrine, it assumed this form at some stage before direct records are available. Uddyotakara (*circa* 650 A.D.), (137) a later philosopher who belonged to the Naiyāyayika school at a point where it had already borrowed the Vaiśeṣika physics, argued that matter could not be infinitely divisible, and that you must assume some unit to account for the variation in mass between, say, a mote in a sunbeam and the Himalayan range. (138) But the Vijñāna Vāda Buddhists had already made short work of the Vaiśeṣika atom long before this time, on very much the same sort of arguments as Śaṃkara was to use later, and it appears that the Vaiśeṣikas were never able to offer a cogent philosophical defence of this most typical part of their doctrine in its classical form. (139)

The Sāṃkhya world-view had been evolutionary and had implied continuity. Matter and mind were assumed to emerge from, to abide in and eventually to merge back into, their imperceptible ground, non-conscious Nature, which persisted through all change as the one ocean persists through all the modifications of its surface into waves, bubbles and foam. The Vaiśeṣikas, however, did not accept the notion of Nature or Primary Matter that spontaneously unfolded its riches for the benefit of the soul. Yet their world-view was not purely mechanistic either, as spontaneous activity was attributed to the primary atoms.(140) It paid attention to the element of discontinuity in our experience, though not stressing it exclusively in the matter of the Buddhist schools. For the Vaiśeṣika, all change results from movement amongst eternal, qualitatively changeless atoms. It is abrupt and momentary in character, though our cognitive apparatus cannot record the changes at the speed with which they actually occur. Changes in the world can be induced by the willed activity (prayatna) of the individual, though he has to contend with the natural properties of the atoms, and, in the more developed forms of the system, with the occult latent force of past actions and with the will of God. The introduction of occult forces and of God into what was originally a purely naturalistic system requires a little explanation.

As the idea of rebirth, and the idea of escape from the sufferings of rebirth, came to dominate in India, every philosophical system had to adapt itself to this end if it was to have any appeal to the people and to survive. The Vaiśeṣikas eventually included a theory of liberation in their doctrine, and even an appeal to God as efficient cause or controller of the play of the atoms. But these were mere external embellishments, coming as afterthoughts added onto the old naturalistic system. The notion of God played no part in that form of the Vaiśeṣika system attacked by Śaṃkara. But all post-Upanishadic philosophers were required to explain how a person's deeds could be performed and disappear and yet give rise to morally appropriate effects at widely separated intervals of time and in new births. To explain this, the Vaiśeṣikas appealed to the concept of "adṛṣṭa", or the hidden power of deeds to bring about their morally appropriate fruit at some future time or in some future birth. The notion of occult force (adṛṣṭa) was not a fruitful concept in a naturalistic system. If you introduce what is fundamentally an ethical concept into a naturalistic system, it tends to stifle enquiry. When the spirit of enquiry flags, one can then always appeal to "adṛṣṭa" or occult forces and feel that one is in possession of an answer to one's problem that is in conformity with one's system.

(XI.4) REFUTATION OF NON-VEDIC WORLD-VIEWS

One of the important results of the acceptance of the theory of occult force was its effect on the Vaiśeṣika theory of the soul. The latter had originally been conceived, in the manner of the Jainas, as co-terminous with the body. But it now had to be assumed to be omnipresent in order to experience the various results of its deeds wherever they might occur. With the soul all-pervading, and therefore motionless, the root of its activity could no longer be seen in movement, but was traced to will or effort (prayatna). Willing, feeling, knowing and desiring were not conceived as processes *going on* in the soul, but as qualities that momentarily emerged in it at the appropriate stimulus. The element of "momentariness" that so often crops up in the doctrine derived partly from Buddhist inspiration, and was responsible for Śaṃkara referring to the Vaiśeṣikas as "semi-nihilists" (ardha-vaināśika), although they were thorough-going realists by European standards. Although the soul (ātman) of the Vaiśeṣika theory is omnipresent, it stands in complete contrast with the Self or Atman of the Advaitin. The Advaitin aims to realize in immediate experience his true nature as the Self of all. The soul as conceived by the Vaiśeṣika is an individual object amidst the world of objects. However, it is conceived as imperceptible, and our knowledge of it is said to be confined to inference. (141)

Another very important innovation of the Vaiśeṣika doctrine, first found in the surviving literature in the Daśapadārtha Śāstra of Candramati (*circa* 500 A.D.), is the introduction of a doctrine of categories. According to the final form of the doctrine, the world is explicable only if one admits that what it contains falls into six separate categories, namely substance, quality, movement, class-character, particular character and inherence. The list has awkward features, but marks an important step in the shift from the inspired but somewhat rhapsodic outpourings of the ancient Vedic teachers to the drier, shallower but more precise formulations of the scholastic period of Indian thought. In the ancient Vedic texts, qualities, processes and relations had been freely conceived as material substances. (142) To the Vaiśeṣika it gradually became clear that all other categories, apart from substance, only exist in substances. And it was also recognized that there are no substances without qualities. (143) The world, however, cannot be reduced to substances and qualities alone. For a substance can, for instance, undergo change without losing or gaining qualities, and this change must be set down as a different category, other than quality, labelled "movement" or "karma" in the system. It, too, can only exist in a substance.

But what about the relation connecting qualities and the other categories with substances? When substances, particularly atoms or groups of atoms come into relation, the relation is spoken of as "contact" (saṃyoga), which is a quality, and which is defined as the coming together of what were previously separate. But, according to Vaiśeṣika doctrine, all other categories apart from substance are dependent for their existence on substances and therefore inseparable (ayuta-siddha) from the substances in which they exist. As they are inseparable from the substances in which they exist, the relation connecting them with these substances cannot be the quality "contact", since the latter is defined as the coming together of things that were previously separate. So the relation connecting a substance with the other categories that exist in it is not the quality "contact", but must constitute a new category, namely "inherence" (samavāya). But as every category, including inherence, was conceived by the Vaiśeṣikas as a kind of object or thing, their theory that a special category called "inherence" was needed to connect a substance with all other categories that inhered in it fell into infinite regress, because a fresh instance of inherence would be required to connect the inherence, which was after all a separate category itself, with the substance, and a fresh inherence to connect the new inherence and so to infinity. We shall find (144) that for Śaṃkara the categories themselves were mere thought-constructions, a new and empty kind of mythology. This was not because Śaṃkara did not see any value in the substance-attribute interpretation of the world, but because the Vaiśeṣikas regarded all their categories as *absolutely* distinct from one another, and in this form he regarded the whole doctrine as logically untenable. In particular, if the quality was totally distinct from the substance, its existence could not be dependent on the latter as the Vaiśeṣikas maintained.

The Vaiśeṣika's concept of inherence lent itself conveniently to Śaṃkara's dialectical attack because "inherence" was regarded by its proponents as a kind of *thing*. How could it function as the needed connection between two terms when it was a kind of *thing*, separate from all other things, which itself needed to be connected to the terms? The thorough-going realism of the Vaiśeṣikas was connected with their invention of a theory of the categories. (145) After this, they were no longer naive realists but conscious realists, aware that they were choosing to be such. They made anything that can be known and named into an objective reality, including even non-existence (abhāva). Just as we find no difficulty in thinking of ourselves as sometimes being "faced by" an "awkward silence" or a "surprising absence of self-control" or a "dearth of good vegetables", so the Vaiśeṣika, on not finding a pot in the corner where he expected to find it, felt himself to be somehow physically face to face with the "absence" or "non-existence" of the pot. Because they made non-existence into a kind of reality, they were able to define several kinds of it. The non-existence of a pot previous to its production from clay was labelled "previous non-existence", its non-existence after destruction "non-existence due to destruction", its difference from a clay bowl "mutual non-existence". As we have already seen, Śaṃkara rejected the theory of different types of non-existence on the ground that anything that could have distinct varieties must be existent and so could not be non-existence. (146)

Another point on which Śaṃkara attacked the Vaiśeṣikas was their theory of causality, which was opposed to that of "Sat-Kārya Vāda", which, as we have seen, (147) he considered a useful basis for explaining the world-appearance from the standpoint of nescience. The details of the Vaiśeṣikas' complicated theory of causality need not detain us here. But a word should be said on the reasons why they came to contradict Sat-Kārya Vāda. According to the mature Vaiśeṣika view, the whole was different from the sum of its parts. For the qualities and universal characters and so on inhering in the whole are not the same as those inhering in the parts. From the connection of the parts arises something completely new, the whole, which comes from the parts. The substance of the whole proceeds from the substances of the parts, and the qualities, etc., of the whole proceed from the qualities inhering in the parts. Whatever "proceeds from" anything else is totally distinct from that thing. Unlike the atoms of which it is ultimately composed, the whole is transient, and disappears with the separation of the parts. On account of their theory that the whole was something *new*, over and above the parts, that *came into being*, the Vaiśeṣikas contradicted the Sāṃkhya view that the effect lay already present, though latent, in its material cause before production. They held the opposite view that the effect is not in any sense existent before its production (Asat-Kārya Vāda). (148)

Śaṃkara could find little merit in the Vaiśeṣikas' teaching. He may have borrowed from Praśastapāda a proof of the existence of the Self. (149) But he had no use for theorists who not merely neglected, but consciously contradicted, the doctrine of the non-dual Self taught in the Upanishads, believing themselves able to determine the nature of the Self, the Knower of Knowing, with the mere weapons of perception and inference alone. As we shall see, (150) he referred to their congeners, the Logicians, as "the riff-raff of the Brahminical and other castes, whose minds have been deranged by sophistical reasoning, pitiable in condition and quite cut off from the traditional interpretation of the Veda." Neither the metaphysics of the Vaiśeṣikas, nor their psychology, nor their theory of the Self, nor their theory of atoms satisfied the test of internal consistency. So in order to preserve the students of Advaita from the influence of heresies, he stated the main points of their theories and subjected them to critical scrutiny in the Extracts set out below.

TEXTS REFUTING THE VAIŚEṢIKAS

1. But we must begin by defending the doctrine of those who hold to the Vedic Absolute (brahmavādin) against a charge brought against them by the Atomists. The Atomists, for their part, hold as follows. They maintain that the qualities which inhere intimately in a causal substance each bring into being a new quality of a similar kind in the effect-substance. We see, for instance, that a white cloth issues from white threads and does not issue from threads of any other colour. Therefore, if a conscious principle like the Absolute is taken to be the (material) cause of the world, consciousness ought to inhere intimately in the

effect, the world, too. But as this is seen not to be the case, it follows that a conscious principle such as the Vedic Absolute cannot be the (material) cause of the world. The author of the Brahma Sūtras refutes this supposition of the Vaiśeṣikas, using their own logical methods.

Their doctrine is as follows. They say that (before the world-manifestation at the beginning of the world-period) the primary atoms (paramāṇu) remain without producing any effects for a certain time, each with its peculiar property such as colour (or touch or taste or odour as the case might be) and having the dimensions of a sphere of infinitesimal size. Afterwards, under the influence of the latent effects of past actions (adṛṣṭa) and other forces, these primary atoms enter into contact with one another and produce the entire world of effects, beginning with the atomic compounds.

In this process, the qualities inherent in the material causes produce corresponding new qualities in the effects. When two primary atoms combine to produce a binary atomic compound, the particular qualities of colours such as white, etc., inhering in the primary atoms produce a new instance of the same colour in the atomic compound. The particular quality pertaining to the primary atoms of having the dimensions of an infinitesimal sphere, however, does not produce a like quality in the binary atomic compound. The latter is taken to be of different dimensions, since they speak of it as characterized by minute size and shortness. When two binary atomic compounds combine to produce a quaternary atomic compound, (151) they also reproduce their own qualities, such as whiteness or other colour-quality, in the quaternary compound. But minute size and shortness, though inhering in the binary atomic compound, are not reproduced in the quaternary atomic compound, since the latter is taken to have the dimensions "big size" and "length". The same process also occurs when a plurality of primary atoms, or a plurality of binary atomic compounds, or a single primary atom in combination with a single binary atomic compound, produce their effects.

Thus you (Vaiśeṣika) hold that binary atomic compounds, which are minute in size and short in shape, arise from primary atoms, which are infinitesimal in size and spherical in shape. Also that ternary and other (i.e. quaternary) atomic compounds, which are actually "large" and "long" and not infinitesimal and spherical, proceed ultimately from primary atoms which are infinitesmal and spherical. Also that from binary atomic compounds, which are minute and short, arise ternary atomic compounds which are "large" and "long" and not "minute" and "short". If, then, we Advaitins maintain that the universe, as a non-conscious effect, arises from the conscious principle, the Vedic Absolute, what have you got to complain about?

The Vaiśeṣika will perhaps say that effect-substances such as the binary atomic compounds are characterized by positive dimensions which are contradictory to those of their material cause (the primary atoms), so that the infinitesimal size and spherical shape of the cause *cannot* be reproduced in the effects. But the universe (the Vaiśeṣika would say) is not characterized in this way by any positive quality that is contradictory to consciousness and would therefore render impossible the reproduction in the effect of the quality of consciousness present in the cause. There is no such thing as a positive quality labelled "non-consciousness" that could exclude consciousness. For non-consciousness is the mere negation of consciousness. The case of consciousness in the Absolute, therefore, is not parallel with that of the infinitesimal size and spherical shape in the primary atoms. So consciousness ought to appear in the effect of the

Absolute, the universe.

But (we Advaitins) contend that this is not right. Infinitesimal size and spherical shape, though found in the cause, are not, on your view, reproduced in the effect. And in our view the consciousness-nature of the cause (the Absolute) is not reproduced in the effect. So far the two cases are parallel. Now, the cause whereby infinitesimal size and spherical shape are not reproduced in the effect cannot be the fact that the effect is characterized by other (and contradictory) dimensions. The fact is that the reproduction of infinitesimal size and spherical shape should be able to take place *before* the introduction of different dimensions. For the Vaiśeṣika doctrine assumes that after the effect-substance has been produced it remains for an instant (kṣaṇa-mātra) without qualities before any qualities are introduced. Nor can you say that the reason why the infinitesimal size and spherical shape in the cause do not produce dimensions similar to their own in the effect is that they reproduce dissimilar ones. For your system maintains that the dissimilar dimensions in the effect arise from something else. It is said by Kaṇāda,"'Largeness' arises from the presence of largeness or plurality in the cause and from (the results of the) new association of parts," (152) and "The (small) atom is the opposite of that" (153) and "And this also explains 'being long' and 'being short'." (154) Nor can it be urged that plurality and largeness in the cause produce like qualities in the effect on account of some peculiar proximity, while infinitesimal size and spherical shape do not. For in the production either of a new substance or of a new quality *all* the qualities of the cause without exception inhere in their substratum (*viz.* the material cause). Thus the fact that the infinitesimal size and spherical shape of the primary atoms does not give rise to like qualities in the effect is due to their very nature (and not to the operation of any external cause). Hence it is permissible for us, also, to say that the conscious principle, the Vedic Absolute, gives rise to its effect (the world) without reproducing in that effect its own characteristic nature of consciousness.

Moreover, there is no universal law that causes produce effects of like nature with themselves. For (on the Vaiśeṣika view) contact (saṃyoga), an attribute, is seen to produce substances (when atomic compounds come into contact), which (constitute a different category and therefore) are by nature different from itself. (155) Nor can you object that it is not right to cite an example about an attribute (such as "contact") when the subject under discussion (the Absolute) is a substance. For the attribute was only cited with the limited purpose of illustrating the production of effects of different nature from their causes. There is no reason for any such restriction as "only substances may be cited to show anything about substances, only attributes may be cited to show anything about attributes." The author of your own Sūtras himself cited an attribute to prove a point about a substance. "Because the contact between the perceptible and the imperceptible is itself imperceptible, it follows that the body does not consist of the five elements." (156) The contact between the earth and the ether, which are respectively perceptible and imperceptible, is itself imperceptible. In the same way, if the body did inhere in the five elements, some of which are perceptible (earth, water and fire) and some not (ether and wind), (157) it would itself be imperceptible. But it is in fact perceptible. So it cannot be made up out of the five elements (and is in fact composed of the earth-element alone). (158) The author of the Vaiśeṣika Sūtras is prepared to argue thus, even though (on his own system) contact is an attribute and the body a substance. (Hence we were justified in arguing in terms of the Vaiśeṣika's own system on the analogy of the attribute "contact" producing effects (substances) different in nature from itself that the Upanishadic Absolute might well produce non-conscious objects, though itself conscious). (159)

* * * * *

2. Now the author of the Sūtras proceeds to refute the theory of atomism. That doctrine arises as follows. In the world, substances composed of parts, such as cloths, etc., are seen to be frequently produced from the component substances, such as the threads that make them up, aided by the relation "contact". From this we infer that everything composed of parts is produced in the same way from further component substances. The point where this division into parts and wholes stops is the primary atom (paramāṇu), the ultimate irreducible limit of the process of division. (160)

This whole universe, consisting of mountains and oceans and all else, is a whole consisting of parts. And because it has parts, it has a beginning and an end (in time). And since no effect can exist without a cause, Kaṇāda holds that the primary atoms are the (material) cause of the universe. Because the four familiar elements, earth, water, fire and wind are found to have parts, the existence of four different kinds of primary atoms corresponding to them is further assumed. And since these mark the ultimate irreducible limit of the process of division, they cannot be subdivided further. When earth and the other elements perish, all things are separated back into their component primary elements, and this is the "time of dissolution" (pralaya-kāla). Then, at the time of cosmic projection, action rises up in the wind-atoms under the impulse of the latent effects of action that has gone before. That action has the result of joining the atom which is its seat with another, by which process, through such intermediary stages as those of the binary atomic compound etc., wind is produced. And it is the same with the production of fire, of water, of earth and also of the human body with its sense-organs. In fact, the whole universe develops from atoms in this way. The followers of Kaṇāda maintain that the colours and other qualities in the binary atomic compounds proceed from the colours, etc., in the primary atoms, in the same way that the colour of a cloth proceeds from the colour of its threads.

Against all this, we have the following to say. It must be admitted at the outset that the contact that supervenes between atoms, (initially separate during the period of world-dissolution), must be due to action, for threads and the like are only seen to come into contact under the stress of action. And action, being itself an effect, presupposes some efficient cause (nimitta). And unless you admit all this, you cannot account for the initial occurrence of action at all. But even if an efficient cause were assumed, it would have to be taken as effort or impact or some other known cause of action. And since, as we shall show, none of these are possible in terms of the Vaiśeṣika system, no initial action could occur in the atoms.

There cannot, indeed, be any effort on the part of the soul in the time of world-dissolution, as there are then no bodies, and effort, which (according to the Vaiśeṣika) is an attribute of the soul, can occur only when there is contact between the soul and the mind when the latter is active within the body. This is also enough to refute the possibility of impact or any other known cause of action. For all operate after the emergence of the universe: they cannot be the cause of the initial action (of the atoms). It might perhaps be replied that it is the latent force of actions earlier performed that institutes the initial action. But this would have to inhere either in the soul or in the atoms. In neither case, however, would the latent force be able to serve as the efficient cause to introduce action into the atoms, since it is non-conscious. We have already explained, in dealing with the Sāṃkhya system, (161) how no non-conscious principle can either act or prompt to action independently unless it is under the control of some conscious being. And since no consciousness arises in the soul during the time of world-dissolution (according to the Vaiśeṣikas), it must be counted as non-conscious. Moreover, if the latent force were supposed to inhere in the soul, it could not be the efficient cause of action in the atoms, as it would not be related to them. And if you say that the atoms are related to the soul (puruṣa) which is in its turn associated with the latent force, then, since the relation of the latent force (as the efficient cause of action) with the atoms would be constant, and there would be no other cause to prevent it, their action ought to be constant (which would imply the impossibility of world-periods and so contradict the Vaiśeṣika system). Thus it has been shown that no initial action can arise in the atoms, for the lack of any specific efficient cause. And if there is no contact there can be none of the whole complex of effects which are supposed to proceed from it, beginning with the binary atomic compound.

Moreover, if there were to be contact between one atom and another it would have to be either total or partial. If it were total, the atoms would have to conglomerate into a single mass (so that all their parts would be in contact). And this would result in all compounds remaining the size of a single atom. Moreover, we should be involved in direct contradiction with experience, for contact is invariably observed to take place between two substances which both have (their surfaces divided into) parts. If, on the other hand, contact between atoms be taken as partial, it would follow that the atoms had parts, which is self-contradictory. If it be said that surfaces divided into parts may be *imagined* in the primary atoms, then, since what is imagined is not real, the contact would not be real either, and there would be no "non-inherent cause" (162) for the production of any real effect. And without any non-inherent cause the whole complex of effects beginning with the binary atomic compound could not arise.

We have seen how there could be no action to produce contact of atoms at the beginning of the projection of the world in any world-period for lack of any efficient cause. In the same way, it also follows that there could be no action in the atoms to produce final separation at the time of world-dissolution. For we can point to no conceivable specific cause for this. The latent force of actions previously performed cannot be cited as such, for it exists to produce further experience, not world-dissolution. So we have to conclude that (when a world-period either begins or ends) there cannot be any action to produce either any initial contact or final separation of the atoms, for lack of any efficient cause. There being no initial contact or final separation, there could not be the world-projection or world-dissolution either, for they depend on them. So the doctrine that atoms are the material cause of the world is wrong. (163)

* * * * *

3. The phrase in the present aphorism, "And also because they admit inherence (samavāya)" refers back to the "There can be no creation and dissolution" in the previous aphorism, (164) and thus the present aphorism carries on the subject of refuting atomism.

You (Vaiśeṣika) maintain that an absolutely distinct binary atomic compound (dvyaṇuka) arises from (the combination of) two atoms and inheres in them. But no one who maintains this thesis can make out a case for the causality of atoms.

You ask, "Why not?" Well, the author of the Sūtras gives the reason "Because there would result infinite regress by parity of reasoning." The binary atomic compound, being absolutely distinct from the two atoms from which it is produced, has to be connected to them by the relation of inherence. (165) But the relation of inherence is itself likewise absolutely distinct from the two terms it connects. It has, therefore, to be connected with them by a fresh relation of inherence, as, like the atoms themselves, it is absolutely distinct from what it is related to. And as each fresh relation assumed would require fresh relations to connect it to its terms, the result would be infinite regress.

To this it might be objected that inherence was directly perceived as constantly connected with its terms, never as either unrelated or requiring to be related through a fresh relation, so that no fresh relations had to be assumed to connect it to its terms, such as would lead to infinite regress.

But this would not be right. For if it were, the relation of contact (saṃyoga) would be in constant relation with its terms, just like the relation of inherence, and there would be no need to assume the latter. (166) If you now maintain that contact *does* need the relation of inherence to connect it to its terms because it is different from them, then the relation of inherence, being likewise different from the terms it connects, will also require a fresh relation to become connected with them. Nor will it avail to say that contact requires a relation to connect it to its terms because it is an attribute, whereas inherence is not an attribute (but a separate category) and so does not. (167) For in truth the reason for dependence on a fresh relation to become connected with its terms is the same in both cases, (168) (namely, the fact of being absolutely distinct from the terms the relations are required to connect). The fact that one of the two relations, (*viz.* contact) is termed an attribute (while the other, inherence, constitutes a separate category of its own) has no bearing on the issue (which is governed by the fact that both are relations entirely distinct from the terms that they are required to connect). Therefore whoever accepts the relation of inherence as a principle distinct from the terms it unites is involved in infinite regress. In a doctrine that becomes involved in infinite regress, the failure to establish one (link in the chain of causation) results in the collapse of the entire edifice, and it could not even be shown that a binary atomic compound arises from two atoms. So this is another ground for the failure of the doctrine of atomism.

Consider also the following. The atoms must be either ever active by nature, or ever actionless by nature, or both, or neither, there being no remaining alternative. But not one of the four hypotheses can be made out to be the case. If they were active by nature they would be eternally active, and the world-dissolution could never set in. If they were actionless by nature they would remain actionless for ever, and creation would never take place. And to suppose that they are both active and actionless by nature is evidently self-contradictory. If they were supposed to be neither active nor actionless by nature, we should have to assume that both activity and rest were introduced causally from without. But in that case, since the latent force of action previously performed, or any other such causal force, (169) would always be in proximity, they would be eternally in motion. And if the latent force of action and other such external causes played no part, it would mean that the atoms could never acquire action. So that is another reason why the doctrine of atoms is invalid.

Now, the Vaiśeṣikas have another quite unsupported theory. Substances with parts, they think, cannot be subdivided into further parts indefinitely. The ultimate indivisibles are the primary atoms. They are of four different kinds (constituting the four elements wind, water, fire and earth), and are associated with colour and other properties (such as touch, taste and odour) They are eternal, and from them proceed both the fourfold elements, with their colour and other properties, and also the world of objects composed of those elements.

From the fact of their being credited with colour and other properties, it is clear that these primary atoms can be neither atomic nor eternal. That is to say, the primary atoms would turn out on this doctrine to be gross and impermanent in comparison with the ultimate world-cause beyond them, so that the teaching of the Vaiśeṣikas would imply the opposite of what they intended. Why is this so? Because it is what we actually find in the world. Whenever we see an object in the world that has colour and other properties, it is invariably grosser and less permanent than its (material) cause. The cloth is gross and impermanent in comparison with the threads of which it is made. And the threads, in their turn, are gross and impermanent in comparison with the yarn. Now, these primary atoms, as conceived by the Vaiśeṣikas, have colour and other properties. It follows, therefore, that they, too, must have material causes, and must be gross and impermanent in comparison with them.

No doubt they argue that primary atoms must be eternal, in the aphorism "whatever exists and has no cause is eternal." (170) But our arguments have shown that this will not apply to the atoms. The primary atoms must have a cause, for the reason we have already given. (171) It is true that they give another reason, too, why the primary atoms must be eternal, namely, "If nothing were permanent, there could be no specific denials of the permanence of individual things." (172) But even this will not suffice to give certain proof that the primary atoms must be eternal. It is only if there were no permanent entity *at all* that it would be meaningless to speak of impermanence: it does not follow that the *primary atoms* have to be assumed to be eternal to avoid this absurdity. There is also another eternal entity, the supreme cause of all, the Vedic Absolute (brahman).

No entity can be established as real through the mere fact that words are used to refer to it. For words acquire significance and meanings acquire validity only by referring to what has already been established as real by other means of knowledge.

The Vaiśeṣikas mention a third reason (for the eterntiy of their atoms), too, in the aphorism "And absence of knowledge." (173) If this Sūtra be interpreted to imply that we had "absence of knowledge," that is, no direct perception of the real (and eternal) material causes of perceptible effects (i.e. no perception of the eternal atoms), then the binary atomic compounds (since they are also the imperceptible material causes of perceptible effects) would have to be classed as eternal (like the atoms, and this would not agree with the Vaiśeṣika system). (174) Perhaps, to avoid this, they will introduce the qualification "excluding composite substances." (175) "But we shall then be left with "having no cause" as the reason for eternality. (But this interpretation of the Sūtra must be incorrect), as the same point has been made at Vaiśeṣika Sūtra IV.i.1 (176) and the present Sūtra cannot be interpreted as a mere useless repetition.

Perhaps, then, the attempt will be made to interpret the aphorism to mean that we are ignorant of any cause of the destruction of anything real, except the separation of its component parts or their destruction, and as neither of these applies to the atom it must be eternal. But this would be wrong, as there is no rule that these are the only two ways in which an atom can be destroyed. Such a rule would only hold good where the only kind of causality admitted was that in which a plurality of causal substances combined together as parts to produce a new substance as whole. The case is quite otherwise, however, where the cause is taken to be a universal, in itself free from all particular qualifications, which assumes new states (avasthā) involving particularity. (177) For in this case "destruction" need mean no more than the dissolution of some concrete form assumed by the cause, like the dissolution of the solidity of a pat of sacrificial butter (in the fire, implying the liquefaction but not the destruction of the butter.) Therefore it is as we have said: because the primary atoms are credited with colour and other properties, the doctrine of the Vaiśeṣikas turns out to imply the opposite of what they intended. (178) And so for this reason again, the doctrine of the Atomists is unfounded.

Now, the elements are thought of in the world as being four. Earth is the grossest, having the attributes of odour, taste, colour and tangibility. Water is more subtle, having only the qualities of colour, taste and tangibility. Fire is yet subtler, having only colour and tangibility. And wind is the subtlest, having tangibility alone. These four are thought of as progressing in order from the more gross to the more subtle, according to whether they contain more or less sensory attributes. A question, then, arises for the Vaiśeṣika. Should he or should he not assume that the atoms from which the four elements are respectively composed show a similar progression from more to less sensory attributes?

Well, as the author of our own Sūtras says, either view involves inextricable faults or reasoning. Suppose you assume a progression from more attributes to less, then where there are more attributes there will be a material accumulation and the "atoms" will no longer be atomic. You cannot deny that accretion of attributes implies accretion of mass, for the latter is seen to accompany accretion of attributes amongst the effects of atoms, the elements. (179)

But what if, in order to avoid any progression in the attributes of the different kinds of atoms, you decline to assume that the classes of atoms from which the four elements are respectively composed show a corresponding progression from more attributes to less? If all the atoms were assumed to have but one attribute each, then there could not be the sensation of touch in fire, nor of colour and tangibility in water, nor of taste, colour and tangibility in earth. (180) For the qualities of the effects (perceptible elements) follow those of the material cause (primary atoms). If, on the other hand, each atom had all four attributes then one ought to perceive odour in water, odour and taste in fire, and odour and colour and taste in wind. But this is not found to be the case. So on this ground also the doctrine of the Atomists fails. (181)

* * * * *

4. The doctrine (of the Sāṃkhyas) that Nature is the cause of the world has been adopted by certain true experts in the Vedic teaching like Manu, by way of illustrating particular aspects of the received doctrine, such as the reality of the effect before production (Sat-kārya Vāda), etc. But this other doctrine (of the Vaiśeṣikas) that everything proceeds from primary atoms has not been accepted by any properly instructed person in relation to any aspect, so that it is in utter discredit with Vedic teachers.

Moreover, the Vaiśeṣikas believe in six "categories" (padārtha), mere scholastic constructions, called substance, quality, movement, universal character, particular character and inherence (samavāya), each absolutely distinct from the others and having different characteristics, as distinct as "man", "horse" and "hare". They hold this, and in the same breath maintain the contradictory proposition that whatever is not itself substance is dependent on substance. (182)

Now, this is not right. Why not? Because in the world things that are distinct from one another like hares, grass and trees are not mutually dependent for their existence. And in the same way, it would follow that if substance and all the other categories were completely distinct from one another in nature, qualities and the rest could not be dependent for their existence on substance (as the Vaiśeṣikas maintain).

Or suppose that the existence of the other categories *does* depend on substance. In that case, when the substance exists, they will exist, and, when it does not exist, they will not exist. And from this it would follow that all that really exists is the substance itself, being characterized by a number of different words in accordance with its different states. It would be like a person called Devadatta, who, remaining one and the same, is spoken of and thought of differently when he assumes different roles. But if this were so, the Vaiśeṣikas would find themselves to have contradicted their own position and to have adopted that of the Sāṃkhyas. (183)

But, you will say, is it not a fact that smoke is quite different from fire and yet is seen to be dependent on it? But in the case of fire and smoke (184) the difference is guaranteed by direct perception. But what about such cases as "white blanket," "brown cow," "blue lotus"? (185) Here all that is perceived is a substance having such and such a distinctive quality. Hence substance and quality are never perceived as distinct in the way fire and smoke are. Hence it follows that the quality *is* the substance. And this also shows that the other categories, movement, universal character, particular character and inherence are also of the nature of substance.

The Vaiśeṣikas will perhaps re-affirm that the other categories *are* different from substance, claiming that the reason why the other categories are dependent on substance is that they are "inseparable" (ayuta-siddha) from it.(186) If so, the inseparability must be inseparability either of place or of time or of nature. But in none of these modes can inseparability be defended. If the other categories were inseparable from substance in place, this would contradict other Vaiśeṣika tenets. What they say implies that a cloth made of threads occupies the place of the threads only and not the place of the cloth, while the attributes of the cloth, like whiteness, occupy the place of the cloth only, and not that of the threads. For they say, "Substances produce a *new* substance, attributes a *new* attribute." (187) The threads, as causal substances, produce the cloth, the effect-substance. And the attributes belonging to the threads, white colour and so on, produce a new example of the attribute of colour and so on in the effect-substance, the cloth. This is their view. But if the substance and its attributes occupy an identical spatial position, this view stands contradicted.

Perhaps, then, it will be said that inseparability means inseparability in time. But this would mean that the left and right horn of a cow (which come into existence simultaneously) would have to be regarded as "inseparable" (which is ridiculous, because it would mean that one horn could not continue to subsist if the other were destroyed). If, on the other hand, inseparability meant non-difference of nature, then substance and quality could not be distinct in nature, because the quality is apprehended as one with the substance.

The Vaiśeṣikas also maintain that when separable entities are related, we have contact, whereas inseparable entities are connected by inherence (samavāya). But this view is wrong. For a (material) cause must exist before its effect, and cannot be inseparable from it. Perhaps they will say that they took only one of the two terms related by inherence as inseparable, and that inherence relates an inseparable effect with its (material) cause. But even on this supposition, there cannot be a relation between a not-yet-existent effect and its material cause, for a relation presupposes the prior existence of the two terms to be related. If they reply that the effect comes into being first, and is then connected afterwards, their case is no better. For if it be taken that the effect comes into being before it is related to the cause, then their other statement "There can be no entry into contact or disjunction of an effect and its material cause because they are inseparable" (188) falls to the ground. (Nor can they avoid this consequence by appeal to the principle that, because contact presupposes movement, the relation of cause and effect cannot be contact and so must be something different, namely inherence). For just as they maintain that the relation of an effect-substance, which has just been produced and has not yet acquired motion, with all-pervading (and therefore motionless) substances like the ether is one of contact and not inherence, even so, the relation of the effect-substance to its material cause may be one of contact and not inherence (even though movement be absent).

Further, there is nothing to show that a relation, whether of contact or inherence, could subsist apart from its terms. It cannot be argued that the existence of the name and idea of contact over and above the names and ideas of the related terms proves that such contact or inherence actually *exist* in separation. For we see that one thing, while remaining one and the same, can be spoken of and thought of in a variety of different ways in a relative sense, whether in regard to the different aspects of its own nature, or on account of its relationships with others. Thus Devadatta, though himself one and the same, may be spoken of and conceived in the world in different ways, according to whether special account is taken of this or that aspect of his own nature or of his relationship with others, so that he may come to be known at different times as "man", "Brahmin", "learned", "generous", "a child", "a youth", "an old man", "a father", "a son", "a grand-son", "a brother", "a son-in-law." And in the same way, one and the same digit, according to changes in the position where it lies, can find itself spoken of or thought of as one, ten, a hundred or a thousand, etc. And it is just in this way that two related things come to be referred to and thought of not only as themselves but also as "in contact" or "in inherence", without the implication that "contact" or "inherence" are themselves "objects" (vastu) separate from the related things. Thus we conclude that these relations cannot exist as separate realities, because we do not perceive it. (189) Nor is there any question of the name and idea of these relations applying permanently to the things connected by them, as we have already said that one and the same thing gets different names and notions associated with it in a relative sense, both on account of its own nature (as subject to development) and also on account of its different relationships with others.

A further flaw in the Vaiśeṣika system is that, as atoms, souls and minds (190) have no external surfaces, they cannot enter into contact as the system demands, (191) for the only instances of contact observed are those between pairs of substances that both have surfaces. Nor will it do to say that atoms, minds and souls have imaginary surfaces, as, if it were possible to bring things into existence by the mere power of the imagination, everyone would realize his every desire. For there would be no reason for any restrictions of the form "Only this non-existent entity, illogical or logical, can be brought into existence through imagination, and the rest not." And imagination is an arbitrary process which can wax abundant. Once imagination were allowed free sway, what would there be to stop anyone invoking a hundred or a thousand imaginary entities beyond even the six categories imagined by the Vaiśeṣikas? The result would be that whatever anyone wanted would happen. One compassionately inclined person could wish away all transmigratory existence on the ground that it was nothing more than a great source of suffering to living creatures. And another person, attached to the gaieties of the world, might wish back into rebirth even the liberated ones. Who could stop them?

And there is another point. Two partless primary atoms could no more enter into contact with a binary atomic compound, which has parts, than they can with the ether. Ether and the primary atoms, as ultimate constituents of the elements, do not enter into contact with one another like paint and wood.

The Vaiśeṣikas will perhaps say that as the (material) cause and its effect can only be conceived as container and contained, the relation called "inherence" must necessarily be assumed. But such a view is wrong, as it involves the fallacy of mutual dependence. It can only be established that (the material) cause and its effect are container and contained if it is already known that they are different. And they can only be established as different if it is already known that they are container and contained. The two propositions are in vicious inter-dependence, giving rise to the situation of the dish and the plum-tree. (192) The followers of the Upanishads (Vedānta Vādin), for their part, do not accept either the difference of the cause and the effect or their standing as container and contained, since they maintain that the effect is but a particular state of the cause.

And there is a further point. Since the primary atoms are limited in size, they must (face in all directions in space and therefore) have as many parts as there are spatial directions, (193) whether these be reckoned as six, eight or ten. And (because they have parts) they must be impermanent, (194) so that the assumption of the Vaiśeṣikas that the primary atoms are eternal and partless cannot stand. Nor will it avail him to rejoin that what we take to be parts, different from one another since they correspond to the differences of the various spatial directions, are in fact themselves primary atoms. For his atoms will still be impermanent. Everything undergoes dissolution into its subtler material cause in a hierarchical series leading to the ultimate (indestructible) cause of all. In comparison with the binary atomic compound, earth is the grossest substance of all.

It is taken by the Vaiśeṣikas as a reality, yet it is admitted to perish. And the subtler and yet more subtle substances (the other three elements, water, fire and wind), being of the same general nature as earth (i.e. being material elements coming to form one world-system), must also perish. Similarly, the binary atomic compounds must perish. And finally even the primary atoms themselves, since they are of the same nature as earth (i.e. material) must also perish. And it will not be right to say that destruction never means more than mutual separation of the parts. For we have already shown how destruction may take the form of dissolution, like the dissolution of the solidity in sacrificial butter (under the heat of the fire). Sacrificial butter and gold and other substances, though not losing their parts under the heat of fire, become liquid and lose their solidity. Similarly, the primary atoms dissolve into the supreme Cause and lose their determinate form. And in the same way it is wrong to think that new effects are brought into being *only* by the entry into contact of the parts. For we see that milk and water, for instance, give rise to such new effects as curds and ice without the accretion of new parts.

And where the Sūtra ends by referring to "complete disregard", it means that the Vaiśeṣika doctrine is a mere patchwork of empty rational constructions that stand in contradiction to the Vedic doctrine that the Lord (īśvara) is the cause of the world. (195) It has not been in any way accepted by qualified persons learned in the Veda, like Manu. (196) Those who wish for their own good should therefore disregard completely this doctrine that primary atoms are the (material) cause of the world. (197)

* * * * *

5. The doctrine of the Vaiśeṣikas and others (198) that desire and the other mental phenomena (199) inhere in the soul is also wrong. For impressions, (200) which are the cause of memory, cannot inhere in the soul, which (on the Vaiśeṣika view is all-pervading and) contains no divisions. (201) And because (according to the Vaiśeṣikas) mind and soul are only in the relation of contact (while memory is in the different relation of inherence within the soul as its attribute, the mind would have no control over memory and) one could not be sure what was and what was not a memory, as anything might be a memory, or again all memories might rise up at the same time.

Nor is the doctrine of the contact of the souls with other entities like the mind tenable, as they each belong to a separate class and are both inaccessible to the sense of touch. (202)

Nor can the other categories such as attribute, etc., consisting of colour, etc., and the categories of movement, universal character, particular character and inherence as conceived by our opponents (the Vaiśeṣikas) really be different from substances (as they suppose, because they maintain at the same time that they are inseparable from them.) For if attributes were totally distinct from substances, and the attributes of the soul, such as desire, totally distinct from the soul, such attributes could not be in any way connected with their substances. If they claim that inseparables (ayuta-siddha) can be conceived without contradiction as different and held together by the relation of inherence, this is wrong in terms of their own system. For on this basis there could not be the relation of (inseparable) inherence between the soul, previously established as eternal, and such transient things as the mental phenomena like desire, etc., though this is demanded by the system. Or, to put it another way, if the mental phenomena like desire *were* in the relation of inseparability (ayuta-siddhatva) with the soul, they would be constant and eternal concomitants like other things that are inseparable from it, such as its infinite size. And this is not acceptable, as it would mean that the soul could never acquire liberation. (203)

Another point is that if the relation of inherence is different from substance, then the Vaiśeṣika ought to state the nature of the connecting relation that unites it to substance. As the two are different, there will have to be a connecting relation, just as there is between a substance and an attribute. If they reply that there is no need to state any such thing, as inherence is an eternal relation, then it would be impossible to maintain that there was any difference between different things connected by the relation of inherence, as they would be related eternally. (204) And if the substance and the other categories were altogether different from one another (as the Vaiśeṣika tries to maintain), they could not stand as possessor and possessed, any more than a pair of substances of which one had the property of touch and the other (such as the ether) not.

Another point is that if the soul really possessed transient qualities like desire and the rest, which are subject to variations of intensity, it would itself be non-eternal. It would be hard to see why it should not have the defects of having parts and being subject to change, like the physical body or like a fruit.

On the other hand the Kārikā (now under comment) suggests that the defects of the soul, such as pleasure and pain, etc., are the result of external adjuncts such as the mind which have been attributed to it through nescience, like the impurities of smoke and dust attributed through ignorance to the pure ether of the sky. If this is accepted, there is nothing to contradict the practical experience of bondage and liberation. For all disputants accept empirical experience as set up by nescience, and reject it as the final truth. So the assumption in some of the rationalist schools of philosophy that there is more than one self (205) is unnecessary and untenable. (206)

* * * * *

6. (As for the Vaiśeṣikas), while agreeing (with the Sāṃkhyas) that souls are many and all-pervading, they make them into material substances, *per se* non-conscious, like pots and walls. And they regard the individual soul's instrument of cognition, the mind (manas), as atomic in size and *per se* non-conscious likewise. And they maintain that desire and the other eight qualities of the individual soul (207) arise in it privately through the contact of the mind-substance with the soul-substance. And these private qualities inhere individually in each separate soul-substance, without there being any intermixture with any other soul. And this, they say, constitutes the transmigratory life (saṃsāra) of each individual soul; while liberation consists in the absence of the rise of any of these nine qualities in the individual soul....

And the Vaiśeṣikas further claim that any given mind is related to one soul only. But the fact is that any given mind must on their principles be in immediate contact with all the other individual souls as well, as (they regard the latter as all-pervading and) all are in equal proximity to it. Now, when the cause is the same, the effect will be the same. And from this it follows that when any single soul experiences pleasure or pain, all the other souls must do so too (on the basis of the Vaiśeṣika theory that souls are many and all-pervading)....

Nor can the Vaiśeṣika appeal to the principle of the occult force (adṛṣṭa) latent in deeds. For all of his plurality of individual souls are all-pervading like the ether. They are in proximity with all bodies equally, without so much as a distinction of a "within or without". And yet they claim that merit and demerit as an occult force can be built up (by the individual) through thought, word and deed. In the case of the Sāṃkhyas, the difficulty is that action lies with Nature and not with the individual soul. Since it lies with Nature, it affects the whole of Nature, and cannot determine the future pleasure or pain of this or that particular individual soul. But in the case of the Vaiśeṣikas, the difficulty is the same one that we mentioned earlier. There is no way of determining "This particular merit and demerit belongs to this particular individual soul" because it will have been performed in conditions where every individual soul is in contact with every mind.

Perhaps the Vaiśeṣika will argue that every soul acts upon its own individual resolves, such as "Let me obtain such and such a result," Let me avoid such and such," "I will make such and such an effort," "I will do such and such," and that the occult future results of their deeds accrues to each soul individually on the basis of these individual resolves. But the author of the Sūtras replies, "No." Any mind is equally connected with all souls (on the principles of the Vaiśeṣikas). Since all minds are in proximity with all souls (because all souls are all-pervading), it is impossible to establish any rule about what actions result (in what future experience for whom). Hence the fallacy remains (namely, that on the principles of the Vaiśeṣika and Sāṃkhya systems it is not possible to explain why some souls experience pleasure while others experience pain.)

Finally, the Vaiśeṣika might argue as follows. He might say that, even though each soul is all-pervading, contact with the mind, which is after all tied to a particular body, will only occur in that part of the soul which is enclosed within that body. Hence the resolves and their execution and the later experience of pleasure and pain through merit and demerit all pertain to that part of the soul only. (208)

But the author of the Sūtras replies that this theory will not succeed either. For, because all souls are all-pervading, they are present in all bodies. Now, the Vaiśeṣikas cannot assume that there is any part of the soul marked off by the body (since in terms of their own system the soul is eternal and could not have parts). Even if the partless soul were imagined to have such a part, it could not be established that (such an imaginary part) was a real agent producing real effects, from the mere fact of its being something imaginary. And again, since the body would be in proximity with all souls (they being all-pervading), it would be impossible to say that it was born as the body of any one particular soul rather than of any of the others.

Or let us assume for argument's sake that the merit and demerit of a given act lie in that place within a given (all-pervading) soul that did the action. Then (the absurd result would follow that) it should be logically possible that two souls that have the same experience of pleasure and pain could experience it in the same body. For merit and demerit can be earned by two souls through acts committed in the same place. We see, for instance, that sometimes Devadatta experiences a certain degree of pleasure and pain at a given spot and that his body vacates that spot, while Yajñadatta enters that spot and is seen by others to experience pleasure and pain to the same degree. And that would not be possible (in terms of the present assumption) unless Devadatta and Yajñadatta had earned this particular piece of merit at the same place.

Furthermore, one who maintains that a soul can have spatial parts will not (on the basis of this theory) be able to experience joy in heaven. (209) For his merit and demerit will exist in that part of his soul that is spatially delimited by his earthly body, whether Brahminical or of other caste, while experience of heaven and the like would take place in some other (very distant) part of his all-pervading soul.

Moreover, the whole theory of a plurality of all-pervading souls is untenable, as there is no example to support such a conception. I ask you, can you point to any example of things which are many yet which occupy the same space? You cannot appeal to the fact that different qualities like colour and odour can exist in the same substance. For though they may be non-different from one another in so far as they inhere in the same substance, they are different from each other by nature, whereas the many souls of your system are not different from each other by nature. Nor can you say that your souls are different from one another on the ground (of the doctrine of your system) that every substance has a particular character which marks it off from all else. For the notions of "difference" and "particular character" are inter-dependent. (210) Nor can you adduce the example of the ether being all-pervading along with the other (all-pervading) entities. (211) For the Upanishadic Absolutist (brahma-vadin) takes all such entities as illusory effects. Therefore it stands proved that only the (Upanishadic) doctrine of the one Self is free from all fallacies. (212)

* * * * *

7. As the heat of the fire cannot be illumined by the light of the fire, since both are attributes inhering in a common substratum, so cognition, as conceived by Kaṇāda and his followers (the Vaiśeṣikas), will not be able to reveal pleasure and other mental phenomena (213), for the latter are all attributes inhering in the same substratum as knowledge (*viz.* the soul as conceived by the Vaiśeṣikas). Moreover, since pleasure and cognition both depend (in the Vaiśeṣika theory) on contact with the mind for coming into existence, (and the mind in the Vaiśeṣika system is atomic and capable of revealing only one quality of the soul at a time), it will follow that cognition and pleasure cannot both be in relation with the soul simultaneously, and this is another reason why, if the Vaiśeṣika system were right, pleasure could never be perceived. The same is true of the other mental phenomena besides pleasure. Being classed as different from cognition, they will not (in terms of the system) be in existence at the same time as it is. Nor can it be said that the mere relation of these phenomena with the soul constitutes their being cognized, for their being cognized is a special qualification over and above their mere existence. That it is only through the special qualification wrought by cognition that they can be cognized at all is also clear from such memories as "Pleasure was cognized by me." For the soul *per se* is without cognition, on the Vaiśeṣika's conception of it. (214)

And the fact that the soul, as the Vaiśeṣika conceives it, is without modification is a further proof that pleasure and the rest cannot be its attributes (as the system makes them out to be). And since the Vaiśeṣika holds that the attributes of the soul (such as the mental phenomena) are altogether distinct from the soul (though they are attributes arising in it from some accidental external stimulus), why should they not belong to another soul or another mind? There is nothing to show it could be otherwise. (215)

* * * * *

8. Alternatively, there is a third view. When the soul (ātman) acts, it is an active substance, and when it does not act it is a non-active substance. On this view, it can abandon action entirely. The peculiar point about this third view is that the soul is not a continually active entity, nor a passive entity prompted to act by the latent force of (past) action, but a substance so organized that when there is no action in it action can nevertheless arise, and when there *is* action in it, action can break off. The substance then persists in its pure state, but with the potentiality (śakti) of action. And this, say the followers of Kaṇāda (Vaiśeṣikas), is the true nature of the agent. And they ask what could possibly be wrong with such a theory.

Well, what is wrong is this, namely that it is not the teaching of the Lord. How do we know? Because the Lord said, "There can be no being of the non-existent" and so forth. (216) This doctrine of the Vaiśeṣikas speaks of the (coming into) being of the non-existent and the passing into non-being of the existent.

If you say, "Well, granting that it is not the teaching of the Lord, is there anything wrong with it logically?", we say that there is, in as much as it is contradicted by all the means of knowledge. (217) How? Well, the doctrine maintains that substances, beginning with the binary atomic compounds, are absolutely non-existent before they are produced, and after remaining in being for a time, become completely non-existent. Thus the non-existent is born as existent, and the existent lapses into non-existence, non-being becomes being and being becomes non-being. When non-being comes into being, it must be produced through the usual complex of causes admitted by the school, the inherent, the non-inherent and the efficient, (218) though it is (at the time) as non-existent as the horns of a hare. But one cannot affirm that non-being can be produced or be subject to causation in this way, for such a thing is never found in the case of what is totally non-existent, like the horns of a hare. If (as on our own view((219) the pot and the like (effects) are taken to be already in being before they are produced, then it is quite logical to maintain that they just require some (efficient) cause to bring them into manifestation.

Further, if the non-existent could become existent and the existent non-existent, no one could place reliance on the ordinary means of knowledge anywhere. For one could never be certain that the existent was existent or the non-existent non-existent.

And there is another point. The Vaiśeṣikas maintain that the notion "It is produced" means that some new substance, from the binary atomic compound upwards, is in relation with its causes and with the universal called Existence (sattā). Before production it is non-existent. And after production it is brought into relation with its material causes, the primary atoms, and with the universal called Existence, through the operation of the whole complex of its causes. It is then said to be "related" and to enjoy intimate relation with its inherent (material) cause. But how, will they kindly tell us, could there be an existent cause of the non-existent? Or how could the non-existent be in relation with anything? No one could logically conceive how (something utterly non-existent like) the son of a barren woman could be related with existence or could have a cause.

Now, it might be maintained that the Vaiśeṣikas do not in fact assume that non-being comes into relation with anything as we have represented them as doing. All that they do is to affirm that all composite substances, from the binary atomic compounds upwards, inhere in their material causes, and that it is as existent entities that they do so. But this will not do. For they do not admit the existence of the said composite substances before relation with the causes. The Vaiśeṣikas in no way admit the existence of the pot before the operation of the potter, the wheel and the stick. Nor will they allow that all that happens is that the (already pre-existent) clay assumes the form of the pot. (220) It follows, therefore, that they must affirm that the non-existent enters into relation with the cause, as this is the only alternative left.

Nor will it do to say that the non-existent can enter into a relation of inherence without contradiction. For a relation of inherence is never found in the case of (utterly non-existent things like) the son of a barren woman and the like. And it will not help to say that it is the "non-existence of the pot previous to its production" that is related to the cause of the pot, and not (anything *totally* non-existent like) the son of a barren woman. For both the non-existence of the pot previous to its production and the barren woman's son are alike non-existence, and there would be the difficulty of explaining how one kind of non-existence could be different from another. For no one can point to any (positive) characteristic that would establish any distinction between the non-existence of one, the non-existence of two, the non-existence of everything, the non-existence after destruction, mutual non-existence and total non-existence.

And since there are no differences within non-existence, the following way of speaking is not right either. It is not right to say that first the non-existence of the pot previous to its production attains to existence as the pot through the operation of the potter and the rest, and that that enters into relation with Existence in the form of its material cause, the raw fragments of clay, and is thus able to sustain the whole causal process, while at the same time denying that the "non-existence after destruction" of that self-same pot can be subject to any causal process (which would bring it back into being again), on the ground that the only form of non-existence that is subject to modification through causal processes like production is the "non-existence previous to production" of substances from the binary atomic compounds upwards. For both the "non-existence previous to production" and the "non-existence after destruction" are alike non-existence. And there is no difference between one kind of non-existence and another. For instance, there is no difference between non-existence after destruction and total non-existence.

If, finally, the Vaiśeṣika should deny that he maintains that the non-existence of the effect previous to its production gives way to existence, then it would follow that it was existence that was attaining to existence, as if (what was already) a pot could become a pot or (what was already) a cloth could become a cloth. But this is just as much in contradiction with the deliverances of the ordinary empirical means of knowledge as is the view that non-existence attains to existence. (221)

* * * * *

9. Where the text says, "One only" it means that here there is nothing which does not fall

within the range of the effects of the Absolute.

And when it says, "Without a second," it has to be understood as the negation of any second thing operating as an additional cause supporting Existence, and itself other than Existence, on the analogy of the efficient cause, the potter, moulding the clay into a pot.

Objection: But is it not a fact that, even on the thesis of the Vaiśeṣikas, (222) everything is correlated with Existence, for (in their view) the word and the idea "Existence" accompanies all categories such as substance and quality, as when we speak of an "existent substance," and "existent quality" or an "existent movement"?

Answer: This might be true as regards the present, but, as regards the past, the Vaiśeṣikas do not admit that any given effect was existent before its production, for they explicitly maintain the opposite view, namely that the effect was non-existent before production. And they are by no means reconciled to the (Upanishadic) doctrine that Existence, one only with a second, existed before the production of the universe. Thus the Existence of which the Upanishad speaks (in the text at present under comment), and which it illustrates from clay and other such examples, is different from "Existence" as imagined by the Vaiśeṣikas. (223)

* * * * *

10. As for the argument that the origin of the ether was rationally impossible and that the texts teaching it ought for this reason to be interpreted figuratively – to this we reply that there is no ground for supposing the origination of the ether to be impossible. (On the contrary, reason teaches that the ether *must* be an effect and so have a beginning). For it is an observed

fact in the world that being distinct implies being a modification. Pots and basins and buckets, for instance, though made of clay, are mutually distinct. Similarly, arm-bands and bracelets and ear-rings, though all made of gold, are mutually distinct, as are needles and arrows and swords made of iron. But that (i.e. the Self) which is not a product of modification is never found to be distinct from anything else. The ether, however, is known to be distinct from earth and the other elements. Hence it, too, must be a product of modification. And space, time and the primary atoms (of the Vaiśeṣika system) must also be effects. . .

A further objection was raised (by the Vaiśeṣikas), who said that the ether could not have a beginning, because being caused and having a beginning demands an "inherent cause", consisting of a plurality of substances of a like kind (such as we find in the case of threads being woven into cloth), and that this was not possible in the case of the ether. (224) To this we (Advaitins) reply that there is no law that only causes of like kind produce effects, and not dissimilar ones. The threads and the relation of contact binding them are causes of the cloth (on the Vaiśeṣika view), but they are not of like kind, (225) for one is a substance and the other an attribute. (226) Nor is there any rule that the instrumental causes, such as the shuttle and the loom, should be of like kind. Nor will it avail you to say that the maxim that origination proceeds only from causes of like kind applies only to material causes (as understood by the Vaiśeṣikas). For a rope will sometimes be found to have been woven from strands consisting of substances of different kinds, such as cotton yarn and cow's hair. Blankets, too, are sometimes woven as patchworks of cotton and wool. If, on the other hand, you take very widely applicable characteristics like "exist" or "being a substance" as criteria of "being of like kind", then the rule becomes meaningless, as on this basis everything is of like kind with everything else.

Nor is there in fact any law that it is only groups of substances that produce origination and not single substances. For you (Vaiśeṣikas) admit that the primary atom and the (atomic) mind produce their own initial movement unaided and without connection with other substances. It will not help you to point out that movement is not a substance, and to claim that the law that only groups of substances and not single substances produce effects applies only to the production of substances. For we have the example (quoted by the Sāṃkhyas) of the transformation (of milk into curds). Your law would only hold if it was invariably in conjunction with some other substance that a substance originated an effect. But in fact it is admitted that one substance alone may constitute its own effect if it assumes some new state. Sometimes transformation of several different substances into one occurs, as in the case of earth and seed and other factors transforming themselves into a sprout. But sometimes it is one substance alone that transforms itself into the effect, as when, for instance, milk transforms itself into curds. There is no divine edict saying that only a multiplicity of causes can produce an effect. Hence we must conclude, on the authority of the Vedic texts, that the universe arose from the one principle, the Absolute, and that the ether and other elements were produced serially in order. Hence the author of the Sūtras remarked earlier, "If you say 'No, because we find an assemblage of several causes,' we reply that you are wrong, as is shown by the case of milk." (227)

Nor was there any justification for the claim that (the ether could not have had a beginning because) it would be impossible to point to any difference between the situation before it began and the situation after. (228) For we have to conclude that the distinction (namely, the possession of the property of sound) whereby the ether is now found to be distinct from the earth and the other elements did not exist before creation. (229) (As for the authority of revelation), the texts show that the nature of the Absolute is quite independent of earth and the other gross elements, as a passage like "not gross, not subtle" shows. (230) And the same text shows that the nature of the Absolute is likewise independent of the ether, as is clear from the words, "It exists without ether." (231) Hence our view that the Absolute existed without the ether before creation stands.

It was also argued that the ether is different in nature from earth and the other gross elements, therefore it could not have had a beginning. But this argument was also wrong. For a mere logical inference about the impossibility of the production of some entity may itself be erroneous if it stands in contradiction with Vedic texts. (232) And we have ourselves, moreover, given positive logical arguments in favour of the view that the ether has a beginning. And we might now throw in another, like: "The ether is non-eternal, because it is the seat of non-eternal attributes (such as sound), like the (admittedly non-eternal) pot." Nor can this argument be demolished by the alleged contrary example of the soul (ātman). (233) For no one who follows the Upanishads can accept that the "Ātman" (as there understood) is the seat of qualities. Nor can anyone who holds (like us Advaitins) that the ether has a beginning accept (with the Vaiśeṣikas) that it is infinite in extent. (234)

* * * * *

11. Even from the standpoint of ordinary secular reasoning the notion that the Self is afflicted with pain cannot stand. To begin with, one cannot attribute pain, which is an object of perception, to the Self, for the latter is not an object of perception.

Objection: Well, cannot the Self have the quality of pain in just the same way as the ether, (which is not an object of perception according to the Logicians of the Nyāya and Vaiśeṣika schools), has the quality of sound? (235)

Answer: No, because pleasure and pain on the one hand, and the Self on the other, cannot both be the object of the same cognition. The cognition which perceives pleasure has an immediately perceptible object. It cannot also have the Self for its object, since the latter (according to you) is an eternal entity accessible only through inference. And if it could, then, because the Self is one, there could be no knowing subject for that cognition. (236)

Objection: Even if the Self is only one, it can still be subject and object of illumination, like a lamp. (237)

Answer: No. It is logically impossible that the Self (taken as a whole) should be subject and object of the same act at the same time. And it is impossible to split it into parts, as it is partless. (238) And this (239) also shows the untenability of the (Vijñāna Vāda Buddhist) view that consciousness splits into subject and object.

Now, on your (Vaiśeṣika) view, pain is an object of perception, and the (eternal) Self is an object of inference. But we cannot from this infer that they are respectively attribute and subject. For pain is invariably an object of perception and belongs to the same domain as colour and form. (240) If pain really accrued to the Self through contact with the mind (as the Vaiśeṣikas hold), it would follow that the Self had parts and was subject to modification and was therefore transient. For no attribute is ever found to accrue to a substance, or to be given up by it without the substance being altered thereby. Nor does anything that is partless ever undergo alteration, while nothing that is capable of acquiring an impermanent quality is itself permanent. Those who follow Vedic revelation cannot admit that the ether is an eternal substance having the impermanent quality of sound, as they do not admit the eternity of the ether, (241) and there is no other example of an impermanent quality inhering in an eternal substance.

Objection: Well, even if a thing is subject to alteration, it will still be eternal if it is invariably perceived.

Answer: No, because a substance cannot undergo alteration except through alteration of its parts.

Objection: Even if something has parts, it can still be eternal.

Answer: No. The parts of whatever has parts must have first come together, and will therefore later be sundered.

Objection: Not so, as there are impregnable substances like the thunderbolt of Indra.

Answer: No, for we must assume that that, too, was composed from parts (and will therefore one day decompose). Therefore the thesis that the Self has pain and other impermanent qualities cannot be made out.

Objection: Well, if the supreme Self is not the one who experiences pain, and there is no other being who could experience pain, then there would be no purpose in taking up the study of the Vedic texts with a view to bring pain to an end (so that your explanation of the Vedic texts ends up by making them useless).

Answer: Not so. For the purpose of such study is to remove the erroneous notion introduced by nescience that one is subject to pain, like the removal of the villager's error about himself which prevented him from rightly counting the numbers. (242) We admit that the Self suffers from *imagined* pain. (243)

5. REFUTATION OF THE BUDDHISTS

The Buddha died *circa* 478 B.C. His followers at various times in the centuries to follow called councils to hammer out doctrine and establish canonical texts. Buddha taught, not in Sanskrit, the language of the priests and the educated classes, but most probably in Māgadhī, the vernacular dialect of Magadha (modern Bihar). What was remembered of the personal teachings he gave was embodied in the Sutta Piṭaka of the Canon (Sutta = Sanskrit Sūtra, Piṭaka = basket), while the disciplinary rules were embodied in the Vinaya Piṭaka. Buddha himself discouraged philosophical speculation. But Buddhism could not survive in competition with other faiths unless it offered some kind of rational grounding for its teachings, and gradually dogmatic treatises came to be composed and to be embodied in a third part of the Canon called the Abhidamma (Sanskrit Abhidharma) Piṭaka. Some time during the reign of Aśoka (the estimated date for the event is 242 B.C.), the teaching was taken to Ceylon, where the Canon has been preserved in the form accepted by the then dominant school (Thera Vādins) in a dialect which is probably close to the Māgadhī of the Buddha and which has since become known as "Pālī". (244)

(XI.5) REFUTATION OF NON-VEDIC WORLD-VIEWS

Śaṃkara and the other non-Buddhist philosophers of the mainland of India were not much concerned with the Pālī Cannon, and it is doubtful if Śaṃkara even knew of its existence. (245) The Buddhist "realists" with whom the philosophers on the mainland were chiefly concerned, however, were a sub-sect of the same school which dominated in Ceylon. Known as the Sarvāstivādins, they were already existent in the time of Aśoka. Their numbers were greatest in north-west India, in Kashmir, in Afghanistan and in the cities on the silk-route leading between India and China. Their Teachers taught and wrote in Sanskrit, and though the original Sanskrit versions of their texts have been almost entirely lost, the Chinese versions have in some cases survived. For example, the Jñāna Prasthāna, the most important of their Abhidharma treatises, is still preserved in Chinese. A great Commentary (Vibhāṣā) on this work was composed in Kashmir some time after 200 A.D., and those amongst the Sarvāstivādins who followed this Vibhāṣā came to be known as the Vaibhāṣikas. Another branch of the Sarvāstivāda school affected to ignore the Abhidharma literature, including the Vibhāṣā, and to hold fast to the word of the Buddha as preserved in the Sūtras. This school was accordingly known as the Sautrāntikas. In fact, however, their doctrine became interwined with that of the Abhidharma literature of the Vaibhāṣikas through their very efforts to critize it. Vasubandhu the Later, (*circa* 400 - 480 A.D.), the author of the only surviving large-scale exposition of the Vaibhāṣika doctrine, the Abhidharma Kośa, is described by his follower Yaśomitra as a Sautrāntika, (246) and on some points he criticizes the Vaibhāṣikas in that work from the Sautrāntika standpoint. Some hold that Śaṃkara's Commentary on the section of the Brahma Sūtras dealing with the Buddhist "realists" (II.ii.18-27) is concerned with the Vaibhāṣikas throughout, while others hold that the Commentary on the last two Sūtras of the group passes over to a criticism of the Sautrāntikas.

The original insistence of the Sautrāntikas on the Sūtras to the exclusion of the Abhidharma was symptomatic of a new trend that began to appear amongst the Buddhist schools about the beginning of the Christian era. The goal of the earlier teaching had been personal release. The new schools looked down on this doctrine and called it the "Small Ferry" (Hīnayāna). In their own doctrine, the "Large Ferry" (Mahāyāna), the adept defers personal release and remains in the world as a Bodhisattva in order to work compassionately for the removal of suffering from all living creatures. New Sūtras appeared in which the Buddha unfolded his "deeper" doctrine that was said to have been hitherto withheld from circulation because it would not have been understood. The Prajñā Pāramitā Sūtra in its various recensions is an example. The new doctrine diminished the distinction between layman and monk and taught that the Buddha-nature (tathāgata-garbha) was latent in all creatures. The accompanying philosophical development was at first "nihilistic" in tendency. The Mahāyāna emphasis on the new Sūtra literature involved the refutation of the philosophical constructions of the Abhidharma treatises of the Hīnayāna schools. Their conceptions were refuted dialectically by Nāgārjuna (*circa* 200 A.D.) and his followers of the Mādhyamaka (Middle Path) school, who soon extended the dialectic to take care of the Sāṃkhyas, Vaiśeṣikas and other prominent Brahminical and non-Brahminical schools. (247)

The Buddha had called his path a "Middle Way", and for the authors of the new Mahāyāna Sūtras the Middle Way and the path to truth lay through the rejection of all pairs of opposite notions. Nāgārjuna fastened exclusively onto the negative side of the new teaching. He did not follow the new Sūtras in speaking positively of the

Buddha-nature as the root of all appearances (dharma-dhātu): he spoke only of the extinction of all plurality. (248) In regard to the objects of the world-appearance, the Middle Way, according to him, consisted in saying that they were neither existent nor non-existent but "empty". The extinction of all plurality (nirvāṇa) is itself neither being nor non-being, as being and non-being are but two opposites which themselves belong to the world of plurality and appearance. The enlightened man is not deluded by the play of appearances and is aware of their emptiness (śūnyatā).

Nāgārjuna did not care to explain how the world of appearance could have come into being, even as appearance. Maitreyanātha (perhaps early fourth century A.D.), the earliest great Teacher of the Yogācāra or Vijñāna Vāda school whose name has survived, and who stands to Nāgārjuna somewhat in the same relation that Śaṃkara stands to Gauḍapāda, wished to make some provision for the explanation of the world-appearance and therefore interpreted the Void of the Sūtras, not as absence of essence, but as a positively existent principle of consciousness, marked by the absence of duality (advaya). Even before Maitreyanātha, it had been taught in the Bodhisattva Bhūmi Śāstra that the world is not being, because all appearance of plurality is false, but that it is not non-being either, since there is a reality on which appearance is superimposed (samāropa). (249) Maitreyanātha's pupil Asaṅga (fourth century) was especially concerned with the practical aspects of the path and with easing the transition from belief in traditional dogma to realization that all was empty, and he re-introduced many of the "factors of existence" (dharma) from the Abhidharma treatises of the Hīnayāna Teachers, adding the important one of the "storehouse consciousness" (ālaya-vijñana). The term "storehouse consciousness" did not imply any permanent or substantial entity, but expressed the theory that the future experiences of an individual would not be conditioned by objects lying outside consciousness. They would be conditioned, rather, by the seeds (bīja) and impressions (vāsanā) left by his past experiences, which continued to dwell in latent form in the series of momentary flashes that constituted the true nature both of himself as an individual soul and of the world he experienced.

By Śaṃkara's day, the main centre for the development and propagation of Yogācāra teaching had long been the "university" of Nālandā, not far from Pāṭaliputra (the modern Patna), the ancient but by Śaṃkara's time already derelict capital of Magadha. The outstanding Teacher of the period immediately preceding Śaṃkara was Dharmakīrti (*floruit circa* 650 A.D.), whose Pramāṇa Vārttika, itself a kind of free verse commentary on the Pramāṇa Samuccaya of Diṅnāga, is quoted by Śaṃkara and by his pupil Sureśvara. A short logical work of Dharmakīrti, the Nyāya Bindu, has survived in the original Sanskrit, and formed the basis of Stcherbatsky's well-known exposition of the philosopher. Tibetan translations of Dharmakīrti's more substantial works, the Pramāṇa Vārttika and Pramāṇa Viniścaya, have also survived, and in the course of various journeys to Nepal and Tibet between 1934 and 1938 Paṇḍita Rāhula Sāṃkṛtyāyana pulled off the remarkable *coup* of recovering the Sanskrit original of the Pramāṇa Vārttika and other related literature, in manuscripts which had apparently lain in Buddhist monasteries venerated but untouched since being deposited there by Indian copyists in the thirteenth century A.D. or earlier. (250)

We have had occasion to note that Śaṃkara's handling of Buddhist technical terms in his Commentary on Gauḍapāda's Kārikās suggests that he was not familiar with the early Mādhyamika and Yogācāra texts in which Gauḍapāda was interested.(251) Holes have also been picked in his statement of Vaibhāṣika doctrine, (252) but we have to admit that our present-day knowledge of Vaibhāṣika teaching is incomplete, that Śaṃkara's statements of their doctrine was partially conditioned by the wording of the Brahma Sūtras and perhaps by written (but now lost) or unwritten traditions about Vaibhāṣika doctrine current amongs the Vedantins of his day, and finally that he was more concerned with protecting the students of Advaita from the seductions of a non-Vedic path than with an objective statement of what the opponents actually said. Similarly, it was necessary for him to adopt a polemical stance against the Mādhyamika Buddhists. With the hindsight of many centuries, it is today often claimed that, in the case of Nāgārjuna at least, their aim was not to deny being but to avoid any affirmation of it that would reduce it to an object, and it has indeed been argued that they played their part in preparing the way for Śaṃkara's own doctrine. (253) But Śaṃkara was concerned with synthesizing the Upanishadic, Brahma Sūtra and Gīta teaching, and for this purpose the purely negative rational dialectic of Nāgārjuna was not the right instrument. He therefore denounced the Mādhyamika teaching as unqualified negation and hence as contradicting all the means of knowledge (which affirm being) and as involving the absurdity of an attempt to negate the negator.

The greater part of what Śaṃkara has to say against the Buddhists, however, is said in criticism of the Vijñāna Vāda in the form in which that doctrine was propagated by Dharmakīrti, (254) and this is the only form of the Buddhist doctrine with which we can be certain that he had some measure of direct acquaintance. The Yogācāra or Vijñāna Vāda tradition, as maintained by Dharmakīrti, derived, through Diṅṅāga, partly from Vasubandhu the Later, and was influenced by Sautrāntika teaching. (255) If the Sāṃkhyas saw all change as occurring within one identical substance, and if the Vaiśeṣikas saw change as the coming together and parting of eternal changeless atoms, the Sautrāntikas, for their part, took the fact of change very seriously, and, as a result, denied that anything had any duration or substantiality anywhere. They were left with a staccato series of momentary "factors of existence" (dharma), each distinct from its successor in the chain, but succeeding one another so fast as to set up the appearance of a permanent observer (soul) inhabiting a world of solid, enduring objects. There being no material causality, all causality was held to be efficient causality, and all "factors of existence", including cognitions, were conditioned to come into momentary existence by other momentary "factors of existence" that had gone before. The external (non-mental) factors had their direct (hetu-pratyaya) and indirect (adhipati-pratyaya) causes. Mental factors (*viz.* "ideas" in the Lockean sense) were conditioned partly by the immediately preceding mental factor in the series (samanantara-pratyaya) and partly by external factors as objects (ālambana-pratyaya). The object is in one sense given in perception, since it conditions the idea. Yet it is (paradoxically) not perceived, as, being momentary, it has already gone out of existence before perception can take place, like a distant star that may continue to be "perceived" in the world long after it is actually extinct. Perception is in fact pervaded through and through by imaginative construction (vikalpa). (256)

The Sautrāntika doctrine, however, underwent an idealistic transmutation at the hands of Diṅnāga and the logicians of his school. To begin with, extension as well as duration was shorn away from the objective reals, which were now reduced to unique point-instants. (257) It was still maintained that they were in some sense "given" in perception, but all *representation* was now said to proceed through universal ideas, which were taken to be mere imaginative constructs. Only the unique point-instants are real, and all universals are fictions; but the latter are nevertheless the only basis of practical experience and activity in ordinary life. Each real point-instant being unique, individuals can only be grouped into classes on the basis of exclusion (apoha) of anything else. The individuals forming a class are alike only in being distinct from all other reals outside the class, and all *representation* of their behaviour depends on universal ideas proceeding from imaginative construction. Dharmakīrti raised the question of how, if the reals are unique point-instants, universal ideas can come to be applied to them at all. As so often in considering the teachings of this school, one is reminded here also of Kant, who composed the most difficult section of the Critique of Pure Reason in an effort to explain how the universal and necessary *a priori* concepts of the understanding could be applied to the raw data of sense, which were totally disparate from them in kind. Dharmakīrti, however, merely says that this is a problem that is only raised in theory, never in practice. Things which, because they produce a given effect in practice, can be distinguished from what does not produce it, are given a common name for purposes of communication. (258)

But the object was not only reduced to a unique point-instant. It was also declared non-different from the cognition whereby it was perceived. As the object is never perceived without the cognition, it cannot be proved to be anything different from the cognition. (259) You cannot argue that, because when a healthy eye and light are present we sometimes see a pillar and sometimes do not, it follows that cognitions must be determined by an object that is external to consciousness (i.e. the presence of the objective pillar), for cognitions can very well (on the Sautrāntika theory) be determined by the immediately preceding cognition. (260) Knowledge is self-luminous. It is illogical to suppose that it could illumine a non-luminous object. It is the momentary cognition itself which assumes the form of an objective characteristic, say blue, under the impulse of the impregnations of previous experience. (261) A cognition cannot be experienced by anything else beyond itself (say an eternal Witness), (262) as the same objection would arise, namely that one thing cannot be aware of another that is different in kind. (263) The fact of hallucinations shows that there can very well be the erroneous notion that an external object is present when only a cognition that has assumed the form of an external object is present. (264) Though consciousness is in truth without parts, it is taken by deluded people to be divided into three as object, idea and act of self-illumination. (265)

Śaṃkara was committed by the text of the Brahma Sūtras to state and attack the doctrine of the Sarvāstivādin "realists", the Vijñāna Vādin "idealists" and the Mādhyamika "nihilists" in that order. The Extracts that follow are grouped as A, B, C and D. Group A consists merely of two short personal observations about the Buddha. The vehement hostility of the first, conditioned partly by the straightforward denunciation in the Sūtra on which Śaṃkara was commenting, stands in some contrast to the more lenient attitude displayed in the second. The remaining three Groups, B, C and D, give the statement and refutation of the three above-mentioned schools of Buddhism as found in the Brahma Sūtra Commentary, along with further material from outside the Brahma Sūtra Commentary placed in its appropriate Group. Group B covers the Sarvāstivāda, Group C the Vijñāna Vādins and Group D the Mādhyamikas. The refutation of the Mādhyamikas given in the Brahma Sūtra Commentary is perfunctory, but it will be seen that there are more detailed attacks on this school in the Praśna and Chāndogya Upanishad Commentaries.

TEXTS REFUTING THE BUDDHISTS: GROUP A, THE BUDDHA

1. And the Buddha, by teaching three mutually contradictory doctrines emphasizing the reality of the external object, of Consciousness and of the Void respectively, showed himself to be a mere loose talker. Or it may be that he was consumed with hatred for the people and taught them contradictory doctrines in the hope that it would confuse them. (266) In any case, there must be no respect for this Buddhist teaching on the part of those who seek their true spiritual welfare. (267)

2. This non-dual principle of reality, void of knowledge, knower and known, has (as the Ācārya Gauḍapāda says) "not been declared by the Buddha." It is true that in refuting the existence of external objects, and in supposing that Consciousness alone existed, he has said something close to the truth. But the true non-dual principle of reality can nevertheeless only be found through the Upanishads. (268)

TEXTS REFUTING THE BUDDHISTS: GROUP B, THE SARVĀSTIVĀDINS

3. We have said that no attention should be paid to the doctrine of the Vaiśeṣikas because it contradicts the Veda, is supported by vulnerable arguments and has not been adopted by any of the great Vedic sages of the past. It has been called a semi-nihilist doctrine because it is *like* the doctrine of the Nihilists, (269) so it follows that the tradition that holds that *everything* is perishable (i.e. the Buddhist tradition, which unlike that of the Vaiśeṣikas,

denied the existence of *any* permanent substance) should be avoided even more carefully. This is what we now propose to show.

The "Nihilist" (Buddhist) doctrine has several different forms, either because it really is conceived in different ways or else because it is taught in different ways to pupils of different capacities. Amongst the various schools, the following three chief ones are found. There are some who maintain that everything exists (Sarvāstivādins), some who maintain that only Consciousness exists (Vijñāna Vādins), and some who teach the doctrine that all is void (Mādhyamikas). Of those who teach that everything exists, (270) some (271) admit the existence both of internal (mental) and also external realities. They admit the existence of elements external to consciousness and of products of those elements, and also of minds and of mental components. For the moment we will confine our refutation to them.

In their doctrine, the elements are earth, water, fire and wind. The products are the four qualities, odour, taste, colour and touch, and the senses that perceive them, namely the senses of smell, taste, sight and touch. They hold that the four different kinds of primary atoms, the earth-atoms, water-atoms, fire-atoms and wind-atoms, being respectively solid, liquid, fiery and kinetic, combine to form the earth and other perceptible elements. There are also (as the basis for the appearance of an experiencing individual) the five "groups" (skandha, of momentary factors of existence, dharma). These are formed respectively of the sense-organs and their objects (rūpa), (272) consciousness of objects associated with ego-feeling (vijñāna), consciousness of objects associated with the feelings of pleasure, pain and indifference (vedanā), determinate consciousness of objects (samjñā) and the various drives and passions (saṃskāra). And they believe that these groups combine to form the basis of all individual experience.

On this we make the following observation. Our opponents hold to the existence of two separate aggregates, each having their peculiar causes. One is the aggregate forming the elements and the products of the elements, which has atoms for its ultimate material cause. The other is the aggregate formed by the five "groups", which has the "groups" for its material cause. They speak, indeed, of an aggregate arising from each of these two causes (i.e. atoms and "groups"), but , says the Sūtra, "They have no right to do so." That is, no aggregate is rationally possible (under their terms). Why not? Because the things entering into aggregate are non-conscious, since the mind (as they conceive it) could only acquire the light of consciousness if the aggregate were already assured. They do not admit any other conscious principle such as an experiencer (a permanent conscious individual soul) or a controlling God who should exist permanently and effect the aggregation. If, however, they claim that aggregation is a spontaneous activity, it is clear that such spontaneous activity could never come to an end (and this contradicts their doctrine of nirvāṇa or release). (273) Appeal to the existence of "currents of consciousness" (āśaya) (274) will not help either, as the latter are indeterminable as either different or non-different (from the series of pulses constituting the current). (275) The theory also breaks down because the currents themselves are assumed to have the form of a series of discontinuous momentary flashes, so that they would be actionless (276) and unable to promote action in others. Therefore the formation of aggregates would not be possible on the principles of the system.

To this the Buddhist might reply that although no permanent conscious being effecting aggregation is admitted, whether as the experiencer or the controller, still, empirical experience is explicable on the basis of the causal chain (pratītya-samutpāda) beginning with nescience. And if empirical experience is explained, nothing else is required. The factors of empirical experience, which begin with nescience, and each of which is the cause of the next member of the series, are found taught in various ways in Buddhist works, sometimes briefly, sometimes in more detail. One finds such a list as nescience (avidyā), the will to sense-experience which leads to the formation of an empirical personality in a future birth (saṃskāra), consciousness as the core of the individual (vijñāna), (277) the psycho-physical organism in its rudimentary state (nāma-rūpa), (278) the six areas of contact (or sense-experience) (ṣaḍ-āyatana), sensation (sparśa), pleasure-pain feeling (vedanā), thirst (tṛṣṇā), activity based on thirst (upādāna), changeful bodily existence (bhava), resulting from the merit and demerit of activity, birth, old-age, death, grief, lamentation, pain and despair. No one, they claim, can possibly deny this chain of causation beginning with nescience. (279) And once the whole causal chain beginning with nescience is admitted to exist, and to be revolving continually like a wheel with buckets at a well, it is found to imply that the formation of aggregates must be possible. (280)

But this is not right, as the causes so far mentioned lead to production (of the next effect in the series) only (and not to aggregation of any kind). An aggregate could be admitted if an intelligible cause were assigned for it. But it is not. Nescience and the rest may cause one another mutually in your cycle, but they only cause the *rise* of the next link in the chain. There is nothing to show that anything could be the cause of an aggregate. True, you claimed that if nescience and the rest were admitted, an aggregate was necessarily implied. To this, however, we reply as follows. If you mean that nescience and the rest cannot arise except in the presence of some aggregate and so are dependent on it, then (if you wish to defend your system) you still have to explain what could be the cause of the aggregate. (281) Now, we have already shown in the course of our criticism of the Vaiśeṣikas that aggregation is unintelligible even when supported by such assumptions as that of the existence of eternal atoms along with eternal individual experiencers who serve as permanent *loci* for the conservation of the effects of past action. So it will be all the less intelligible in a theory in which only atoms of momentary existence are admitted, without any permanent experiencer or any permanent *locus* for anything. If the Buddhist now claims that it is this causal chain beginning with nescience that is the cause of aggregation, we ask how this causal chain could ever be the cause of aggregation when it depends on aggregation for its own existence. (282)

Perhaps you will now try to counter by saying that in this beginningless world-process (saṃsāra) the aggregates beget one another of their own accord in a temporal series, and that nescience and the rest pertain to them. In that case, we ask: Does each new aggregate arise from the previous one regularly, and is it strictly similar to it in kind? Or is it that there is no regularity about the process, so that the new aggregate could be either similar to the previous one or different? If the new aggregate were regularly similar to the previous one, the human individual (pudgala) could never attain birth as a god or an animal or sojourn in hell (as the Vaibhāṣika doctrine maintains he can). If, on the other hand, there were no regularity in the process, the human individual could suddenly become an elephant for a moment, and then a god, and then go back to being a man. So both of the alternative consequences (of taking the aggregates as causing one another spontaneously) result in a contradiction with the tenets of the Vaibhāṣika school.

Further, you hold the view that the aggregate that exists in experience is not "an experiencer" in the sense of constituting a permanent substance. But on this basis experience cannot be anything that is sought by anything else: experience must be for the sake of experience. And so liberation, too, will have to be for the sake of liberation. There cannot be anyone else, any seeker of liberation (mumukṣu). If there were anyone who sought either experience or liberation, he would have to exist at the time of his experience of liberation. And if he did this, that would contradict the dogma that all is momentary. So the Sūtra means that even if nescience and the rest (of the Buddhist's causal chain) could cause each other to come into existence, there still could not be an aggregate. For the latter cannot be established when no experiencer is admitted.

It has been shown that it would not follow, from the fact that nescience and the rest of the causal chain could produce effects, that aggregates existed. Now (in Sūtra 20) the further point is made that even this mere production of effects is impossible. The upholders of the doctrine that everything undergoes destruction every moment maintain that when each new momentary apparition comes into being the previous one is destroyed. But no one who holds this doctrine can establish a causal connection between one moment and the next. For the earlier moment cannot possibly serve as the cause for the later one when it either has already been destroyed or is in the course of being destroyed, as it will then have been swallowed up by non-being.

The Buddhist will perhaps reply that he means that the cause of the later moment is the first moment in its completed state, and regarded as now momentarily) existent. This, however, will not agree with his system, as to assume that anything existent went into action (to produce its successor) would imply its relation with a later moment. (283) Nor will it help him to say that the "existence" is itself the activity. For no effect can come into being that is not in some way charged with the nature of its cause. And if he admits this, then the nature of the cause will persist into the time of the effect, and this will amount to a rejection of the doctrine of universal momentariness. And if he claims that causation can take place without the effect being charged with the nature of the cause, he falls into the doctrine that anything might be the cause of anything.

Consider again. The rise and destruction of a thing might be taken either as constituting the nature of the thing itself or as another state of the thing or as a different thing. But none of these conceptions are intelligible. If they constituted the very nature of the thing itself, then the words "thing", "rise" and "destruction" would be synonyms. One is therefore driven to assume that there must be some difference, and one might suppose that the words "rise" and "destruction" were names of earlier and later states of the thing, while the thing itself actually continued to exist in between them. But even this would go against the assumption that the thing was momentary, as the thing would then be in relation with three separate moments, the beginning, the middle and the end. Well, let us suppose finally that the rise and destruction of the thing were absolutely distinct from it, as distinct as horse and buffalo. But then the thing would be quite unrelated to rise and destruction, and so eternal, (and not, as the Buddhist dogma requires, momentary). And if it were said that perceiving the thing constituted its rise, and not perceiving it its destruction, then, as perception and non-perception are attributes of the perceiver and not of the thing perceived, the thing would again be eternal. So this is another reason why the Buddhist doctrine is untenable.

We have shown that, on the doctrine that everything suffers destruction after existing for a single moment, no previous moment can be the cause of a later one, because it has already been destroyed before the latter comes into existence. Perhaps the Buddhist might rejoin that the effect comes into being even when the cause has already gone out of existence. But this will result in contradiction with his own tenets. The particular tenet that will be contradicted is his doctrine that phenomena arise through the co-operation of four causal factors. (284) And if they could arise without a cause, then anything could arise out of anything, there being nothing to prevent this absurd consequence. And if they say that the first moment lasts until the production of the next it would mean that the cause and the effect would be simulta--neous, and that would be against the tenets of the system. For their doctrine is that all causal forces are momentary. (285)

The Nihilists (Buddhists in general) suppose that all "factors of existence" other than "the three" are composite and momentary. They call "the three" the suppression through knowledge of experience arising through passion, (286) the suppression of experience without knowledge (287) and space (ākāśa). They regard these three as mere negations of empirical phenomena and as of inexplicable nature. (288) For they say that "suppression through knowledge" is the conscious destruction of positive experience, "suppression of experience without knowledge" is non-conscious destruction of positive experience, and "space" is mere absence of destruction. The Sūtras will be refuting their conception of space later; for the present, they go on to refute the two "suppressions".

The Sūtra says, "Suppression can never occur, either with or without knowledge." That is to say, it is impossible. And it is impossible, the Sūtra says, because there can be no extermination. For these "suppressions", with or without knowledge, must relate either to a causal series or to a permanent substance. But they cannot relate to a causal series. For no causal series can ever be exterminated, since its members give rise to one another in an uninterrupted causal sequence. But they cannot relate to a permanent substance either. For there cannot be any such thing as an "inexplicable" but total destruction of a permanent reality, for here recognition reveals an unbroken element persisting continuously amidst the various changing states. (289) Even in those states where the identity is not clearly recognized, we may infer its presence by analogy, on the ground that we have perceived the persistence of an unbroken element in other substances. So the hypothesis of the two "suppressions" put forward by the opponent cannot stand.

And then that "suppression of nescience and the rest of the causal chain," which the opponent imagines he included in "suppression through knowledge", must either arise from right knowledge, together with its auxiliaries, or else just arise automatically of its own accord. On the first supposition there would be a contradiction of the fundamental dogma of the school that destruction invariably takes place uncaused. (290) If the second view were true it would mean that the spiritual path (291) and the teaching were useless. So, as the Sūtra puts it, on either supposition this doctrine is wrong.

(XI.5) REFUTATION OF NON-VEDIC WORLD-VIEWS (TEXTS)

Now, we have already seen that they regard the two "suppressions" and space as "inexplicable", (292) and we have refuted the view that the two suppressions could have this "inexplicable" existence that is attributed to them. We now proceed to refute the view that space could have an "inexplicable" existence.

To begin with, it is in any case wrong to attempt to maintain that space has an "inexplicable" existence, as it is taught as an existent reality, just as the two suppressions are. And space is known to be a reality on the authority of Vedic revelation in such texts as "The ether arose from the Absolute." (293) To those, however, who do not accept such revelation (i.e. the Buddhists) we must say that space has to be inferred to be a reality from the fact that it is the vehicle of sound, for we see that it is only real substances, like earth and the rest, which support their peculiar attributes like odour and so on. Moreover, he who maintains that space is nothing more than the absence of destruction (294) finds himself also maintaining that when one bird is flying in the sky this represents an obstruction, so that no other bird who wanted to get up and fly could do so, and there would no longer be any space. (295) Nor could you reply that the second bird could fly wherever there was no obstruction. For space would then have to be taken as that positive entity that served as the *locus* of specific cases of absence of destruction, not as mere absence of destruction. (296)

Moreover, in maintaining that space is mere absence of destruction, the Buddhist contradicts his own fundamental tenets. For there is a passage in their traditions (297) where a series of questions and answers follows from the question "On what, holy One, does the earth rest?", in which the last question is "On what does the wind rest?" The answer given to this question is, "Wind rests on space." This would be impossible if space were not a positive reality, so this is another reason why they are wrong when they say that space is not such.

Again, they contradict themselves when they maintain that "the three" consisting of the two suppressions and space are "inexplicable", and not positive realities, and yet are eternal. For what is not a positive reality cannot be either eternal or non-eternal, since attributes can only be predicated of a subject if they are taken to inhere in some real principle. And if substance and attribute were here in evidence, "the three" would be realities like a pot, and hence not "inexplicable".

Further, because the Nihilist (Buddhist in general) holds that everything is momentary, he must hold that the perceiver, too, is momentary. But the perceiver cannot be momentary. And this is so, as the Sūtra puts it, "On account of remembrance of one's past experiences." Remembrance means in this case the reproduction of an experience one had in the past. It can take place only if the one remembering is the same as the one who had the experience, for we do not find that one person can remember the experience of another. How, for instance, could one have such experiences as "Formerly I saw that, now I see this," unless it was one and the same person seeing on both occasions? Indeed, everyone in the world is familiar with the experience of recognition in the form "It is the same I who formerly saw that who now sees this," which amounts to a direct perception that the one who now sees and the one who formerly saw are one and the same. If the agent had been different in the two cases, the feeling would have been, "It is I who remember, and it was someone else who saw." But no one ever has this feeling. When such a feeling does arise, people feel that the one who remembers and the one who saw are different, and express it by saying, "I remember that he saw that." But in the other case, even the Nihilist (Buddhist in general) himself recognizes himself as the one sole agent in the remembering and the seeing, and says, "I saw this." He can no more deny his own act of seeing and say "It was not I" than he could deny that fire was luminous and hot. And this being so, the Nihilist cannot very well deny that, as the connection of one and the same person with the two separate moments of seeing and remembering has been established, it will follow that the doctrine of universal momentariness has been undermined.

But one might go further and ask the Nihilist why he does not feel thoroughly ashamed to go on recognizing himself as the agent in every successive cognition right up to his dying breath, and to remember all his past cognitions from birth on as having had himself as agent, while continuing to adhere to his doctrine that everything goes to destruction the moment it arises? He might perhaps rejoin that all this comes about through similarity. (298) One might then reply to him that the notion "this is like that" shows that similarity involves two entities. But as the Nihilist cannot admit that there is a single perceiver who could perceive the two similar things, his claim that recognition is based on similarity is just babble. If, on the other hand, there were really a single perceiver able to perceive the similarity of two moments, then there would be one person persisting during two moments, which would contradict the principle of universal momentariness.

He might perhaps claim that the notion "this is like that" was just a fresh cognition, and not based on the perception of an earlier and a later content. But this would be wrong. If we had to reckon with a fresh cognition revealing similarity which was quite different from what was meant by "this and that," this would render the sentence "this is like that" meaningless. All we would be able to do would be to assert similarity (without specifying what was similar to what). For if a body of people engaged in a discussion decide to reject what is otherwise universally accepted as true, then no demonstration or refutation that is made within that circle will constitute an intelligible proposition, either for the speaker himself or for the other disputants. One should only advance that of which one can say, "This is verily so." Anyone who speaks of anything else is merely proclaiming his own verbosity.

Nor, indeed, can any empirical experience (which depends on recognition of ourselves and objects) be explained on the basis of similarity. For in recognizing a thing, what we recognize is the thing itself, and not something "like it". It is true that in the case of external objects we are liable to error and might sometimes have the doubt "This is either that same thing or something like it." But in the case of ourselves as knowing subjects we never experience any such doubt as "I am either that same 'I' or something like it." For we have the definite conviction "It is that same I who saw something yesterday who remembers the fact today." So this is another way in which the Nihilist doctrine breaks down.

And there is yet another point in which it fails. Because they do not admit any persistent material cause, they are reduced to the doctrine that being originates from non-being. They expound the doctrine of the origination of being from non-being according to the maxim "Because no effect arises until its cause has been destroyed." (299) The shoot, they believe, springs forth from the seed only after the latter has been destroyed, curds come only when the milk has been destroyed, a pot only when the lump of clay has been destroyed. If the effect arose from a changeless and indestructible (kūṭastha) cause, they say, then anything could come from anything, without distinction. And therefore they maintain that because the shoot arises from the seed only when the latter has already been swallowed up in non-being, it follows that being originates from non-being.

To this the Sūtra replies as follows. "The existent (sat) does not arise from the non-existent (asat), because this is never actually found to occur." "Being" (bhāva) does not arise from non-being. If it did, then, since non-being is void of any distinctions, it would be meaningless to distinguish one cause from another. There is no difference between the "non-being" of such things as destroyed seeds on the one hand, and the non-being of imaginary creatures like the "horned hare" (300) on the other, for both non-beings are alike in point of having no definable nature (svabhāva). (301) When no distinction in the cause can be established it is impossible to explain how shoots arise only from seeds, or curds only from milk, or how causation follows any rules whatever. If, on the contrary, undifferentiated non-being be accepted as the cause, then the shoots and other empirically real effects could as well be regarded as arising from non-existent creatures of imagination. But this is not found to be the case in our actual experience. If, on the other hand, non-being is assumed to be characterized by distinctions, as a blue lotus, for instance, is characterized by blue colour, then, from the mere fact of possessing distinctions, non-being would automatically become being, just like a blue lotus.

In fact, however, non-being cannot be the cause of the origination of anything, from the mere fact of its being non-being, like the horns of a hare. And if being did arise from non-being, then every effect would invariably be associated with non-being. But this, also, is not found to be the case, for every reality (vastu) is seen to have its own positively existent nature. Nor does anyone maintain that effects like clay dishes, invariably associated as they are with their material cause clay, are really associated with something different, like threads. The world at large takes effects invariably associated with clay as being in fact modifications of clay.

The point, too, about how being must originate from non-being because nothing can arise from an indestructible cause, and without the destruction of its cause, was not sound. For it is found that substances of durable nature like gold are causes of such effects as ornaments, and recognized as persisting in them permanently. Even in cases such as the seed, where the whole nature of the cause seems to suffer destruction, we cannot admit that it is the earlier condition of the seed passing into destruction that constitutes the cause of the later condition. For in our submission it is those parts of the seed or other such material cause that are *not* destroyed that constitute the cause of the shoot or other such product. Hence, because existent things are not found to arise from non-existent ones like the horned hare, while they are found to rise from existent ones like gold, this doctrine that being arises from non-being is erroneous.

Not only this, the Nihilists throw the whole world into confusion by claiming in one breath that mind and mental phenomena arise from the four causal factors, (302) and that the material elements and their products arise from the primary atoms, (303) while claiming in the next that being arises from non-being, thus contradicting their own special theories.

A further point is that if being really arose from non-being, lazy people who were not prepared to make efforts to gain a particular end might gain it all the same, as non-being is not hard of acquisition. The farmer who did not work in his fields would still get his crop. The potter who made no effort to fashion his clay would still get his pitcher. Even he who wove no thread on the loom would get cloth, just like the industrious weaver. Nobody would need to make the slightest effort to attain either heaven or liberation. Few would be found to champion so unreasonable a thesis! And for this reason also the doctrine that being arises from non-being falls to the ground. (304)

* * * * *

4. The Buddhists maintain that knowledge and its objects are momentary in the most radical sense. They consist in nothing but a chain of separate momentary "factors of existence" (dharma). The notion of a permanent object (or subject) arises from the similarity of the different members of the chain, as in the case where the notion of a single permanent substance, a flame of a lamp, arises (from what is really but a swift succession of similar but different flashes). To put this notion of permanence to an end is (according to them) the highest goal of man. Some of them hold that matter (in its atomic and momentary form) exists, accompanied by cognition, which is different from it, but assumes its form. (305) Others hold that nothing over and above cognition exists. (306) It is the inconsistencies of the former school that we now proceed to expose here.

On their view, there can be no memory. For they maintain that all cognition acquires its form from the external object, and is momentary in character. If every cognition were momentary, no cognition could ever receive an impression (saṃskāra) (from another). Nor is there any basis for asserting similarity, (307) as no permanent support exists anywhere (to connect two things so that they can be compared and seen to be similar). Or if it were admitted, this would undermine the dogma that all is momentary. And that they do not want.

Moreover, if all the momentary "factors of existence" ceased on the instant of their own accord, (308) the holy texts of the Buddhists teaching how to bring them to an end would stand exposed as useless. If everything were exhausted in its own (momentary) nature, nothing would depend on anything else for annihilation. If, on the other hand, they were to affirm that it could be causally dependent on some different chain of "factors", then, if all things were momentary, anything could depend on anything. (309) But the rule actually found in the world is that causal dependence occurs when two entities co-exist in time (310) and stand in some mutual relation through which one undergoes development. (311)

TEXTS REFUTING THE BUDDHISTS: GROUP C, THE VIJÑĀNA VĀDINS

5. The defects of the doctrine of the Buddhist realists, such as their failure to give a coherent account of the rise of phenomena, having been exposed, the Buddhist idealist now takes up the challenge. It appears, he says, that some of the pupils of the Buddha had an obsession about the reality or external objects, and that this realist doctrine was devised in accordance

with their special needs. But it is not what the Buddha really intended to teach as the final truth. The doctrine he really meant to teach as the final truth was that of the sole reality of cognition (vijñāna-skandha). In this Vijñāna Vāda, the whole drama of empirical cognition is explained as internal and as taking place within the mind, including not only the mental process of the act of knowing but the object and resultant-cognition as well. For even if there were such a thing as an external object, the whole process of cognition could not begin until it had entered the mind.

But how (one may ask) can one be sure that all the factors of empirical experience are thus internal and that no object external to consciousness exists? Because, they reply, the existence of an object external to cognition would be impossible. For, if an external object were admitted, it would have to consist either in the primary atoms or else in aggregates of them grouped in the form of pillars and other such objects that we find in the world. But what in fact is it that is mentally represented as pillars and the like? It cannot be the primary atoms, as these are not capable of being represented in knowledge at all. But it cannot be objects like pillars conceived as aggregates of atoms either, for these (are not genuine entities as they) cannot be determined as either different or non-different from the primary atoms. (312) Universals and other such categories are refuted on similar lines. (313)

They make the further claim that, as bare awareness, cognition has no particular form. Cognition particularized towards individual objects – such as cognition of a pillar, of a wall, of a pot or of a cloth – could not arise without some latent principle of differentiation being present within cognition itself, from which we are bound to conclude that cognition possesses an inherent tendency to simulate objects. This much admitted, however, it follows that the form of the object is already included in cognition, and the assumption of objects outside it becomes pointless.

Again, the non-difference of the object and the cognition follows also from the law of simultaneous apprehension (sahopalambha-niyama), since neither of them is apprehended without the other. (314) And this would not be intelligible if they were different by nature, as there would then be nothing to prevent them from appearing separately. So this (says the Vijñāna Vādin) is another reason for the non-existence of external objects.

The nature of experience of objects in the waking state has to be seen to be analogous to the experience of dreams and the like. For just as in the case of dream-fantasy, or of a mirage, or of the hallucinatory vision of a castle in the sky, consciousness assumes the twin form of subject and object without the actual presence of any external object, so does it also do the same, we must conclude, in the case of objects like pillars in the waking state. For the dream-cognition and the waking-cognition are alike in point of being cognitions.

Perhaps it will be asked how cognitions could vary amongst themselves if there were no external objects. On account of variety in the latent impressions (vāsanā) resulting from previous experience, they reply. Transmigration is a beginningless process. Cognitions and impressions give rise to one another mutually like seed and sprout, so there is nothing to prevent variety of experience. Reasoning by the method of agreement and difference also shows that the variety in experience is to be accounted for on the basis of latent impressions only. Both you, as realist, and myself, as idealist, admit that in dream and similar states the variety of the experience is caused by latent impressions, without the presence of external objects. All that I do is to deny that the variety in experience is *ever* caused by an external object: it is *always* caused by latent impressions. So here is another argument for the non-existence of external objects.

Faced with all this, we (Advaitins) reply, in the words of the Sūtra, "It cannot be that external objects do not exist, for we actually apprehend them." The fact is, the non-existence of external objects cannot be proved. Why not? The words of the Sūtra "Because we actually apprehend them" give the reason. In every cognition an external object is apprehended, whether it be a pillar, a pot or a cloth. What is actually apprehended cannot be non-existent. When a person is actually in the course of eating and deriving satisfaction from his food he does not say, "I am not eating or deriving satisfaction." How, then, can one accept the word of a person who says, "I am not apprehending any external object and no such thing as an external object exists," while he is actually in the process of perceiving objects through sense-contact?

We shall perhaps hear the Vijñāna Vādin say, "I do not say that I do not apprehend anything. What I say is that I do not apprehend anything except apprehension (consciousness)." True, you say it, because you do not know how to bridle your tongue. But you are not saying anything arrived at through reason. For the mere fact that you admit apprehension forces you to admit the existence of an apprehended object over and above the apprehension. No one apprehends apprehension and calls it a pillar or a wall. What everyone in the world does is to apprehend pillars and walls as objects of apprehension.

Everyone in the world apprehends objects like that, and this is clear from the fact that even those who deny the existence of external objects speak of the internal object, which they admit, as "appearing as if external." This means that they experience consciousness directed to the external like everyone else, as they have to say "as if external" and use the phrase "as if" when they want to try and refute the existence of external objects. If they did not apprehend consciousness directed to the external (and believe that external objects actually existed), how could they say, "as if external"? No one would say, "Viṣṇumitra looks as if he was the son of a barren woman." (315) Those, therefore, who are prepared to admit the truth of what they actually experience will have to agree that it is the external itself that comes into manifestation, not the internal that manifests as if it were external.

The opponent will perhaps rejoin that (whatever be the case with what we actually perceive) the fact that it is the internal that manifests as if it were the external has been well proved on account of the logical impossibility of an external object. (316) But it has *not* been well proved. For the question whether we can speak of the logical possibility or impossibility of a thing depends on the prior question of whether or not the various authoritative means of knowledge have yet been applied to establish its existence. It is not that the question of whether or not we can apply the various authoritative means of knowledge to it depends on the *a priori* logical possibility of the thing. Whatever is apprehended by any of the authoritative means of knowledge, beginning with perception, is possible, from the mere fact of being apprehended. What is impossible is never apprehended by authoritative means of knowledge. In the present case, the external object is apprehended in its true nature by all the authoritative means of knowledge. When it is actually apprehended in this way, how can one say that it is impossible, merely because it is impossible to establish its hypothetical difference or non-difference (from atoms)?

Nor would the annihilation of the external object result from the fact that cognition corresponds in form to the object. For without an external object, it could not correspond to one, while we have the already established fact that the object is actually apprehended as external to cognition. As for the law of simultaneous apprehension (of idea and object), it should be accepted as proving, not that the idea and the object are identical, but that the object is the cause of the idea. And such distinctions as "cognition of the pot" and "cognition of the cloth" pertain to the successive qualifications only, to the pot and the cloth, not to cognition, the thing qualified. (317) It is like the case when we have the two ideas "the white cow" and "the black cow". Here there is a distinction between the qualifying attributes "whiteness" and "blackness", while that which they qualify, the universal "cowhood", remains the same. Here, what remains one is evidently different from what are two, and those that are two are different from that which remains one. In the same way, object and cognition must be different (since the object remains the same while the cognitions of it may be of different kinds). This is how we should interpret the experience of perceiving the pot and then remembering it. For here there is a distinction between the two things (in this case) *qualified*, while that which qualifies them, the pot, is the same. Or again there are two perceptions of the smell of the milk and the taste of the milk. Here again there is a distinction between the two things that are qualified, perception of smell and perception of taste, but that which qualifies them, the milk, remains the same (and so must be different from them). In this way the object must be different from the cognition of it.

Another point is that since any two successive cognitions will be exhausted in their own (momentary) manifestation, they will not be able to stand to each other as subject and object of perception. This, however, is enough to undermine a great many dogmas of the school – the doctrines, for instance, that consciousness includes distinctions, that the "factors of existence" (dharma) are momentary, etc., (319) the doctrine of the unique particular essence (sva-lakṣaṇa), and the general essence (sāmānya-lakṣaṇa), (320) the doctrine that one separate cognition can impregnate another with an impression and that the other can receive it, (321) also the doctrines of affliction through nescience, the good path, the evil path, bondage, liberation and so forth.

And here is another point. If a person is prepared to admit the existence of a series of cognitions, why should he not admit the existence of external objects like pillars and walls in the same way? Perhaps he will say that cognitions are matters of direct experience (whereas external objects are mere mental constructs). But he really ought to admit that the external objects are experienced as well. To this he will reply that a cognition, being luminous like a lamp, reveals itself by its own power, whereas this is not the case with the external object. But to say this is to accept the self-contradictory notion that a thing could act on itself, like fire burning itself, while rejecting the common experience of everybody that an external object is perceived by a cognition that is different from the object, an experience that is in no way inherently contradictory. This is proof of deep sagacity indeed. Even if it were admitted that cognition took place without external objects, it could not be that they were self-revealed, for the notion of action on oneself is inherently contradictory.

The opponent will perhaps counter this with the remark that if a cognition has to be cognized by another cognition, different from itself, (322) that other cognition will have to be cognized by another again and so on, leading to infinite regress. Nor is this all. Knowledge indubitably reveals things, like a lamp. To assume a further cognition to reveal a cognition would therefore be meaningless, because, since both cognitions would have the function of revealing, they could not stand mutually as revealer and revealed.

But both these contentions are wrong. For when once a cognition is actually perceived, no demand to perceive the Witness of that cognition arises, so that there is no occasion to speak of an infinite regress. And the Witness and the cognition *can* stand as perceiver and perceived, since they are different in nature. And the Witness is self-established, so that its existence cannot be denied.

And there is another point. To claim that a cognition is like a lamp, and that cognitions are therefore able to manifest of their own accord without depending on anything else to illumine them, is as much as to affirm that they are inaccessible to any means of knowledge and have no one to know them. It would be like talking of the radiance of a thousand lamps that were enclosed invisibly in the hollows of a thick mass of rock (323). Nor can you accept this and tell me that, since cognitions are self-luminous experience by their very nature, I am here only adopting your own view. For lamps and the like are only found to be manifest to some knowing subject, who is other than themselves, and who is equipped with eyes to see them. Like them, cognitions too, require to be illumined. Hence we conclude that they, too, like lamps, are manifest only when there is a subject to know them.

The opponent may now say that if I claim that the Witness, as the knower in question, is self-established and itself illumines the cognition by its own power, I am only restating his own doctrine (of the self-luminosity of knowledge) in different language and with different arguments. But this is wrong, as knowledge as he understands it (the mere series of particular cognitions) is marked by origination, destruction, plurality and other such characteristics. So our point that the individual cognition, even though (it reveals things) like a lamp, itself requires to be known by something else, stands proved.

The idealist has claimed that cognition of objects like pillars takes place in the waking state without the presence of any external object, just like those of dream and similar states, since the two classes of cognition (those of dream and waking) are identical in point of being cognitions. This point has to be answered. And what we say on this point is that the cognitions of waking experience are *not* the same as those of dream and similar states. Why not? Because, as the Sūtra says, they have different characteristics. The dream and the waking states do have different characteristics indeed. Can you give us an example of how? Yes, the dream-world is subject to cancellation, the waking world not. When a man awakes, what he experienced in dreams stands cancelled, as when he says, for instance, "I had the illusory experience of meeting a great man, I did not really meet a great man at all, but my mind was overcome by sleep and that was how the erroneous notion arose." In the case of magic (hypnotic) displays, too, the same sort of "cancellations" occur afterwards. But pillars and other objects experienced in the waking state are not subject to cancellation in this way, either in the waking or in any other state. (324)

Another point is that vision of dreams belongs to the general class of memory-experience, whereas waking experience is genuine perception. The difference between memory and perception is something that is directly perceived. The one is not attended by the presence of the object, whereas the other is, as is clear, for instance, when we say, "I was thinking of my dear son. I do not see him, though I wish to see him." This being so, it follows that we directly experience the difference between waking cognition (perception) and dream cognition (of the class of memory). And nobody who does this can say that waking cognition is false from the mere fact of its being cognition, like dream cognition. Those who lay claim to wisdom should not try to gainsay their own direct experience through mere verbal argument.

Again, it is just the very person who cannot show that the cognitions of waking experience are intrinsically void of all external support who wants to prove that they are so on account of their similarity with dream cognitions. But if a certain characteristic is not able to belong to something intrinsically, it will not be enabled to do so by that thing's similarity to anything else. Fire, being experienced as hot, will not become cold on account of any incidental similarity to water! That waking and dream have mutually different characteristics we have already explained.

It was also said that the variety in cognition could be explained by the variety of latent impressions giving rise to it, even if there were no external objects. This, too, must be answered. And in this connection we say that, if our opponent's view were to be accepted, it would follow that latent impressions could not come into being at all, as they do not accept cognition of external objects. Latent impressions, different for each object, are formed as a result of cognizing objects. How else could different latent impressions be formed if objects were not cognized? If the opponent tries to say that they form a beginningless series, he will not be able to prove his case. He will have a mere infinite progression without any firm basis anywhere, each link in the chain as blind and dark as the other, and without any possibility of explaining the fact of empirical experience.

The idealist also produced an argument based on agreement and difference that was supposed to show that all our cognitions derive from latent impressions and not from objects. (325) But if what has just been said is true, it will be seen that this argument, too, has already been refuted. For, without cognition of objects, formation of latent impressions is impossible. And since one has to admit that objects (when perceived for the first time) are perceived without latent impressions, and that latent impressions cannot be formed without prior cognition of objects, the real force of the argument from agreement and difference is to show that the object does exist (independently outside the mind and its impressions).

Latent impressions (vāsanā), moreover, are a sub-species of impressions in general (saṃskāra). (326) Impressions (saṃskāra) are inconceivable without a substratum in which they inhere. And this is supported by universal worldly belief. But there cannot on your view be any substratum in which impressions could adhere, since you maintain that no such thing is truly cognized.

It is true that the Buddhist idealist assumes the existence of a "storehouse consciousness" (ālayavijñāna) to serve as a substratum for the latent impressions. But because it is assumed to be passing in and out of existence every moment it has no fixed nature, and can no more serve as a substratum for the latent impressions than the series of (momentary) (pravṛtti-vijñāna) representations themselves. Without a single continuous principle persisting in past, present and future, or an immutable Witness of all objects, one cannot account for ordinary empirical experience, which implies the various activities of accumulating, recalling and synthesizing latent impressions that arise in different times and places. If the "storehouse consciousness" were taken as being something permanent and fixed it would contradict one of the root dogmas of the system. (327) As the Buddhist idealists (Vijñāna Vādins) agree with the Buddhist realists (Sarvāstivādins) that all is momentary, the refutations of the latter doctrine given earlier at Sūtra II.ii.20 apply here also. (328)

* * * * *

6. Here the Buddhist interposes and denies that any Self of the nature of light exists, other than the mind yet similar to it in kind (329) and capable of illumining it. For we have no knowledge of any illuminating principle over and above the intellect, either through perception or through inference. It is not as if there could be a separate mind operating at the same time as the first one. You (Advaitin) have said that if in cases like that of the pot and the light illumining it (and assuming its form), the illuminator and the illumined, though different, are not discerned as such, this is due to their high degree of similarity. In this case, we (Vijñāna Vādins) reply, since the light and the pot, etc., are known (in certain circumstances) to be

different, (330) we can very well speak of the similarity of the two different things where they coalesce. But in the case of the mind, we are not aware either through perception or inference of any other light illuminating it, as we are in the case of a light illumining a pot. There is just the mind, itself of the nature of consciousness, assuming both its own form and that of the object and acting as illuminator. So the conclusion stands that no one can establish either through inference or perception the existence of any separate light illumining the mind.

And when we spoke just now of the "similarity" of the object, such as the pot, and the light illumining it, conceived according to the Advaitin's example as separate entities mingling as illuminated and illuminator, this we only admitted for argument's sake. The pot or other object and its illuminator are not really different. In truth, the pot itself, as associated with light, is luminous. For the pot is reproduced anew each moment. It is consciousness itself that manifests in the form of the pot or other object associated with light. This being so, everything is of the nature of consciousness, and there is no example of an external object at all.

First of all the Buddhists form a theory in this way that consciousness itself assumes the form of both subject and object. And then they have another theory that it later (loses this dualistic form and) becomes pure. Some of them say that even in its pure form, free from subject-object division, consciousness still goes on rising and falling every moment. Others say that even the pulsations come to an end. While yet others, the Mādhyamikas, say that consciousness, having at first been obscured (saṃvṛta), (331) is later freed from all objective and subjective elements, and then it is just an empty void like the pots and other objects which had manifested in it.

All these theories of those who deny that any Self of the form of light exists over and above the mind are obstacles to the Vedic path of beatitude. Against those Buddhists who admit an external object (Vaibhāṣikas) we argue as follows. It is clear at the outset that an object like a pot cannot illuminate itself. A pot or the like standing in darkness never illumines itself. It is invariably the case that the pot is seen in light, illumined by association with the light of a lamp or the like. Though the pot and the light mingle, they are different from one another. For the two are perceived sometimes together and sometimes apart, like pot and a rope. And as they are different, it follows that the pot is illumined by something that is different from itself. The pot does not illumine itself of its own accord.

Perhaps you will ask whether the lamp is not seen to illumine itself. For people in the world do not bring together another lamp to illumine a lamp, as they do to illumine a pot, which suggests that a lamp must illumine itself. (332) But this idea is wrong, as both the pot and the lamp do require to be illumined equally. It is true that the lamp illumines itself at the same time that it illumines other things. But it is in no way different from the objects it illumines in point of itself having to be illumined by consciousness standing beyond it. In this respect, it is exactly like the pot and the rest. This being so it must certainly be regarded as having to be illumined by something other than itself.

Perhaps you will say that the pot, though needing to be illumined by consciousness, requires another light separate from itself in addition, whereas the lamp does not. And from this you might conclude that, though the lamp requires to be illumined by something else (*viz.* consciousness) separate from itself, still, it does also illumine both itself and the pot. But this would be wrong, because there is no difference in the present context between the pot and the lamp, arising either from their intrinsic natures or from external circumstances. (333) Just as the pot has to be illumined by consciousness, so also does the lamp, so that there is no difference from them on that score. And as for the statement that the lamp illumines both itself and the pot, that was just wrong. You ask why? Well, think what is the condition of the lamp when it is out. It then undergoes no change, either through itself or indirectly through anything else (such as the destruction of darkness) Only that can be illumined which is seen to undergo a difference according to whether an illuminator does or does not come near it. But one cannot imagine a lamp either coming or not coming near itself. When (in the case of the lamp itself) this alternative is not possible, it is clearly wrong to say that the lamp illumines itself.

It has been established that there is no difference between a lamp and such objects as pots in point of being illumined by consciousness. The lamp, therefore, cannot be brought up as an example to show that cognition can both be its own illuminator and the object of its own illumination. Cognitions are no different from external objects in point of having to be illumined by consciousness. And if cognition were an object of pure consciousness (as Witness), it would be on the same plane as objects. Assuming that cognition *is* in some sense an object for consciousness, are we to say that cognition is an object for some principle (like itself) that is itself an object, or is it not rather that cognition is an object for some (separate) principle of consciousness that is essentially a subject? On this doubtful question one must reason by analogy with what one finds elsewhere, and not in contradiction with it. On this basis we should have to say that lamps, as external objects, are perceptible only to some subject separate from themselves. And hence we should conclude that cognition, too, since it is an object for consciousness, must be an object for some principle of consciousness that is different from itself, even though it is itself an illuminator like a lamp. And that separate subject which takes cognition for its object, since it must be different from cognition, must be the Self of the nature of light.

But will not the conception of a separate principle taking cognizance of cognition lead to infinite regress? (334) No, for all that we have done is to demonstrate logically that if it is something known, that which knows it must be a separate principle. One cannot determine through mere logical reasoning whether, in any particular case, there actually *is* either a knower or a separate knower knowing that knower. (335) So the question of infinite regress does not arise.

But, you may ask, if cognition is known by a separate principle, will the latter not depend on separate instruments for that knowledge, and will not this lead to infinite regress? (336) This, however, is not right. For there is no universal rule that knowledge invariably requires instruments. You cannot establish any universal law saying that whenever one thing is known by another there are invariably instruments of knowledge over and above the knowing and known entity, as the case is seen to vary. In what way? Well, take the case of a pot. It has to be perceived by something different from itself, and here there has to be an instrument over and above the knower and the known in the form of a lamp or other means of light. The lamp or other means of light cannot be regarded either as a part of the pot or of the perceiving eye. And though the lamp is in the same case as the pot in that it requires to be seen by the eye, nevertheless the eye itself does not here require any external auxiliary in the form of light apart from the lamp. So one cannot establish any universal rule that, whenever one thing has knowledge of another, there is also an instrument of knowledge that is different from either. So if cognition were taken to be known by a separate knowing principle, this could never be shown to involve infinite regress, either through the need for an instrument of knowledge or through the need for a fresh principle to know the knower. So the existence of the Self as a principle of light over and above the empirical cognition stands proved.

The Buddhist will perhaps object that no external object over and above cognition exists at all, neither the pot and the like nor the lamp. For the principle holds, he will say, that whatever is never perceived apart from something is itself only that thing, (337) as, for example, the pots and cloths and other objects in dream-cognition. Because the pot and the lamp seen in dream are not perceived anywhere apart from the dream-cognition, they are accepted as simply *being* the dream-cognition and nothing else. And we ought to conclude in the same way that, in the waking state also, the pot and the lamp and so on, since they are not apprehended anywhere except in the waking-condition, simply are consciousness in the waking state and nothing else. So no external objects such as a pot or a lamp exist. All is mere cognition and nothing else. As for the statement that, since cognition requires to be illumined by a separate principle, there exists another light over and above cognition illumining the pot and the rest – that statement (says the Vijñāna Vādin) was wrong. For it is impossible to support it by any example, since all is mere cognition and nothing more.

All this, however, is wrong. For you yourselves admit the existence of external objects in a certain sense. You do not deny their existence absolutely. And if you try to claim that you do, we say that you are wrong. You speak of the cognition, the pot and the lamp. Because these different words must have different meanings, it follows that you are forced to admit the existence of objects separate from cognition in a certain sense. If no object separate from cognition were admitted, then the words "cognition", "pot", "cloth" and the rest would all mean the same thing, and would have to be regarded as synonyms. But on this view the end and the means would be identical, and all your traditional teachings based on a distinction between means and ends would be reduced to absurdity, and their author (the Buddha) convicted of ignorance.

Nor is this all. You admit the existence over and above cognition of champion, opponent, theory and error in debate. You cannot say that champion, opponent, theory and error are all your own cognition and nothing more. For anyone engaged in debate has to refute the opponent together with the latter's theories and errors, and no one can admit that he has to refute either his own cognition or himself, for this would undermine all human experience. Nor can the opponent and his theories and errors be accepted as being known to himself alone. They must be accepted as being known by someone different from him. And hence it follows that every other object in the waking state is known by someone different from itself, simply because it is an object of waking experience, just like such objects of waking experience as the opponent in debate and his theories and errors, to use a simple enough illustration: and (on your own theories) one stream of cognitions (person or object) has to be known by another that is different from itself, and one cognition has to be known by another that is different from itself. So it follows that not even the Buddhist idealist himself can refute the existence of a separate light over and above cognition.

Nor can this argument be set aside on the ground that there is nothing else but bare cognition in dream. For the non-existence of one thing can only be established on the basis of the positive existence of another. You yourselves affirm the presence of *cognition* of objects in dream. It is only on the basis of the presence of cognition of objects *as a real fact* at other times that you have been able to deny the presence of external objects in dream. Whether the external objects are absent or present in dream, in either case your argument will depend on cognition of external objects as a real fact. And this you cannot refute, as there is no argument that could refute it. (338) This is also enough to refute the doctrine (of the Mādhyamikas) that all is the void. And it also invalidates the Mīmāṃsakas' thesis that the Self is actually *perceived* as the inmost Self and not as "me". (339)

The view put forth earlier that the pot, together with the light illumining it, was reproduced anew and different every moment, was wrong. For it is recognized at other times as "This is that very pot." Nor can it be said that this is only a fancied recognition resting on mere similarity, as in the case of hair or nails that have been cut and have regrown. (340) For even in the case of the hair and the nails, it is impossible to show that their existence comes and goes momentarily, while there is the added difficulty that the new hair and nails each share the same class character with the old. When hair and nails have been cut and have regrown, then, since the class character of hair and nails is always one and the same, the recognition of the new hair and nails as such based on it is undubitably correct.

When we see the hair and nails that have been cut and have regrown we do not think of the new hair and nails as being individually the same as the old ones. When we see someone's hair and nails after a long time still the same as before, we think that they are *like* what he had before, not that they *are* what he had before. But in the case of pots and other such permanent entities we feel, "That is the same" so that the example of what happens in the case of hair and nails was inappropriate to refute recognition of permanent objects.

When a thing is immediately recognized in perception as "This is that same," it cannot be shown to be different by mere dialectical argument, since inferences that contradict direct perception are radically fallacious.

Moreover, from the standpoint of the Buddhist, the notion of similarity is unfounded, as he maintains that recognition is momentary in character. Only he can have the notion of similarity who first sees one thing and then later another. But in the Buddhist hypothesis the one who sees one thing does not himself last over for another moment to see anything else. For if cognition be momentary, whatever sees anything once must itself be exhausted in that cognition. But the notion of similarity involves the idea, "This is similar to that." "That" represents a memory of what has been seen before. "This" represents a present perception. If one could remember what one had seen in the past as "that" and then continue on in existence until the present moment when one was aware of "this", that would undermine the dogma of universal momentariness. If, on the other hand, there were one separate memory-cognition "that", and after it disappeared there arose and disappeared another momentary cognition of a present object as "this", then the notion of similarity would be unfounded. For there would be no one person with the notion

"This is like that." The different elements of the cognition would belong to different knowers.

Communication would also be impossible. If a cognition were exhausted in the perception of its object, one could not communicate such ideas as "I see this" or "I see that," as the person who had the experience would not last until the moment of communication. Or if he did, it would undermine the dogma of universal momentariness. Perhaps the Buddhist will say that the communication is not made by the one who had the experience, and that the notion of similarity does not occur to the same person who had the memory. But that would mean that everything would be blind darkness, like a man blind from birth describing a particular shade of colour and having a feeling of its similarity with something else. This would include objects of the Buddhist's reverence, such as the guidance found in the scriptural traditions of the omniscient one (the Buddha), which is a consequence he would not wish. The twin defects in the doctrine of universal momentariness of visitation by the fruits of deeds one has not done, and of not receiving the fruits of deeds that one has done, are too obvious to be dwelt on further here. (341)

Perhaps the Buddhist will say that what enables communication of what has been seen in the past to take place is the rise of a single cognition which is connected with the past and the future in the sense of being a link in a series, and that the expression "This is like that" is to be explained on similar lines. But this cannot be right. For the present and the past pertain to different moments of time. The present cognition would stand for one link in the series, the past cognition for another: and the two would belong to different moments of time. If you had a single cognition in the form of a series which embraced the objects of both these cognitions, then, because one cognition would fulfil two moments, the doctrine of universal momentariness would be undermined. And it would also undermine all empirical experience in general by rendering impossible such distinctions as "mine" and "yours".

And if all were just self-revealed cognition and nothing more, and if cognition were taken to have the nature of pure awareness and light as its essence, and if there existed nothing beyond it to cognize it, then many of the characteristic Buddhist beliefs about it would be unjustifiable — the beliefs, namely, that it is non-constant, of the nature of pain, empty (śūnya) and not-self. Nor could cognition then have a variety of different elements of mutually contradictory nature, like a pomegranate (as their theory of experience demands). For its essence would be pure light. And if non-constancy and pain, etc., were taken as elements of cognition, the fact that they were experienced would still make them into objects and so separate from cognition.

If, on the other hand, non-constancy and pain, etc., really were one with cognition, then it would be wrong to suppose it could ever lose them and become cleansed. Being cleansed means losing impurities externally acquired, as in the case of removing rust forming on steel mirrors, etc. But fire is never seen to be "cleansed" of its natural light and heat.... Granted that the red colour of certain flowers is seen to pass into the cloth in the process of dyeing, yet even here we must infer that the flower acquired the colour from some external source. For it is seen that alteration can be produced in the attributes of flowers and fruits, etc., by artificial treatment of the seeds. So it remains true that cognition conceived on the Buddhist model could never be "cleansed" (as their theory of liberation demands that it should be).

Moreover, the "defilement" involved in manifestation as object and subject, which they attribute to cognition, is unintelligible in view of the fact that cognition (as they conceive it) cannot come into contact with any external factor. The existent cannot come into contact with the non-existent! And where there is no contact with any external factor, whatever attribute is seen to belong to anything belongs to it by nature, and the thing cannot be "cleansed" of it. It is (an essential characteristic) like the heat of fire or the brilliance of the sun. Therefore this fancy that cognition could undergo defilement and cleansing of that defilement without contact with any external factor is seen to be just a blind traditional superstition, bereft of any real evidence.

They suppose that the extinction (nirvāṇa) of cognition constitutes the highest human goal. But this theory is also wrong, as their view does not allow for the presence of anyone to reap the proposed advantage. A person who has been pricked by a thorn can (by removing it) reap the advantage of the cessation of the pain it was causing. But if the person who had been pricked by a thorn were to die, there would be no one to reap that advantage. To speak of the highest human goal, when all has been extinguished and there is no one to reap the advantage, is nonsense. The Buddhist uses the word "human" and so refers to some being, a self, a consciousness, and supposes that it has a "highest goal". But if this "human being" is extinguished, whose is this "highest goal" that it should remain a human goal at all? But if one holds that, over and above cognition, there exists a Self who can witness many objects, one can explain everything, including memory of what has been seen before and the rise and fall of pain. For defilement will result from contact with some external factor, and cleansing will result in the loss of that (externally acquired) defilement. (342)

* * * * *

7. To this a Vijñāna Vādin might object: Tell me, why do you need to say that empirical experience (anubhūti) occurs to a Witness who is different from it (and witnesses it as an object)? If you (Advaitin) say that experience depends on an experiencer, we (Vijñāna Vādins) reply that on our view the experience is itself the experiencer. "That which is really undifferentiated, of the nature of cognition (buddhi), appears through erroneous vision as if it had the distinctions of knower, knowing and known." (343) Those who hold with us that (momentary) consciousness is the only reality maintain that consciousness alone is the act and also the factors of the act (namely agent, action and object).

To this the Advaitin would reply: If consciousness were both real and subject to momentary destruction (as you hold it to be) then it would require an agent to bring it into being. If you reply that consciousness (does not require an agent to bring it into being since it) has no characteristics at all, you contradict your own fundamental doctrine (that it consists in momentary flashes). If you say that characteristics such as "existence" consist merely in the absence of opposite characteristics such as non-existence, we reply that in that case it becomes impossible for you to establish your view that consciousness is subject to momentary destruction. For you maintain that it is of unique nature (sva-lakṣaṇa). (344)

You say that the cessation (after a moment's existence) of the unique particular is its "destruction". And of "destruction" you give the (circular) definition "absence of non-destruction". Of cowhood, also, you give the (circular) definition "absence of non-cow". But this will not serve for a definition of cowhood. (345) Even that which is called a moment (kṣaṇa) is on your view only the non-existence of its other (the non-momentary).

Although there are no distinctions in non-existence, you want to try to introduce them through name. But how can plurality be introduced into what is essentially one merely through distinctions based on name? If a word signifies no more than the non-existence of things different from that which it designates, how can it apply to a (particular such as) an individual cow? A non-existence cannot create any distinction, nor is it in any sense a particular. You maintain that names and universals, as mere negations, are nothing distinct from consciousness.If you admit, (and, of course, you do admit them) perception and inference in practical experience, then you must necessarily admit that they occur through distinctions, such as those of action, its factors and results. Colours, like blue and yellow, and objects like a pot, must be accepted as distinctions occurring in empirical consciousness; and one must also accept the existence of that (changeless principle) through which they are experienced. And just as the cognition must be different from the colours and other objects, since it is the perceiver and they are the objects of the perception, so must there stand another (principle, the Self), since it illumines the cognitions like a lamp. (346)

* * * * *

8. Now the Kārikās raise a further objection, only in order to strengthen the (Vijñāna Vāda) doctrine they have already stated. We maintain

(says the objector against the Vijñāna Vāda position) that our ordinary consciousness of the world is knowledge caused by and associated with an external object. It has an object that is different from itself. Consciousness of the ether and the other elements composing the world could not occur without the existence of an object, as it presupposes some cause. Otherwise duality, in the form of sound and touch and blue and yellow and red, could not exist. And yet it does exist, because we perceive it. And it is because we perceive it that we have to accept the doctrine of the other school (347) – the doctrine, namely, that an external object exists over and above cognition. For consciousness, which is of the nature of pure light and nothing more, could not become variegated through its own nature without the variety of external objects in the form of blue and yellow colour, etc. It could no more become variegated without objects than a crystal could without association with blue and yellow external adjuncts (upādhi).

And there is another reason, also, why the external object, repeatedly spoken of by the other school as existing over and above the cognition, must in fact exist. This is the fact of pain. One experiences pain caused by burns from (coming into contact with) fire and the like. If external objects like fire did not exist over and above cognition to cause burning and the like, no one would experience pain. But people do experience it. So on this ground, also, we maintain that external objects exist. That is, if there were only bare consciousness and nothing more, the rise of pain would not be intelligible. For it is not experienced elsewhere (i.e. where there is no special cause for it). (348)

To this we (Vijñāna Vādins) reply as follows. (349) It is true that you hold that, from the standpoint of abstract reasoning about the experience of duality and pain, empirical consciousness implies an external cause. Good luck to you with your belief that abstract reasoning supplies the clue to reality as it actually is. Do you want us to explain the point further? All right. We do not admit that the supposed objects of consciousness, such as the pot and the like, condition empirical consciousness, or that they are objects, or that they are objects of consciousness, or that they are the cause of consciousness assuming variegated forms. Why not? Because we look at the matter from the standpoint (not of abstract reasoning but) of metaphysical reality. Viewed from that standpoint, the pot is seen to be but a form of the clay and nothing over and above the clay. It is not anything completely different, in the sense, for instance, that a buffalo is something completely different from a horse. Nor is a cloth anything above its component threads, nor are the threads anything above the yarns and fibres of which they are made up. And one may continue the analysis right up to the point where words and ideas fail, without finding any external cause for anything anywhere.

Or it may be that the author (Gauḍapāda) meant to say, "Because we (i.e. the Vijñāna Vādins) look at the matter from the standpoint that nothing (objective) is a metaphysical reality, (350) and hence do not admit that empirical consciousness is conditioned by an external object, for the reason, that is, that the external object would be like a snake superimposed on a rope. The so-called "condition" would then be no condition. For it would simply be an object of erroneous cognition, and we know that it actually is so from the fact that it does not exist when erroneous cognition is not in play. Those who are in dreamless sleep or in the state of intense meditative concentration (samādhi) or who are liberated do not experience erroneous cognition, and neither do they perceive any external object over and above the Self. The visions of a raving lunatic are not accepted as constituting reality by the sane. (351) And this is itself enough to refute the notion that we either perceive duality or experience pain.

From the fact that nothing external exists to condition empirical consciousness further consequences flow. Cognition does not come into contact with any external object, nor are its representations of the object in any way given to it from without. For all is non-existent in waking, too, just as in dream, as our earlier arguments have shown. Nor is representation of the object anything other than bare cognition. For it is cognition itself that manifests as the object, such as the pot, exactly as in dream.

Now, the point might be raised that if the mind were to represent a pot when there was no pot, that would amount to an illusion, and in that case we ought to be able to say what was not an illusion. By way of reply, we re-affirm that the mind does not come into contact with any external object to condition it in any of the three divisions of time – past, present or future. If it did so at any time, the experience would be real and not an illusion, and the representation of the pot, etc., when there was no pot, would amount to an illusion by comparison. But in actual fact the mind never does come into contact with an object. Gauḍapāda, still expounding Vijñāna Vāda, goes on to say "How could that mind undergo an illusion, since there is nothing to condition it?" meaning that it cannot do so at all. It is the very nature of the mind that it should simulate the nature of an object like a pot, even when there is no object there to condition it.

Now, in the passage beginning at Kārikā 25 (352) and ending here, the Teacher (Gauḍapāda) has approved and followed the words of the

Vijñāna Vādin Buddhists in which they refute the doctrine of their opponents, the (Buddhist) realists. But now in the present verse he proceeds to use their arguments to refute their own doctrine. When the Vijñāna Vādins maintain that the mind represents the pot, etc., when there is no pot, we accept this, but only from the standpoint of the highest reality. So the Teacher (Gauḍapāda) says, "Therefore." Therefore, he means, the "origination" of a representation in the mind must be explained on the basis "Nothing originates," so that the mind itself only *appears* to undergo origination and does not really originate, just as no object of cognition *really* originates. (353)

The Teacher therefore refers now to "those who see origination in the mind." He means the Vijñāna Vādins, who hold that the mind comes and goes in momentary flashes, is characterized by pain and "emptiness" and is not-self. He says that when they claim to be able to see the true nature of the mind through the mind itself, although this is in fact impossible, it is as if they were claiming to "trace the footprints of birds in the sky." He means that they are even more reckless than the others, the dualists. (354)

TEXTS REFUTING THE BUDDHISTS: GROUP D, THE MĀDHYAMIKAS

9. The Absolute (brahman), the non-dual reality, being void of all distinctions and of direction, location, quality, movement, and the results of deeds, appears to persons of small intellect as non-existent. (355)

* * * * *

10. But as the doctrine of the Void is negated by all the empirical means of knowledge (356) no effort is wasted on its refutation here. (357) This ordinary empirical experience of the world, solidly established as it is through all the various means of knowledge, cannot be argued away (through mere dialectical argument) without prior knowledge (through Vedic revelation capped by direct personal experience) of some other real principle. For where no exception can be shown, established rules hold. (358)

* * * * *

11. As for those (Mādhyamikas) who proclaim the doctrine of the Void, seeing everything as empty, they effectively proclaim the emptiness of their own doctrine. They are more reckless (even than the Vijñāna Vādins), and seem to think they can catch hold of the ether by clenching their hands. (359)

* * * * *

12. Some deluded people (the Vijñāna Vāda Buddhists) maintain that consciousness rises up anew every instant in the form of some object and then immediately dies out, like flames flaring up and subsiding again when they encounter the sacrificial butter. Others (the Mādhyamika Buddhists) maintain that when this process has been suppressed all is void. (360) There are others (the Vaiśeṣikas) who maintain that the one who *has* consciousness is the eternal soul, but that consciousness itself is fragmentary, bears on individual objects, is impermanent, and comes into being and passes away. The Materialist maintains that consciousness is a property of matter.

The truth, however, is that it is the Self, as pure Consciousness, which neither increases nor diminishes, that appears to be associated with qualities of name and form, which are in fact only external adjuncts. This we know from such Vedic texts as, "The Absolute is the Real, Knowledge, the Infinite" (361) and "The Absolute is Consciousness" (362) ... and others. Objects change in their nature, while consciousness does not. Things assume different forms, and are known to do so. From the mere fact that they are known as changeful, we conclude that the consciousness that knows them is unchanging.

It is not reasonable to maintain that a reality is known to exist but that there is nothing to know it, any more than it would be reasonable to maintain that a colour was seen but that there was no eye to see it. The known, however, (being transient, invariably) withdraws itself from knowledge, whereas knowledge never withdraws itself from the known. For when one known object disappears, knowledge remains present to illumine another. The view that, because it is not evident in dreamless sleep, knowledge (then) withdraws itself, like the known, is wrong. For, just like a lamp, the function of knowledge is to illumine a knowable object. It is wrong to think that because there is no knowledge in dreamless sleep, knowledge in its pure form is then absent, like objects. For knowledge has the function of manifesting the knowable, as light has the function of illumining objects. Hence it is no more possible to argue for the absence of consciousness in dreamless sleep than it would be to argue for the absence of light when there are no objects for it to illumine. The Nihilist (Mādhyamika) cannot argue the absence of an eye if no colours are seen through the eye on account of thick darkness.

Perhaps I shall be reminded that the Nihilist (Mādhyamika) argues from the non-existence of *any* knowable to the non-existence of knowledge. But, if so, the Nihilist ought to tell us through what it is that he establishes the non-existence of that knowledge whereby he argued the non-existence of knowledge. This non-existence, too, is something that has to be known. It could not be established unless there were knowledge.

Perhaps you will say that knowledge is inseparable from the knowable, and that the non-existence of the knowable would therefore imply the non-existence of knowledge. But this will not do. For the Nihilist regards non-existence as knowable, and even accepts this "knowable non-existence" as eternal. (364) If, in these circumstances, knowledge were assumed to be non-different from the knowable, it, too, would be eternal. And its (knowledge's) non-existence would itself (because knowable) imply knowledge. The "non-existence" of knowledge would thus be purely verbal. On this view, one could not definitely establish as a final truth that knowledge was non-existent or was not eternal. And no harm results to our position if knowledge in fact exists and it is its mere *nominal* non-existence that we have to contend with!

But what if non-existence be knowable but other than knowledge? Here again, no harm results to our position, as the absence of the knowable does not imply the absence of knowledge.

You cannot say that the knowable can exist apart from knowledge, but that knowledge cannot exist apart from the knowable, for a verbal distinction does not amount to a real one. (365) If you start from the position that knowledge and the knowable are the same, then to say that the knowable exists separately from knowledge, while knowledge does not exist separately from the knowable, is a mere verbal quibble. It is like saying that flames exist separately from fire, but that fire does not exist separately from flames. If, on the other hand, you hold that knowledge is different from the knowable, then it is clearly wrong to hold that the non-existence of the knowable implies the non-existence of knowledge.

But is it not a fact that we are not aware of knowledge in the absence of the knowable, so that it does not then exist? No, for we have to admit the presence of knowledge in dreamless sleep. (366) Nor can you retort that in dreamless sleep we have knowledge knowing itself as knowable, (367) because knowledge and the knowable have been proved to be different from one another. For it has already been shown that the knowledge which has non-existence as its object is different from that non-existence, and that knowledge and the known are therefore different. Not even a hundred Nihilists could alter this point, which has already been proved, as if they were raising up the corpse (of an already refuted argument) from the dead.

Perhaps you will say that on my doctrine knowledge must itself be the knowable, and charge me with infinite regress on the ground that any given cognition would have to be known by another, and so on to infinity. But this objection is not right, as one can divide all things into two classes without remainder (i.e. into knowledge and the knowable). Everything that is knowable is knowable for some knowledge. But knowledge itself remains different from the knowable and is knowledge only. This second category, knowledge, is accepted by all philosophers except the Nihilists, and no third category of the form of knowledge to know knowledge is accepted. So there is no occasion for infinite regress.

It may be that the Nihilist will object that if knowledge cannot be known to itself, it cannot be omniscient. But as this is an objection that only faces him, why should we (who accept that knowledge is self-luminous) be expected to contend with it? The objection concerning infinite regress, too, rests on the assumption that knowledge is knowable. And, as knowledge cannot be known as an object by itself, it is *he* who falls into infinite regress, (because he holds that knowledge is knowable, that one cognition is known by another as an object).

Nor do we admit that these difficulties affect us equally. For knowledge is intelligible if it is taken as one. Knowledge is one and the same in all places, at all times and in all conditions of men and other sentient beings. It appears as many and different through differences in the external adjuncts of name and form, etc., with which it is associated, like the sun and other luminous bodies reflected in water-surfaces and elsewhere. Hence these objections do not apply to us. (368)

* * * * *

13. "In this connection, indeed," proceeds the Upanishad – that is, in connection with explaining what preceded the production of the universe – "Some," that is, the Nihilists, "said" by way of an explanation of reality, "Non-being." That is, they explained the condition of this universe before its production as a manifest effect as mere absence of being, in the words, "In the beginning this (the world) was (non-being), one only without a second." The Buddhists, indeed, suppose that, before the production of the world, the truth (tattva) was just mere absence of Being. And they do not admit any positive principle of non-being standing opposed to it, in the manner, for instance, of

the (Hindu) Logicians, who hold that whatever is perceived exists — what is rightly perceived exists as real, what is wrongly perceived exists as unreal.

You might object that in that case they ought not to say "Before (manifestation) this universe was non-being, one only without a second." For by doing this they bring non-being into relation with time by saying "It was," and they bring it into relation with number by saying "without a second." And you would be quite right. For they ought not to do so, as they take non-being as mere absence of existence. What is more, their whole doctrine that all is bare non-being is demonstrably untenable, as it is not reasonable to maintain a doctrine that denies the existence of the person who maintains it. Nor will it help matters to say that the existence *now* of the one who maintains the doctrine is admitted, but not his existence before the rise of the universe. For there is nothing to prove the absence of existence before the rise of the universe.Indeed, the notion that there was non-being before the rise of the universe is nonsensical.

Mīmāṃsaka's Objection: (369) Words denote real universals. (370) So the meaning of the words and also of the whole phrase in the text "This was only non-being in the beginning, one only without a second" is unintelligible. But if so, the text cannot be authoritative

Nihilist's Answer: The objection is wrong. For the purpose of the text is only to negate the *idea* of being. The word 'sat' denotes the universal Being. And the words "one only without a second" are placed in apposition with it. Together these are made the predicate in a sentence beginning "This was...". In a sentence affirming being, the force of a negative particle is to use the positive idea contained in the sentence — here "There was Being, one only without a second" — as the basis from which to divert the sentence away from its original positive meaning. It is as when a person mounted on a horse uses the leverage from his perch on the horse to divert it away from the objects towards which it is heading. It is not that the text just declares that Being (sat) is non-being (abhāva). So the force of the text "(In the beginning) this was verily non-being, etc." is only to correct a wrong human notion. First of all the text proclaims "All this was Being in the beginning, one only without a second." And then, having done so, it can very well correct a misunderstanding in the following sentence. Thus the text about non-being can be shown to be Vedic and authoritative, and the objection was wrong. So (it can quite well be said that) Being arose from total non-being....

The text, having first put forward the chief thesis of the Nihilist, then goes on to refute it. "O, my dear one, what could be the proof that Being arises from non-being?" That is to say, there could be no proof of such a thing. The claim, indeed, is made that the sprout arises from the seed through the destruction of the latter, and hence that it arises from "non-being". But that is really in contravention of their own doctrine. For the component parts that are organized at the seed-stage to form a seed persist also in the sprout: they do not undergo destruction. As for the seed as a composite entity, the Nihilists do not admit the existence of any such entity over and above the component parts,that it could undergo destruction on the rise of the sprout. And if they did admit it, they would contradict their own dogmas.

To this they might reply that they admit as a "surface reality" (saṃvṛti), the existence of the seed as a composite entity over and above the parts, and that this is what undergoes destruction. But what they mean by "surface reality" is by no means clear. Is it being or non-being? If it is non-being, then it is something they cannot illustrate by any example. And if they say it is being, they still cannot claim that the sprout arises from non-being. For it will still arise from the parts of the seed.

If they say that these parts, too, are destroyed, it is wrong. For it is with the parts just as it is with the whole. The Nihilists do not admit any whole in the shape of the seed as a composite entity, so they cannot affirm the destruction of the parts of any whole. In any case, the parts of the seed will have yet finer parts, and these yet finer parts still. The series being endless, nothing can be destroyed anywhere.

The doctrine of the Realists that being arises from being is intelligible. For it can very well be claimed that Being is imperishable, on the ground that all notions are accompanied by the idea of existence. (372) The Nihilist can produce no example of being arising out of non-being. But the Realists can say that the pot arises from the lump of clay, because the pot arises when the lump of clay is present and not otherwise.

If the pot really arose from non-being, the one who wanted a pot would not resort to clay. Further, the notion of, and the term, "non-existence" would then apply to the pot — but as they do not, we can say, on this ground also, that being does not arise from non-being.

Some say that the notion of "clay" is the occasion of the notion "pot", while in reality there is neither real clay nor pot at all. Even on this view, an existent notion "clay" would be the cause of an existent notion "pot", so that there would not be the production of being from non-being.

Objection By The Nihilist: There is only immediate consecution between the idea of the clay and the idea of the pot, which gives the appearance that one is the cause of the other, while there is no genuine relation of causality between them.

Advaitin's Answer: No, for you are quite unable to supply any external example that would prove your doctrine of the immediate consecution of notions. So that is why the texts say, "He said, 'How indeed, my dear one, could it be so?'" That is, how could being arise from non-being? In other words, there is no example which could illustrate how being could arise from non-being. And this is why the text refutes the thesis of those who say that being arises from non-being, and why (Uddālaka) then concludes the statement of the proof of his own view with the words, "(On the) contrary, it was Being only that existed in the beginning, my dear one." (373)

6. REFUTATION OF THE JAINAS

The doctrines of the Jainas were of little direct importance to Śaṃkara, and the only place where he refutes any part of them in detail is his Commentary on the Brahma Sūtras II.ii.33-36. Even here, he does not give a general sketch of their theory, as he had done in the case of the Sāṃkhyas, the Vaiśeṣikas and some of the Buddhist schools, but contents himself mainly in hammering away at two points in it. A few remarks on the history of the Jaina community will perhaps suffice as an introduction to the single appended Extract.

(XI.6) REFUTATION OF NON-VEDIC WORLD-VIEWS

The name "Jaina" derives from the honorific epithet "Jina" or "Victorious One" which was applied to the Teacher whose original name was Vardhamāna, but who was also (and most frequently) surnamed Mahāvīra (Great Hero) or Jñātṛputra (Scion of the Jñātṛ Clan). A "Jaina" is a follower of "Jina" or Mahāvīra, as a Buddhist (Sanskrit "Bauddha") is a follower of Buddha. Mahāvīra may have lived at about the same time and in about the same geographical area as the Buddha, though the two appear never to have met. The early Buddhist canonical literature refers to Mahāvīra as one of the many rival wandering Teachers who were active in the Buddha's day, though in fact he may have lived earlier. Whereas the Buddha taught a doctrine that was based mainly on his own personal experience, Mahāvīra had a more traditional approach and merely renewed and revivified the teachings of the Nirgrantha sect, to which he and his parents belonged. According to later Jaina tradition, this school boasted twenty-four successive Great Teachers or "Passage-Makers" (tīrthakara), of whom only the last two, Pārśva and Mahāvīra himself, are accepted in modern scholarship as historical figures. It is thought that Pārśva may have been active about 750 B.C., but whether he founded the school himself or merely transmitted the doctrine of earlier Teachers is not known for certain.

From time immemorial the Jainas have had a four-fold discipline, one code each for men and women in the renunciate and householder class. The householders supported the renunciates. Although Mahāvīra himself came from noble stock, the emphasis on non-killing in the creed has been held to be responsible for the fact that to this day the householder members of the community tend to pursue commerce and urban professions rather than other callings. An important historical event in the life of the community was the journey south, perhaps a little before 300 B.C., of the monk Bhadrabāhu, who foresaw a famine and set off for the south, taking a large group with him, which eventually settled in Mysore. In course of time the Northern and Southern Communities became separate sects, the southerners known as "Naked Ones" (Digambara) on the ground that their monks held to the full rigour of the ancient renunciate's discipline, whereas the northerners were known as the "White Robed Ones" (Śvetāmbara), because their monks wore a white robe for the sake of decency. Few monks, even of the Digambara sect, walk about naked today.

The Śvetāmbaras, who tended to migrate westwards to Gujerat from the original homeland of Bihar, drew up a Canon of teaching, perhaps some time in the first century A.D., which was held to emanate from Mahāvīra. It was composed in the Ardha-Māgadhī Prākṛta dialect, which has been said to imply that it could not have reproduced Mahāvīra's actual words. (374) The Śvetāmbaras admitted it was incomplete, and the Digambaras regarded it as spurious, and composed their own independent works to replace it. But it is generally admitted that the doctrine of the two sects does not differ in essentials. Unlike the Buddhists, who, artificial revivals apart, have disappeared from India completely, the Jainas have remained in being, a respected and largely well-to-do community of nearly one and a half million. Their ascetic ideals and emphasis on non-violence have been a positive contribution to Indian culture, while certain individuals, particularly Hemacandra of Gujarat (twelfth century A.D.), have made notable contributions to Indian literature and scholarship. If it is true to say that Mahatma Gandhi would not have quite been what he was but for Christianity, it is far more deeply true to say that he would not have been what he was but for the doctrines and practice of the Jainas.

Modern scholars, when reconstructing Jaina philosophy at the sort of stage it would have reached when attacked in the Brahma Sūtras and by Śaṃkara, usually turn to two Prākṛta works, the Tattvārthādhigama Sūtra of Umāsvāti (Śvetāmbara) and the Pravacana Sāra of Kundakunda (Digambara). Of these, the second is tentatively assigned by Frauwallner to the fourth century A.D., and the first to a slightly earlier period. (375) Kumārila complains of the "inexactitude of terminology" in the Jaina works arising from the fact that in his day they were still mainly written in Prākṛta and not Sanskrit. (376) There is no need to describe their doctrines in any detail here. According to the Jainas, the soul is by nature happy, freely active and omniscient, but its powers are stunted by accretions of subtle matter that pour into it as the result of embodiment and of passionate activity. Though the soul is spoken of as "spiritual" it is regarded as attracting to itself a mass of "karma" by its deeds and thoughts, karma being regarded as a quasi-material substance that darkens the soul and causes it to undergo future experiences in new bodies. Reincarnation is a self-perpetuating process until the inrush of subtle matter is halted through moral purity and asceticism. The life of the monk who attains enlightenment carries on until the fall of his body, when the soul rises to a kind of heaven above the universe, where it remains for ever in great felicity.

A pluralistic doctrine that ignored the Veda could never be expected to find favour with the authors of the Brahma Sūtras or with Śaṃkara. Without troubling to summarize and refute the doctrine in any detail, however,they fasten onto two main points, the doctrine of the seven standpoints and the doctrine that the soul was of changeable size and exactly fitted its successive bodies. The doctrine of Seven Possible Standpoints (syād-vāda) seems to have arisen as a systemization of a mental attitude practised amongst Mahāvīra's earliest followers. (376)

It is never right to think "S is P." One must always realize that S could, in certain circumstances and for certain people, be (1) P, (2) not P, (3) either P or not P, (4) neither P nor not-P, (5) either P or else neither P nor not-P, (6) either not-P or else neither P nor not-P, (7) either P or not-P or else neither P nor not-P. Such is the case, for instance, with regard to a drink being hot, relative to various possible circumstances of time and place and different drinkers. (377) This way of arguing can be used to show that an opponent's world-view is wrong because it does not embrace the whole truth, but, as Śaṃkara is not slow to point out, it can be applied equally destructively to the doctrines of the Jainas themselves. It also involves attributing contradictory properties to the same object at the same time, even though the result is admitted to be "indescribable" or "unintelligible". Against the doctrine that the soul is eternal but capable of assuming different sizes, Śaṃkara used the Law of Contradiction as a deadly weapon.

TEXTS REFUTING THE JAINAS

1. The philosophy of the Buddha has now been refuted. We next go on to refute the philosophy of the Naked Ones (Digambara, here a collective name for the Jainas as a whole). The latter accept seven principles, namely soul, non-soul (the totality of inanimate beings), inflow (of particles of subtle matter into the soul leading to obscuration of its powers and to further worldly experience), arrest (of further inflow), destruction (through ascetic practices of the contents of previous inflow), bondage and liberation. To put it briefly, however, there are only two principles, soul and non-soul. For they think all the rest can be somehow included in one or the other of these two.

They have another way of analysing these two principles, namely into five "masses of being" (asti-kāya) – those of soul, matter, cause of movement, cause of arrest of movement and space. All of these include many sub-divisions, which they dilate upon in terms of their own system.

Everywhere they apply their method of the seven standpoints – from one point of view it (anything) exists, from one point of view it does not exist, from one point of view it both exists and does not exist, from one point of view it is indescribable, from one point of view it is existent and indescribable, from one point of view it is non-existent and indescribable, from one point of view it is both existent and non-existent and also indescribable. They apply their method of the seven standpoints even to such items as oneness and eternity.

To all this we reply that the relativism of the Jainas is not justified, because, as the author of the Sūtras puts it, "of the impossibility (of directly contradictory attributes) in one and the same thing." (378) You cannot have contradictory attributes such as 'existent' and 'non-existent' at the same time in the same substance, any more than the same thing can be at the same time hot and cold. The seven principles, which they regard as existent and as having definite natures, must either exist with those natures or not exist. If all that we have is the indefinite knowledge that a certain thing might be of such and such a nature, or of a different nature, or not of that previously assumed nature, then our knowledge is like doubt and has no cogency.

Perhaps you will say that the definite knowledge that a thing is many-sided does not lack cogency, like doubt. But we reply that you are wrong. For even the definite knowledge of one who recklessly extends the principle of relativism to cover all entities is itself an entity, and falls within his own formula, "From one point of view it is, from one point of view it is not, etc.," and is hence itself not of a definite nature. In the same way, both the one who has the definite knowledge, and also the cognition resulting from the process of knowledge, will exist from one standpoint and not from another. This being so, how can a Jaina set himself up as an authority and give teaching, when neither the means of knowledge nor the object of knowledge nor the knower of knowledge nor the knowledge itself can be asserted to have any definite existence? And how could he have pupils who acted on his teaching, seeing that its exact nature could never be definitely ascertained? For people in the world wait until they are sure that something will have an advantageous result for them and then apply themselves calmly to the proper means for attaining that thing: they do not act without such knowledge. One attempting to propagate a science which is itself by its very nature beyond definite determination as "such and such" can expect to find his words neglected like those of a drunkard or a lunatic.

Similar reasoning applies to the five positive categories (of the Jaina system). On the question of whether or not they were really five, they would be five from one point of view and not-five from another point of view, and so either less than five or more than five. Nor can these categories be indescribable. If they were indescribable they could not be mentioned. To be mentioned and indescribable is a contradiction. Even if they could be mentioned, they would (in terms of the system) be determinately known and also not determinately known. And the doctrine would say that the result of determinate knowledge from one point of view was perfect certitude and from another point of view was not, while from one point of view there was imperfect knowledge and from another point of view there was not. But this is not a reasonable and trustworthy view, but rather that of a drunkard or a raving lunatic.

Heaven and liberation, too, from one point of view would exist and from another point of view would not. From one point of view they would be eternal and from another point of view non-eternal. Since their nature could not, on the Jaina view, be definitely ascertained, it would be impossible to work for them as goals. The various classes of souls that their tradition speaks of, too, such as the eternally perfect ones and the rest, could not actually have the characteristics ascribed to them if the Jaina logic were correct. But the truth is that there cannot be contradictory attributes like existence and non-existence in one and the same substance, and this holds whether we are considering souls or any other category of being. When the property of existence is present in a thing, the opposed property of non-existence cannot also be present, and *vice versa*. So that the whole Jaina doctrine is unfounded. And what we have already said is enough to refute the notion that there could be alternative possibilities of a thing being (at the same time) one and many, eternal and non-eternal, distinct from something else and non-distinct. As for their doctrine that aggregates can be formed from those atoms of matter which they call "pudgalas", this has already been refuted by our refutations of atomistic doctrines elsewhere, and we do not need to go over the same ground again here.(379)

Just as the Jainas relativism involves the fallacy of supposing that one and the same thing can have contradictory properties, so also there are fallacies in their view that the Self (ātman) or individual soul (jīva) is of less than infinite extension. The Jainas regard the soul as being of the same dimensions as the body. This implies that the Self is less than the whole of reality, and is limited. And this in turn implies that it is transient, like a pot. Further, it is a fact that bodies are not all the same size. A human soul, being of the size of a human body, should it later take birth as an elephant due to the vicissitudes of merit and demerit, would not fill the whole of the elephant's body. Or if it should take birth as an ant, it could not be compressed into the body of an ant. In fact, the same criticism of this doctrine of the soul would apply in regard to (the different sizes of the body implicit in) youth and old-age in a single birth.

Very well, you will say, but the soul is composed of an infinity of parts. These parts contract in a small body and expand in a big one. But in that case we ask whether these parts of the soul, infinite in number, exclude one another spatially or not. If they do, an infinity of such parts could not be compressed within a limited space. But if they do not exclude one another, then they could all occupy but the space of one part, so that the soul would only be the size of an atom (which is against the doctrines of the system). Nor could it in any circumstances be right to say that an infinity of parts of the soul could be limited to the size of a particular body.

Perhaps you will reply that when the soul obtains a large body it acquires an increment of parts, and when, in turn, it acquires a small body, it undergoes a diminution of parts. But the author of the Sūtras replies that this is not right either. One cannot establish without contradiction that the size of the soul accommodates itself to this or that body in turn by increment or diminution of parts. Because, as the author of the Sūtras goes on to say, it would imply, amongst other fallacies, that the soul underwent modification. A soul that was continually subject to expansion and contraction from the increment and diminution of parts would undeniably be subject to modification, and, being subject to modification, would be transient, like a piece of leather or the like. But this would be in contradiction with the Jaina's doctrine of bondage and release, according to which the soul floats about in the sea of transmigratory life like a bottle-gourd, encased in its eight kinds of deeds (karma), (380) and eventually soars upwards, after cutting its bonds. Furthermore, the parts that accrue or are lost are of the nature of that which comes and goes, and thus no more belong to the true nature of the (eternal) soul than the body and other transient features do. Nor can you say that one particular part constitutes the soul, as it would never be possible to say exactly which part it was. And there is the further difficulty that one cannot explain where these in-coming parts of the soul come from, or what it is into which the parts that are lost are dissolved. They cannot come from the elements or dissolve back into them, as the soul is not material. Nor can one think of any other entity, whether general or particular, which could support the parts of the soul, there being no evidence for the existence of any such thing. Further, if such increments and diminutions really occurred, the soul would be of indeterminable form, as there would be no rule to determine the size of the in-coming and out-going parts. Therefore we must conclude, on account of these and other difficulties, that there cannot be successive increments and diminutions of parts of the soul.

Or else the Sūtra may be interpreted in a different way. The previous Sūtra had objected that, if the soul were of the size of the body, and acquired larger and smaller bodies, it would not be all-pervading, and hence would not be eternal (which the Jainas claim that it is). To this the Jaina now replies that though the soul undergoes successive changes of size, yet it is permament, just as a stream is permament (even though the water in it is always changing). Just as those who wear dyed robes (the Buddhists) speak of the permanence of the *series* of cognitions, even though each individual cognition is transient, so might the Naked Ones (the Jainas) argue here (in a similar way). Against this objection the present Sūtra makes reply and says that if the series (of different sizes in the case of the soul) was not real, there would be no soul. And if it was real, the view would still be wrong, as it would attribute to the soul modifications and other impossibilities.

And a further difficulty lies in the fact that the Jainas hold that the size of the soul acquired on reaching its last state, that of liberation, is permanent. If the size of the last state is permanent, the size of the first and intervening states must equally be permanent, in which case there would be no difference in size between any of them. The soul would then have the size of one body only, and could not obtain fresh bodies of larger or smaller size.

Or we may explain the Sūtra a little differently. The Jaina may be supposed to say (without reference to the size of the body) that the size of the soul in its last state is fixed and permanent and that it must have been the same in its initial and intervening states also. But the soul must then be accepted as being always and without exception, either atomic or infinite in size and not the size of the body (which contradicts the Jainas' own dogmas). And so we conclude that no attention should be paid to the doctrines of the Jainas, as they are as erroneous as those of the Buddhists. (381)

NOTES TO CHAPTER XI

(1) B.S. II.iii.6 (2) *Ibid.* I.ii.17, II.ii.13 (3) *Ibid.* II.i.10, II.i.29. See Belvalkar, Vedanta Philosophy, p.155, cp. also S.L. Pandey, p.158. (4) B.S.Bh. I.iv.15 (5) *Ibid.* (6) B.S.Bh. II.ii.15, cp. below, p.224 (7) B.S.Bh. II.ii.17, cp. below, p.231 (8) Cp. Sac, The Method of the Vedanta (M.V.) p.690 f. (9) *Ibid.* p.706 (10) *Ibid.* p.739 (11) G.K.Bh. IV.1 (introduction) (12) Keith, Sanskrit Literature p.478 (13) B.S.Bh. II.iv.12, Gambhīrānanda p.540 (14) Bh.G.Bh. XVIII.19 (15) Cp. below, p.157 (16) B.S.Bh. III.iii.54, Gambhīrānanda p.742 (17) Cp. below, p.260 (18) p. 93 above (19) The aphorisms of the B.S. are arranged in four "Books" (adhyāya) of four "Quarters" (pāda) each. These are the remarks made to open the Commentary on the second Quarter of the second Book, and they explain why the author of the B.S. waited until this point before he passed over from enquiry into the meaning of certain Upanishadic texts to rational criticism of positions held by other schools. (20) B.S. I.i.5 (21) B.S. Bh. II.ii.1 (22) Praśna Bh.VI.3 (23) The term is used in quite a general sense to mean all those who accept the independent reality of anything apart from their own Self, in particular, of an opponent in debate. The Advaitin does not do so. See next paragraph. (24) G.K.Bh. III. 17 (25) Bṛhad Bh. III.iii.1 (26) B.S.Bh. II.ii.25 (27) B.S.Bh. II.ii.11, closing introductory sentence (28) Vālmīki, Book II Chap.109 (Bombay Recension), trans. H.P. Shastri, Vol.I p.416 (29) The exact sense of the term "lokāyata" here is disputed, as is the date of the Artha Śāstra. (30) The Tattvopaplava Siṃha of Jayarāśi, probably written a little after Śaṃkara's day, though offering homage to Bṛhaspati, legendary founder of the Lokāyata school, is apparently a treatise on

philosophic scepticism rather than on materialism proper. Cp. the summary by W. Ruben, W.Z.K.S.O., 1958, pp.140-153, and the observations at Chattopadhyaya p.221 (31) Kṛṣṇa Miśra, Act II, verses 19-25: V.P. III.xviii.25-28 (32) von Glasenapp, Stufenweg p.32 (33) L. Silburn in Renou and Filliozat, Vol.II. sect.1498. (34) Frauwallner, G.I.P. p.307 f. (35) In accordance with the principle laid down above, p.157, cp. p.151 f., that a school should be critized as far as possible along the lines of its own methods and assumptions, the Materialist is at first attacked from the standpoint of the Vaiśeṣika, who only accepts perception and inference. The Advaitin only comes in with his own position towards the end of the Extract. (36) At death: perhaps also in dreamless sleep and swoon. (37) The Materialist claims that consciousness is a property of the elements and also that it is what perceives the elements. But this is contradictory, because in perceiving the elements it would also have to perceive itself, their property. Nothing can be both the agent and the object of an act of perception at the same time. (38) So far the refutation has been conducted from the standpoint of the Vaiśeṣika. Now the Advaitin's own position is brought forward. (39) I.e. the Advaitin does not hold, with the Vaiśeṣikas, that consciousness is a *property* of the soul, but that it is the non-dual Self in its true nature. (40) B.S.Bh. III.iii.53 and 54 (41) The reference is to the absence of all sense-contacts in the states of dream and dreamless sleep, here contrasted with waking. (42) Which we could not have unless there had been the light of consciousness present in dreamless sleep, distinct from the body and mind, etc., which were not present. (43) And so not subject to perception as an object. (44) Argument by analogy is uncontrolled and always open to abuse. The argument to which the Materialist here objects is the following. The senses, in particular the power of sight, *usually* require an external auxiliary in the form of the sun or the like for their proper functioning. Hence it follows that they *always* need some other auxiliary when no external luminary, etc., is present. (45) A Svabhāva Vādin speaks here. He holds the doctrine that all things act according to their natures. (46) Coolness, we have seen, was taken as an inherent property of water in the classical Hindu physics. (47) Cp. the parallel examples given above, Vol.I p.215 (48) Above, p.163 (49) The Materialist has a difficulty in explaining dream and dreamless sleep. How can the organs be sometimes luminous and sometimes not, contradicting their own nature? The Advaitin does not have this difficulty, as he holds that the organs are always *per se* non-conscious and that it is the light of the Self as pure Consciousness that illumines them from within. The Materialist defends his position by pointing to the example of the firefly. Śaṃkara points out that this example is not relevant, as the firefly is always luminous by nature. So it will not explain how the organs can be luminous in waking but not in dreamless sleep. (50) Bṛhad. Bh. IV.iii.6 (51) Hacker in W.Z.K.S.O., 1961, p.111 (52) Frauwallner, Buddhismus, p.170 (53) The Yoga Bhāṣya is attributed to Vindhyavāsī by Vādirājasūri, cp. Frauwallner, W.Z.K.S.O., 1958, p.114 (54) Frauwallner, G.I.P. I. p.401 (55) See below, p.189. (56) The texts are in Chapters XII.194, XII.247-248 and XII.287 of the M.Bh. Cp. Frauwallner, G.I.P. I. p.288 ff. (57) W.Z.K.S.O., 1960, p.90 (58) Chānd. VI.ii.3 - VI.v.4 (59) Frauwallner, *op. cit.* p.307, cp. Johnston pp.35 ff. and p.71 (60) Frauwallner, *op. cit.* p.118. See M.Bh. XII.232.4 ff. G.P. Ed. Vol. III p.577 (61) Frauwallner, *op. cit.* p.317, Johnston p.52 (62) Above, Vol. I. p.16 (63) References are given in Garbe, p.30 f. (64) Keith, Sāṃkhya System p.25 f. (65) Above, Vol.I, p.17 (66) Johnston p.8 and p.10 (67) Frauwallner, *op. cit.* p.131 f., cp. Johnston p.44. (68) Frauwallner puts this forward as a hypothesis, *op. cit.* p.322 f. (69) Frauwallner, *op. cit.* p.338 (70) Cp. above, Vol.I. p.28 (71) Frauwallner, *op. cit.* p.380 f. (72) The reference is to the three "constituents" (guṇa) of Nature, called sattva, rajas and tamas. But, as will be seen below, Śaṃkara accepts them primarily as mental qualities, which is what they were when they first appeared in the Sāṃkhya doctrine, as mentioned above, p.173. (73) On "vivartate", cp. above, Vol. II. Chap.V, Note 86. (74) I.e. B.S. II.ii.1 (75) According to Belvalkar, the reference is to the words "samanvayāt" at Īśvara Kṛṣṇa verse 15 (76) Seed, soil, water, air, and light, etc., are involved. (Belvalkar) (77) Reading vijñāna-svarūpa-mātra-vyatirekeṇa (78) Īśvara Kṛṣṇa Kārikā 57 (79) Bṛhad. III.vii.4 and

III.viii.9 (80) See B.S. II.i.24 (81) Cp. Īśvara Kṛṣṇa Kārikā 62. "The soul is neither bound nor released, nor does it undergo transformation. That which transmigrates, is bound and released is Nature, appearing in multifarious forms." (82) In the manner proposed at Īśvara Kṛṣṇa Kārikā 58 (83) This famous image, originating, perhaps, from the time of the old Sāṃkhya Teacher Pañcaśikha and found at Īsvara Kṛṣṇa Kārikā 21 used to illustrate the relation between the soul and Nature, has also been widely used to illustrate the relation between the soul and the body, for example in Buddhist literature, in Apocryphal and Talmudic literature, in the Hadith Literature of Islam, in the Brothers of Purity, in Attar's Asrar Namah, in the Gesta Romanorum and in the Eighteenth Century Fables of Gellert. Detailed references in Ritter, p.582. T.L. Joshi p.77 refers to its appearance in Chinese literature in the second century B.C. (84) Cp. Īśvara Kṛṣṇa Kārikā 20 (85) Which would make release impossible. (86) The eleven senses are those familiar to us from Śaṃkara's own teaching, cp. above, Vol. III, p.28 f. Some Sāṃkhya schools reduced the number to seven by treating all five sense-organs of knowledge as modifications of the one sense-organ of touch. (87) A minority view, traceable to Vindhyavāsī, *circa* 425 A.D., cp. Frauwallner, G.I.P. I., p.402. (88) The usual view, cp. Īśvara Kṛṣṇa Kārikā 22. (89) Manas, buddhi, ahaṃkāra — the usual view. (90) The view of Vindhyavāsī. He accepted only a cosmic intellect, which he called "Mahat" and not "Buddhi", and he did not admit a separate buddhi for the individual. The only inner organ attributed to the individual was "mind" (manas). Frauwallner, *op. cit.* p.402 f. (91) The Sāṃkhya's attack here is clearly directed against an earlier form of the Vedanta than Śaṃkara's, not against "non-dualism" in Śaṃkara's sense, but against a "monism" similar to Bhartṛprapañca's doctrine. Cp. the reference, lower down, to water. We have already seen how Bhartṛprapañca appeals to the simile of water and its various manifestations, above, p.78. (92) The appeal is to the principle of "sat-kārya Vāda", for which see above, Vol. II pp.95-119 (93) Cp. Vol. III p.143. (94) The Sāṃkhya attributes contradictory and mutually exclusive characteristics to the soul, as a conscious principle, on the one hand, and to non-conscious Nature and its transformations and "constituents" on the other. The soul and Nature cannot intermix. See Vācaspati Miśra, Tattva Kaumudī Commentary on Īśvara Kṛṣṇa Kārikā 19. (95) The term "sattva" here means the individual mind, according to a technical usage of the school. Cp. Vācaspati's Bhāmatī II.ii.10, buddhi-sattva. (96) I.e. Nature, particularly rajas within Nature. The argument derives point and flavour from the fact that the whole purpose of the Sāṃkhya discipline is to teach liberation. It is a "mokṣa-śāstra". (97) Chānd. VI.i.4 (98) I.e. as mere empirical facts, which do not necessarily turn out to be real when examined critically. (99) B.S.Bh. II.i. 1-10 (100) Śaṃkara himself takes the term "puruṣa" in the Upanishad to mean "the Self" (ātman). Cp. Praśna Bh. III.3, trans. Gambhīrānanda II p.439. See also the following paragraph here, where the terms "ātman" and "puruṣa" are identified. But the Sāṃkhya understands the term "puruṣa" according to the tenets of his own system. For him it is not the one Self of which all plurality is an appearance. It is merely one of a plurality of conscious, all-pervading, non-active entities that stand over against Nature and its transformations. (101) The latter is the Vaiśeṣika hypothesis, cp. the following section of the present chapter. But the last creative Sāṃkhya Teacher of the classical period, Mādhava (*circa* 500 A.D.), accepted an atomic structure for Nature under Vaiśeṣika influence. Frauwallner, *op. cit.* p.407 (102) The Sāṃkhya, of course, admits a plurality of souls. But plurality is in their very nature. It is not supposed to be a defect arising from change. The Sāṃkhya is here arguing against the Vedantin, who cannot afford to admit plurality. (103) Reading avidyā-viṣaya-nāma-rūpopādhi with H.R.Bhagavat (Vol.I p.419),not avidyāyāṃ viṣaya-nāma-rūpa- etc., as in the G.P. Ed. p.110. The bulk of the passage here omitted has already appeared as Extract 2 of section 1 above, p.154 f. (104) Cp. Īśvara Kṛṣṇa 11 (105) Which contradicts the Sāṃkhya system, in which Nature undergoes real transformation for the sake of the experience and final release of the soul. (106) If the Sāṃkhya admits real modification on the part of the soul, he loses the contrast between soul as experiencer and Nature as the object of experience. On this opposition his system greatly depends. (107) The Advaita reasoning is that the Sāṃkhya has been pushed by the argument into having to claim that the soul, although undergoing modification like Nature, is nevertheless an experiencer. His only argument is that, amongst things undergoing modification, the soul is a special case. But this, the Advaitin points out, is no argument at all, as there are many things that are special cases but not experiencers. (108) It is essential to the Sāṃkhya system that Nature should serve the ends of the soul. (109) Bṛhad. II.iv.14 (110) Muṇḍ I.i.4, also of the Atharva Veda. (111) Made by the Sāṃkhya towards the beginning of the present section. (112) Above, p.194 (113) Praśna VI.3, the text at present under comment. (114) Praśna Bh. VI.3 (115) The various degrees of nescience are described amongst the sub-divisions undergone by Nature during its period of manifestation, Īśvara Kṛṣṇa, Kārikā 48. (116) In particular, no God to prompt activity in Nature by the fiat of His will. (117) But this is contradicted by the Sāṃkhya's own tenets, as he admits the periodical rise and dissolution of the universe. (118) As they are opposites in all respects, cp. Īśvara Kṛṣṇa, Kārikā 11. "The manifest universe and Nature, its cause, consist in the three "constituents", lack consciousness of being different, are objects, are universal and not individual in nature, are non-conscious and are substances and have the quality of generating further effects. Spirit is the opposite of all this." (119) U.S. (verse section) XVI.45-50 (120) This passage leads on from where the passage given at Extract 8 of the following section (refuting the Vaiśeṣikas) breaks off. (121) The Sāṃkhya admits real change. (122) Cp. Īśvara Kṛṣṇa, Kārikā 9 (123) Bh.G.Bh. XVIII.48 (124) This piece leads on from Vol. III p.19 f. above, where it was shown that the Advaita theory did not involve any confusion in the distribution of the rewards of acts to their proper agents, even though only one Self was admitted. (125) The Sāṃkhyas claim that through mere proximity (saṃyoga, Īśvara Kṛṣṇa, Kārikā 20, sānnidhya, Vijñāna Bhiksu I.164) the intellect of the individual soul acquires a semblance of consciousness, while the soul, all-pervading, identifies itself with a particular intellect and imagines itself to be an agent. Śaṃkara claims that they lack a clear theory to show how one all-pervading soul comes to identify itself with a particular intellect. (126) Souls, for their part, are actionless and therefore helpless. And if Nature were only intent on showing off its riches it would never arrange for their release. (127) The passage is concerned with revealing the weakness of the Sāṃkhya doctrine on account of its inability to explain karmic retribution without confusion. Cp. Note 124 above. (128) B.S.Bh. II.iii.50 (129) Īṣvara Kṛṣṇa 18 (130) *Ibid.* 62, "Verily no soul is either bound or liberated." (131) G.K.Bh. III.5 (132) Vācaspati's Tattva Kaumudī on Īśvara Kṛṣṇa 8 (133) B.S.Bh. I.iv.1 (134) Bh.G.Bh. XVIII.19 (135) Frauwallner, G.I.P. Vol.II, p.186 (136) See Note 151 below. (137) Frauwallner, *op. cit.* p.22 (138) *Ibid.* p.81 f. (139) *Ibid.* p.83 (140) See below p.247 (141) Frauwallner, *loc. cit.* p.184 (142) von Glasenapp, Entwicklungsstufen p.3 (143) Frauwallner, *op. cit.* p.116 (144) Below, p.227 (145) Frauwallner, *ibid.* p.120 (146) See above, Vol. II p.105 f. (147) Vol.II p.95 ff. (148) Frauwallner, *op. cit.* p.167 (149) Hacker, Vedanta Studien, p.243, claims that the argument for the Self at Bṛhad. Bh.IV.iii.2 owes a debt to Praśasta Pāda p.69, Eng. trans. p.152 ff. (150) See below, Vol.V Chapter XIII section 1 Extract 5. (151) On the standard Vaiśeṣika view, four binary atomic compounds are required to produce a quaternary compound. Śaṃkara's oldest commentator, Vācaspati Miśra, thinks Śaṃkara committed a *lapsus calami* here. But the (unknown) author of the later Prakaṭārtha Vivaraṇa Commentary thought that Śaṃkara was harking back to an older form of the Vaiśeṣika doctrine represented by the Rāvaṇa Commentary on the Vaiśeṣika Sūtras, no longer extant. Cp. Belvalkar, Brahma Sūtras, Part II p.31. Govindānanda's Ratnaprabhā quotes the Prakaṭārtha Vivaraṇa with approval, saying rāvaṇa-praṇīte bhāṣye dṛśyata iti ciraṃtana-vaiśeṣika-dṛṣṭyedam bhāṣyam ity āhuḥ. (152) Vaiśeṣika Sūtra VII.i.9. Differences of manner — as when a ball of cotton is either pressed together or allowed to expand. Belvalkar, *loc cit.* p.34 (153) Vaiśeṣika Sūtra VII.i.10. The surviving Commentators on this Vaiśeṣika Sūtra explain it with the help of an appeal to God, as does Ānandagiri in his sub-commentary on the present passage in Śaṃkara's B.S.Bh. Belvalkar, *loc. cit*, explains the obscure passage roughly as follows. Smallness, the quality of the binary atomic compound, does not arise from the two primary atoms in the same way that largeness arises from plurality.

in the cause in the case of the ternary compound. It arises from their "being two", but this "being two" is not already inherent in their nature, because all grouping is dependent on counting in some mind, in this case that of the Lord. According to Frauwallner (*op. cit.* p.134) the notion that number depended on counting in a mind probably arose among the Vaiśeṣikas comparatively late, after the introduction of the doctrine of the categories *circa* 500 A.D. (154) Vaiśeṣika Sūtra VII.i.17 (155) The contact between the threads is a cause of the cloth because without it there could be no cloth. But it is an attribute (of the threads), and hence distinct in nature from its effect, the cloth, which is a substance. (156) Vaiśeṣika Sūtra IV.ii.2. "Contact" is technically an attribute. (157) The Vaiśeṣikas held that one could "feel" the wind but not "perceive" it, because it was invisible. One has to *reason* that there must be a substance "wind" to cause the feelings associated with a cool breeze, etc. Frauwallner, *op. cit.* p.32 (158) Cp. Frauwallner, *op. cit.* p.43 (159) B.S.Bh. II.ii.11 (160) Cp. Uddyotakara Nyāyavārttikam, IV.ii.16, Kāśī Sanskrit Series Ed. p.510. Frauwallner, *op. cit.* p.81 f. (161) Cp. above, p.180 (162) The inherent cause (samavāyi-kāraṇa) of an effect is the material cause. The non-inherent cause is that which itself inheres in the inherent cause and modifies the effect. For the technicalities, see Frauwallner, *op. cit.* pp.169 ff. (163) B.S.Bh. II.ii.12. The reference two sentences earlier to the "lack of any efficient cause" clearly shows that it was an early atheistic form of the Vaiśeṣika that Śaṇkara was attacking. Cp. above, note 151. (164) Śaṃkara's Commentary to which was given in the previous Extract. (165) If two things are *absolutely distinct*, then, if they are to stand in relation to one another at all, they must be *brought into* relation and *held in* relation to one another by the relation, almost as if the latter were a material tie, like a piece of string. (166) The notion of contact presupposes the coming into contact of terms previously disjunct. This will not do as a description of the relation of a substance with its attributes, as the substance can never be without its essential attributes (e.g. fire can never be without heat). So the Vaiśeṣikas assumed the special category of "inherence" (samavāya) to account for this kind of relation. Śaṃkara argues that if inherence is perceived contact will also be perceived, and the whole assumption of inherence will be superfluous. (167) We have seen that inherence was regarded by the Vaiśeṣika as constituting a special category of its own, not reducible to contact, which is a quality. Above, p.209 (168) I.e. in the cases both of contact and inherence. (169) Govindānanda suggests kāla, time. (170) Vaiśeṣika Sūtra IV.i.1 (171) Because they enter into contact and therefore must have parts. But whatever has parts is composite, and it owes the composition of its parts to an external cause and is subject to dissolution. (172) Vaiśeṣika Sūtra IV.i.4. Śaṃkara's reading and interpretation of the Sūtra are different from those in surviving Vaiśeṣika texts, cp. Gough p.133 and the remarks at Belvalkar, part II p.42. Śaṃkara makes the Vaiśeṣika argue that if nothing were permanent there would be no means of showing that anything was impermanent for lack of a permanent entity to contrast with it. (173) Vaiśeṣika Sūtra IV.i.5. According to the Vaiśeṣika Commentator Śaṃkara Miśra it simply means, "Any inference as to the non-eternality of the atoms is an error." (174) The binary compounds would exist but would have no perceptible cause. As such they would be eternal, cp. Vaiśeṣika Sūtra IV.i.1, quoted at note 170 above. But, on Vaiśeṣika principles, they ought not to be eternal, as they result from a combination of atoms, and, as long as the binary atomic compound exists, the atoms cannot separate and world-dissolution can never be complete. (175) This would eliminate the binary atomic compounds as eternal entities, since they are composite substances, but would leave the simple atoms lying beyond, eternal, correctly in line with the system. (176) In Vaiśeṣika Sūtra IV.i.1, already quoted above, Śaṃkara is arguing that the Vaiśeṣika Sūtra IV.i.5 cannot be explained in a way that would enable world-dissolution to proceed without reducing it to a meaningless repetition of what had already been said at Sūtra IV.i.1. (177) The process of world-manifestation ascribed by the Sāṃkhya to non-conscious Nature and by the Bhedābheda Vādins to the Vedic Absolute (178) That is, they intended to say that the atoms were eternal and that all perishable objects of the world arose through the combination and disjunction of atoms. But because they credit the atoms with colour and other properties, the whole atomistic theory turns out to be indefensible. (179) Earth is grosser than water, fire or wind, so that one cannot help assuming that the earth-atoms, of which it is supposed by the Vaiśeṣikas to be composed, are grosser than the atoms composing the other elements. (180) I.e. there would simply be the resistance to touch in wind, colour in fire, taste in water and odour in earth, these being the *specific* properties of each of the four elements respectively. (181) B.S. Bh. II.ii.13-16 (182) The assumption is contradictory, because if two things are absolutely distinct from one another there cannot be any relation of dependence between them. (183) In that they have given up their doctrine of pluralism. By doing so, they make of all things one substance, the latter being like the Nature of the Sāṃkhyas. (184) It is a case of two *substances*, one of which is dependent on the other. (185) White, brown and blue are here qualities, not substances like smoke. (186) "Any two things are called 'inseparable' when one can only exist as long as the other is not destroyed, e.g. part and whole, attribute and substance, act and agent, class and individual, characteristic and eternal substance." Annambhaṭṭa, Section 79, p.61. Cp. Foucher, p.169 ff. (187)Vaiśeṣika Sūtra I.i.10 (188) Vaiśeṣika Sūtra VII.ii.13, reading "yuta-siddhy-abhāvāt" with the Vaiśeṣika Sūtra text, Ed. Jīvānanda p.153 and Gough p.220, not the ayutya-siddhy-abhāvāt of modern printed texts of the B.S.Bh. (189) Here Śaṃkara uses the term anupalabdhi, which is not enumerated in his one list of the pramāṇas. Cp. above Chap. X, note 156. (190) See Nyāya Sūtra III.ii.59, which expresses the old Vaiśeṣika doctrine that the mind is atomic in size. Souls have no surfaces because they are all-pervading (vibhu). (191) The Vaiśeṣikas held that while two infinite substances, like two souls or like the soul and ether, could not enter into contact, an infinite and a finite substance, such as soul and mind, could. Frauwallner, *op. cit.* p.128. The difficulty that mind and soul are in practice inseparables, and so should be related by the category "inherence" and not by the mere quality "contact", was overcome verbally by saying that they were *potentially* separable (pṛthag-gatimattvam), *ibid.*, p.151 f. Frauwallner clearly feels, with Śaṃkara, that this is a weak part of the Vaiśeṣika doctrine.

NOTES TO CHAPTER XI

(192) A peasant left his dish near a plum-tree. Asked where it was, he replied, "Near the plum-tree." Asked where the plum-tree was, he replied, "Near the dish." (193) This is one of the old Buddhist arguments against the Vaiśeṣika atom. Cp. Ārya Deva, IX.15, quoted Frauwallner, Buddhismus p.220, "That which has an eastern side has an eastern part. That which gives an atom parts renders it 'non-atomic'." (194) Whatever has parts has been composed and will one day be sundered.Cp. Bṛhad. Bh. I.iv.7, trans. Mādhavānanda p.120. (195) As already remarked, Śaṃkara conceived the Vaiśeṣika system as atheistic. It was apparently not until the time of Praśasta Pāda, in the second half of the sixth century A.D., that we have clear evidence of the presence of the idea of God in the system, and then only as efficient cause of the world. For the Vedantin, the Lord is, of course, both the efficient and the material cause of the world. (196) See above, the opening paragraph of the present Extract. (197) B.S.Bh. II.ii.17 (198) Śaṃkara is perhaps referring to the Logicians and Ritualists — (Mīmāṃsaka), who adopted many of the tenets of the Vaiśeṣikas for their world-view. (199) Desire, aversion, joy, pain, cognition, effort, merit (dharma), demerit (adharma), and impressions (saṃskāra). (200) Saṃskāra (201) Within the all-pervading partless soul of the Vaiśeṣikas one cannot conceive any particular area delimited by the body of the individual, seeing that all souls interpenetrate one another spatially. (202) Ānandagiri says that the relation of contact only occurs between beings of similar class which are in principle subject to the sense of touch, like two wrestlers, or two rams, or a rope and a bucket. In any case, it cannot logically be supposed to obtain between the all-pervading soul of the Vaiśeṣika, which has no surface, and the atomic mind, which has no surface either. (203) For the Vaiśeṣika defines liberation as the state in which merit and demerit become exhausted and no further empirical experience ensues. Praśastapāda, trans. Jha p.601. (204) The position is absurd, because it would then be impossible to draw a dividing line and speak of "this substance" and "these attributes". Sac. M.R.V. p.226 (205) The Sāṃkhyas eventually came to hold that there must be a plurality of selves to account for the variety in human experience. They probably

did so when their one-soul doctrine came under criticism from the Vaiśeṣikas, cp. Frauwallner, G.I.P. I p.322 f. The Advaitin accepts only one Self, holding that the distinction in the experiences of the different individual souls arises from external adjuncts set up by nescience. (206) G.K.Bh. III.5 (207) Cp. note 199 above (208) It is argued that the merit or demerit of any given action by any given self is experienced in the place where the act was performed, as no other self could perform that action at that place and time, or experience its occult results at the same place and time. This explains how the merit and demerit of any particular soul accrues to it alone, even though all souls are all-pervading. (209) And as the Vedas, which are right, speak of experience in heaven, this theory must be wrong. (210) The Vaiśeṣika does not admit that his all-pervading individual soul is perceived, so the differentiating character marking it off from other all-pervading souls is not perceived either, while their "having a particular character" is the only ground of their difference. How can he affirm they each have a particular character unless he knows in what way they differ? (211) Govindānanda suggests space and time. (212) B.S.Bh. II.iii.50-53 (selected) (213) For the Advaitin, desire, aversion, joy, pain, cognition, effort, merit, demerit and impressions (saṃskāra) all pertain to the subtle body, and the Self illumining them is untouched by them. For the Vaiśeṣika they are qualities *actually belonging to* the soul-substance, merely occasioned or aroused by the mind as instrument. (214) "But it (the Nyāya-Vaiśesika system) insists that the ideal of life is not reached until we feel convinced that the self is in reality beyond all experience." Hiriyanna, Outlines, p.264. (215) U.S. (verse section) XVI.51-5 (216) Bh.G. II.16 (217) In particular, perception, inference and Vedic revelation. (218) The inherent cause (samavāyi-kāraṇa) of a new substance, the effect, is the collection of substances from which, as material cause, the new whole, as effect, is composed. The whole "inheres" in the parts. The non-inherent cause (asamavāyi-kāraṇa) consists in the qualities that belong to the substances that go to make up the effect. They are the causes of the qualities of the effect, e.g. the blue colour of the threads which is the cause of the blue colour of the cloth composed from the threads. The nomenclature is awkward, because the non-inherent cause (colour of the threads) actually inheres in the inherent cause (the threads), and it is just this fact of inhering in the inherent cause which distinguishes the non-inherent cause from the efficient cause, the weaver, who has no inherent connection with the material from which the effect is composed. Cp. Frauwallner, G.I.P. II p.169 (219) Cp. above, Vol.II Chapter VI Section 1. (220) The Vaiśeṣikas took the *difference* of one thing from another seriously. They could not, in the manner of the Sāṃkhyas and pre-Śaṃkara Vedantins, allow that the pot was no more than the clay in a new form. It was something *over and above* the material from which is was composed. Otherwise, how could you speak of it as an effect, thereby *distinguishing it from* its material cause? (221) Bh.G.Bh. XVIII.48 (222) Who maintain the opposite thesis that the effect does not pre-exist in the cause, but is a new production. (223) Chānd. Bh. VI.ii.1 (224) B.S.Bh. II.iii.3, Gambhīrānanda p.446 (225) The Vaiśeṣika opponent is greeted with examples from empirical experience cited against his doctrine by the Sāṃkhyas. (226) According to the distinction of the categories set up by the Vaiśeṣikas themselves. (227) B.S. II.i.24 (228) To refute the opponent's contention, the Advaitin has only to show that a beginning for the ether is logically *possible*. The way for accepting the authority of the Vedic texts that affirm it is then open, as empirical experience cannot produce evidence to contradict their statements on this subject, since perception and inference based upon it has no access to this abstruse realm. (229) So that, even on the opponent's own premises, the beginning of the ether was a significant event. (230) Bṛhad. III.viii.8 (231) *Ibid.* (232) As this is not a field that stands within the range of perception, and, in Indian logic, reason is based on perception. Reason was regarded as a weak authority when it had to reason by analogy to things lying beyond the range of possible perceptual experience, unless it was engaged in working out the implications of the revealed texts. (233) According to the Vaiśeṣikas, the soul (ātman) is eternal but has impermanent attributes, such as transient cognition, will and desire. (234) B.S.Bh. II.ii.7 (235) The Vaiśeṣikas maintained that sound was a quality of the ether-substance. Praśastapāda p.58 (trans. Jha p.129) Cp. Frauwallner, G.I.P. Vol.II, p.206. See also Nyāya Sūtra II.ii.38. (236) The knowing subject cannot know itself as an object. Cp. Sureśvara, N. Sid. II.27 (237) Which illumines itself, *inter alia*. (238) The example of the lamp could be explained on the basis of the flame, conceived as one part of the lamp, illumining the rest of it. (Mādhavānanda) (239) The fact that the Self is partless. (240) That is to say, the realm of the perceptible, the changing, whereas the Self, according to the Logicians, is an object of inference only, and not of perception. It belongs to a totally different realm. It is the knowing subject, eternal and unchanging. (241) The foundation of the Nyāya doctrine is an ancient, perhaps pre-Upanishadic, Indian tradition of naturalism, in which the elements are not created, but eternal. For the Upanishadic seers, however, all things rose on the basis of the Absolute, and hence had an origin and a beginning. Cp. Taitt II.1. "The ether arose from the Self, wind from ether." (242) Ten villagers crossed a river, and one was deputed to count the party. Because he forgot to count himself, he could only find nine, and had to be *told* "Thou art the tenth." Similarly, for the final rejection of the erroneous notion that the Self is subject to pain, we require to *hear* the truth from the Veda. We have already met the story above, Vol.I, p.155, 160. We shall meet it again in Vol.V Chap. XIII section 1 and Vol.VI Chap. XV section 4. (243) Bṛhad. Bh. I.iv.7 (244) Buddha is thought to have spoken Māgadhī, the language of Bihar. The dialect of the earliest surviving form of the Buddhist Canon, which came later to be called Pālī, was probably based on the spoken dialect of the neighbouring area to the West, between Mathura and Ujjain. S.C. Chatterji thinks that an original Māgadhī Buddhist Canon was remoulded in this dialect because it was more widely understood, being spoken in an area of traffic and trade. Chatterji, p.179 (245) Kumārila could produce quotations in Pālī, but his knowledge of Buddhism and languages was exceptional for a Brahmin of his time.

See Upadhyaya, B.D., Śaṃkara Digvijaya, Bhūmikā p.31. (246) Murti, Central Philosophy p.68 (247) Warder (p.144) contends that Nāgārjuna should not be classified as belonging to the Mahāyāna fold. He admits, however, (*ibid.* p.155) that Nāgārjuna's pupil Ārya Deva "placed the Bodhisattva in the foreground." If the Ratnāvalī is an authentic work of Nāgārjuna, he devoted 102 verses to Bodhisattva practice, cp. Alex Wayman, Journal of Indian Philosophy, Dordrecht, Vol. VI, Dec. 1978, p.416. Most mordern scholars appear to maintain that Nāgārjuna supplied a dialectical support for the doctrine of "emptiness" (śūnyatā) occurring in the Prajñā Pāramitā literature of the Mahāyāna. (248) Cp. Frauwallner, Buddhismus p.174 (249) *Ibid.* p.267 f. (250) Some printed editions of the whole or part of the P.V. are listed at Vetter, Erkenntnisprobleme p.117. (251) Above, Vol.I, p.29 f. (252) Particularly at Yamakami Sogen, pp. 126-142 and 161-169, and at Joshi L.M., p.233 f. Both these authors, however, appear guilty of unwarranted animus against Śaṃkara: on Yamakami Sogen, cp. B.S. Upadhyaya pp. 1007-1009 and S.K.Belvalkar, Brahma Sūtras Part II, references listed there in the Index under the name Sogen. One would expect a fairer account of Śaṃkara's treatment of Sarvāstivāda and Vijñānavāda in the two articles by Professor Nakamura cited by Potter (Nos. 2238 and 2248), but they are inaccessible to most western students because they are in Japanese. (253) Above, Vol.I, p.26. (254) Cp. Ingalls in P.E.W., Jan. 1954, p.300. (255) Cp. Frauwallner in W.Z.K.S.O., 1959 p.126 (256) Cp. Murti, C.P.B. p.82 (257) They are deśānugata as well as kālānugata. Silburn, p.280 (258) Vetter, Erkenntnisprobleme p.53 (259) Vetter, Erkenntnisprobleme, p.78 (260) See below p.278 (261) See below p.288 (262) Cp. Prajñākara Gupta, Commentary ad *loc.* (i.e. III.328) sākṣātkaraṇādikam pratyākhyātam. Śaṃkara's answer to this will be found below, p.283 (263) Vetter, *op. cit.* p.80 (264) Hiriyanna, Essentials p.81 (265) See below, p.299 (266) Cp. Kumārila, Ś.V., Codanā Sūtra verse 140, trans. Jha p.42: "... these may have been composed by Buddha himself...to deceive people." Maṇḍana Miśra (B. Sid. p.96) quotes Kumārila's Ś.V. (Codanā Sūtra verse 96), saying that, as a mere *man*, Buddha could not have had insight into supersensual matters. Śaṃkara is less severe in the following Extract. He seems prepared to respect the Buddhists' own account of the reason for the presence of different schools of Buddhist teaching, namely that it was due to different capacities among the students. Śaṃkara's personal pupil Sureśvara was altogether more sympathetic to the Buddha. Cp. B.B.V. I.iv.410: "Even the Buddha, in declaring that objects were impermanent, painful and without any real essence (śūnya), was clearly striving only to eradicate attachment and other passions, and not to deny the Self." Shortly after Śaṃkara's day the Bhāgavata Purāṇa accepted the Buddha as an Avatāra of Viṣṇu (I.iii.24), born in the Kali Age "to confuse the enemies of the gods." By the time of Jayadeva (c.1200 A.D.), when Buddhism was no longer a threat, Viṣṇu was said to come as Buddha to spread His compassion. (Jaya Deva I.12) But Śaṃkara followed the earlier Vaishnava tradition, where the ten Avatāras of Vishnu began with Haṃsa (the "Holy Swan") and did not include the Buddha. M.Bh. Śānti Parva 339.103-5, G.P. Ed. p.707. (267) B.S.Bh. II.ii.32 (268) G.K.Bh. IV.99 (269) In that it admits only a few eternal entities, like atoms and universals, while the great majority of substances and qualities proceed from the conjunction of atoms, and are followed by their disjunction and are consequently perishable. See Bhāmatī on B.S. II.ii.18. (270) The Sarvāstivādins were subdivided into two main schools called the Vaibhāṣikas and Sautrāntikas. Both these schools adhered to the reality of external objects, though their theories of the nature and the knowledge of objects were different. The Vaibhāsikas held that we had direct knowledge of the objects, while the Sautrāntikas held we only had indirect knowledge of them through inference from the sense-data. (271) I.e. the Vaibhāṣikas as opposed to the Sautrāntikas. (272) The five terms are paraphrased according to Vācaspati's Bhāmatī Comm. *ad loc.* (273) Activity is brought to an end by the destruction of its cause. If activity just sprang up of its own without a cause, nothing could stop it. Liberation,on Buddhist principles, would then be impossible. (274) The sub-commentators see a reference here to the "storehouse consciousness" (ālaya-vijñāna) of the Yogācāras. Though we associate this concept more typically with Mahāyāna authors and not with the Hīnayāna tradition, they may still be correct, as Vasubandhu does indeed introduce this concept into his exposition of the (Hīnayāna) Vaibhāṣika work, the Abhidharma Kośa. See Frauwallner, Buddhismus, p.117. (275) Vasubandhu held that when one thing is not established as identical with or different from a second thing, the first thing does not exist, and is a mere name. Frauwallner, *op. cit.* p.86 ff. See also the present work below, Note 312. (276) What is momentary has not time to act. (277) It is that which enters the womb to form the core of the future personality, Dīgha Nikāya XV.21, ed. Rhys Davids and Carpenter, Vol.II p.63. On Vijñāna in this context cp. Frauwallner, G.I.P. I. p.204, where a connection is traced between its use in early Buddhism and in the Upanishads. (278) That which forms itself in the womb in dependence on the previous entry of "vijñāna". Frauwallner, G.I.P. I, p.205 f. (279) Because misery allied to thirst for more experience is manifest to everyone, and only explicable through a chain of causation beginning with nescience. (280) Once you have admitted the causal cycle beginning with nescience you have admitted the formation of aggregates, as the existence of experiencing individuals, implied by the cycle, implies in turn the formation of aggregates. Further, the immediate experience of the existence of the chain of misery outweighs any negation of its existence based on mere inference. (281) The Buddhist had assumed that the existence of the chains was incontrovertible, and claimed that it implied an aggregate. The Advaitin says here that if it implies an aggregate in the sense of being dependent on one, it will have to be shown how an aggregate can be caused before the cycle can be accepted at all. It is, after all, only a rational construct. (282) Nescience and its effects can only occur to some permanent being who "has nescience", and any such being must be an aggregate. The Buddhist argument is therefore circular. (283) According to the theories of the day, there was a moment when a product came into being and just "existed" before it had time to engage in action of any kind. (284) The four "pratyayas" (cp. above. p.257), here interpreted as the object, the sense-organ, environmental auxiliaries (like light etc.) and previous similar impressions. (285) Hiriyanna, Outlines p.202; Essentials p.79 (286) Pratisaṅkhyā-nirodha. It is not a single event, but a process in which the passions are rooted out one by one, and the further experiences to which they lead are thus blocked. The process ends in Nirvāṇa Cp. Abhidharma Kośa I.6, translated and explained by Frauwallner, Buddhismus, p.130 f. The role of knowledge here is explained at Murti, C.P.B. p.272 (287) Apratisaṅkhyā-nirodha. Sometimes possiblities of experience are blocked by circumstances and not by attainment of wisdom. For instance, one who has embarked on the holy path can no longer be reborn in hell, or as an animal or demon. Suppression of experience in this sense never amounts to the total suppression of all experience, but is grouped with pratisaṅkhyā-nirodha on the ground of its being a reality, yet non-composite and outside time. (288) While the two "suppressions" involve the cessation, either total or partial, of the flux of phenomena, they are themselves in some sense entities, not exactly being or non-being, hence "indescribable" or "unintelligible" as Śaṃkara says. On this point, see Murti C.P.B. p.273. (289) The lump of clay is destroyed to make way for the pot: but it is not total destruction without residue. The clay remains, and may be recognized as identical with the pot. (290) The Vaibhāṣikas held to this principle. Whatever is brought into being perishes automatically on the instant and does not require to be destroyed. "Pratisaṅkhyā-nirodha" is itself "uncaused", it is not anything that is brought into being at a particular point in time. It is simply the state of affairs that remains over when experiences have been blocked. (291) I.e the Noble Eightfold Path (292) Indescribable as being or not-being. See Note 288 above. (293) Taitt. II.1 (294) Gopinath Kaviraj (Bhūmikā p.60) produces evidence to suggest that the Vaibhāṣikas did not think of space as mere absence of obstruction, but as a positive entity in some sense. (295) If space really equalled absence of obstruction, then a single bird flying in the sky, since it would constitute an obstruction, would cancel space and make it impossible for any other bird to fly. (296) A negation is significant only as denying the presence of something in some positive *locus*. Here, space would have to be taken as the positive *locus* in which obstruction is denied. Bhāmatī. (297) It is quoted by Max Müller, S.B.E. Vol.XV, Introduction p.lii. Gopinath Kaviraj (*loc. cit.*) traces the reference to

NOTES TO CHAPTER XI

Yaśomitra's Comm. on Vasubandhu's Abhidharma Kośa (Ed. Wogihara, Tokyo, 1932) I.55.5. It is not certain whether Śaṃkara actually had direct access to the works of Vasubandhu and Yaśomitra or whether he was merely following traditional Vedanta interpretations of the Sūtra under discussion. (298) I.e. that nothing persists as identical, but that because of the mutual similarity of the various members of certain chains of cause and effect we fail to note the difference between each link in the chain and imagine ourselves in the presence of a permanent substance. (299) Cp. Nyāya Sūtra IV.i.14. Some authorities hold that the B.S. here switch their attack from the Vaibhāṣikas to the Sautrāntikas in this and the following Sūtra. See Belvalkar, Brahma Sūtras, Part II, Notes p.88. (300) The horned hare is taken by Śaṃkara as non-being (abhāva) not merely because it is never met with in experience,like the golden mountain, but also because it is a self-contradictory conception, like the square circle. If a creature had a horn, it could not be a hare. (301) Śaṃkara himself, like Bergson, dismisses the concept of non-existence as unintelligible. Cf. the present work, Vol.II. p.105f. (302) For the four causal factors, see above p.257 (303) See above, p.261 (304) B.S.Bh. II.ii.18-27 (305) The Vaibhāṣikas and the Sautrāntikas. (306) The Yogācāras or Vijñānavādins. (307) And so of explaining how the appearance of a permanent substance, like the flame of a light, could arise from the swift succession of momentary flashes that were supposed, on the Vaibhāṣikas' theory, to make it up. (308) Vasubandhu the Later argued that destruction, being merely non-being, could not be caused by action from without. But things evidently pass away. Therefore they must do so by their own very nature. But if they pass away by their own very nature they must do so immediately, as, if they endured at all, there would be nothing in their own nature that could rise up anew to cause their destruction. Cp. Vetter, Erkenntnisprobleme p.15 (309) Such a doctrine would not cover the restriction on causality observed in the world. If it were right, there would be no reason why you could not get curds out of sand as well as getting them out of milk. (310) Even this is impossible on Sarvāstivāda assumptions. (311) The two horns of a cow exist at the same period of time, but in no way modify or condition one another. So a further qualification besides simultaneous existence is required for causality. One has to act on the other. R.T. cites the example of rain and a sprout. The Extract is U.S. XVI. 23-9. (312) If they were distinct from the atoms (i.e. atom-instants) they would be separate realities, which would be against the Buddhist doctrine that everything is momentary. If non-distinct they would no more be able to manifest in knowledge than the atoms themselves. Ānandagiri. (313) Cp. above, p.257 f. (314) This law is defined by Stcherbatsky as "the fact of co-extensiveness of existence and knowledge", Buddhist Logic, II.p.355. (315) A person can only make a comparison if he and his hearers know what the thing in question is being compared to, which must consequently exist. The mere fact that the idealist is forced to speak of objects "appearing as if external" proves that something external to consciousness exists, and that he himself is aware of it. (316) Because it could not logically be conceived as either different or non-different from its component atoms. (317) The Buddhist idealist has suggested the opposite view that what appear to be objects must in fact be modifications of consciousness. See above, p.276 f. (318) Even when the object is the same and there is distinction in the manner of cognition only, it still does not follow that the object is of the nature of cognition. Bhāmatī. (319) Ānandagiri says that "etc." means void of a nature of their own, without a "self". (320) A short chapter is devoted to this distinction, Stcherbatski, Théorie, Chap.VII, pp. 115-123. (321) Criticized by Kumārila, Ś.V., Nirālambana Vāda, verse 182, trans. Jha p.145 (322) This would follow from its not being admitted to reveal itself. (323) That is, cognitions would be lamps in the hollow of a rock in the sense that there would be no one to know them. (324) In dreamless sleep and dream, the objects of the waking world are simply effaced. There is no cancelling-cognition of the form "The objects of waking did not exist and were a mere error." The argument is possibly borrowed from Kumārila, Ś.V. Nirālambana Vāda, verses 87-90, tr. Jha p.133. (325) The argument is: When there are impressions, consciousness undergoes modification; when there are no modifications it does not. So Govindānanda's sub-commentary. (326) Commenting on Yoga

Sūtra II.13, Vyāsa defines the vāsanā as that saṃskāra which produces memory. (327) I.e. the doctrine "Every phenomenon is momentary." (328) Above, p.264 and p.268 with Note 290. The Extract comprises B.S.Bh. II.ii.28-31 (329) I.e. as an illuminator. It is agreed that the mind illumines the object like a lamp: but the Advaitin has also argued that the mind itself requires to be illumined by a separate luminous principle, the Self. On the similarity between the mind and the Self as Witness, cp. above, Vol.III p.54 (330) A pot could be felt by the hand in a dark room where there was no light. (331) Saṃvṛti is defined as "That which covers on all sides" and is equated with ignorance (ajñāna) by Candrakīrti, commenting on Mādhyamika Kārikā XXIV.8. Cp. G.K.IV.57 and 74 (332) The same illustration of the Vijñāna Vādins is attacked at Śānti Deva IX. 18-9 (Matics p.213). (333) The argument will show that neither of them can illumine anything else — i.e. they are the same in their intrinsic nature, and both require illumination from without. (334) That is, if there has to be a separate principle to know cognition, will there not have to be a separate principle to know the first one and another to know that and so to infinity? (335) Appeal must be made not to mere reason but to direct experience, which latter shows that there *is* an ultimate knower, a Witness, itself not known by anything else. (336) The instruments will require to be known, and separate instruments will be required to know the instruments, and yet further instruments will be required for the knowledge of those instruments and so on. (337) The principle known in Buddhism as the Law of Simultaneous Apprehension (sahopalambha-niyama). Cp. above, p.278 (338) The Buddhist claims that there are no external objects in waking any more than there are in dream. But he cannot establish that dream-objects are not external except by contrasting them with objects of the waking world which are. So he cannot establish that the objects of the waking world are mere transformations of self-luminous consciousness. So his argument that mental cognitions are self-luminous and do not require a separate self-luminous Witness to illumine them breaks down. (339) This is a reference to Kumārila's doctrine of knowledge of the self. Extracts devoted to refuting it will be given below, Vol.V Chap. XIII section 1. (340) You "recognize" Tommy's mop of red hair when you see him again after two years – but in fact you have never before seen the new crop he has grown in the meanwhile. (341) The Hindus believe in a permanent soul undergoing transmigration. Its fate in the present life is largely due to its actions and thoughts in former lives, and its present actions and thoughts help to condition its future lives. By denying a permanent soul of any kind, the Buddhists cut at the roots of this belief, and their doctrine was held by the Hindus to undermine moral responsibility generally. (342) Bṛhad. Bh. IV.iii.7 (343) A quotation of Dharmakīrti, P.V. II 354, but reading abhinno for avibhāgo. Following the commentator Bodhanidhi, Professor Mayeda holds that this verse may here be an interpolation. But he points out that Sureśvara quotes it at B.B.V. IV.iii.476. Mayeda, A Thousand Teachings, p.200, Note 101. (344) Dharmakīrti taught that the judgement "This is a bull" had two elements. The first affirmed pure being. The second attributed to it imaginatively a character. But the notion "bull" has no positive meaning: its meaning is only the negation of cow and lion and all other universal ideas except, "bull". (Stcherbatski, Théorie p.154). The real is the unique particular, and all representation of it consists in the false ascription to it of universal terms which have no positive meaning, being derived through negation of other universal terms. (345) Because in order to know non-cow you would already have to know cow *as a positive entity* in order to be able to differentiate non-cow from it. Kunjunni Raja p.87 f. Śaṃkara is possibly here referring to Kumārila's refutation of Dharmakīrti's theory of meaning made at Ś.V. Apoha Vāda section, verses 83 and 84, and using it. (346) U.S. (Verse section) XVIII.141-52. (347) The Vaibhāṣikas (348) E.g. in dreamless sleep. So there is consciousness without pain – a proof that consciousness and pain must be different. (349) The previous objection was against Vijñāna Vāda. The reply begins as Advaita, goes over to Vijñāna Vāda, and finally returns to Advaita. The example which Śaṃkara goes on to give of the pot being nothing over and above the clay into which it can be analysed has been cited by Frauwallner (W.Z.K.S.O., 1959, p.124) from the Nyāyānusāra of the Buddhist (Sautrāntika) author Śrīlata. He later (p.128) cites a passage from Diṅnāga's Hastavāla Prakaraṇa in which the latter argues that the rope is no better than the snake, since it can be analysed into parts and has no existence beyond them. It has no real being but only "nominal being" (prajñapti-sat), i.e. for practical purposes in the world men decide not to analyse it into its component parts to find its true nature, but to designate it arbitrarily as a rope. Thus its "reality" derives from mere naming. Vetter (W.Z.K.S.O. 1968/1969, p.410. footnote 4) remarks that this is not at all unlike the argumentation used by Śaṃkara himself in relation to cloth and threads, etc., at B.S.Bh. II.i.15, Gambhīrānanda p.336. (350) Reading abhūtadarśanāt (not bhūta-darśanāt) (351) Śaṃkara makes the same point at Chānd. Bh. VIII.xii.3 trans. Gambhīrānanda p.659. (352) This is an answer to the opponent's view detailed above, beginning at the third paragraph of the present Extract. (353) The Advaitin accepts the Vijñāna Vādin's arguments in so far as they show that there is no external object. But he goes further and concludes that if the mind appears to represent objects at all, the whole process must be illusory, including the mind itself. Again, from the standpoint of the highest truth, the Eleatic doctrine prevails that it is logically impossible that anything should come into being. Even the "coming into being" or "origination" of an idea in the mind must be an illusion. (354) G.K.Bh.IV. 24-8 (355) Chānd. Bh. VIII. i.1, introduction (351) The Bhāmatī affirms that the reference is to the empirical means of knowledge (laukikāni pramāṇāni) which determine what objects exist and what do not. (357) This sentence recurs word for word at Bṛhad. Bh. IV.iii.7 as well as in the present B.S.Bh. passage, in both cases after the conclusion of the case against the Vijñāna Vādin. It is part of the evidence showing that the two commentaries were by the same author. (358) B.S.Bh. II.ii.31 (359) G.K.Bh. IV.28 (360) That is, Nirvāṇa or liberation implies the extinction or destruction of consciousness. (361) Taitt. II.i.1 (362) Ait. V.3 (363) Objects change and give way to one another. But the fact they they are invariably known shows that the consciousness that illumines them is different from them in kind, and invariable. (364) It was common practice amongst Hindus as well as Jainas, and even with some Buddhists of opposed schools, to attribute crass nihilism to the Mādhyamika (Cp. Hiriyanna, Outlines p.221 f.). And the Mādhyamikas do lend colour to this interpretation by some of their own expressions. For instance, in commenting on Nāgārjuna, M.K. XV.2, Candrakīrti says (Prasannapadā p.265) that the true nature of the things seen through ignorance in ordinary worldly life consists in the fact they they are not born, that they are nothing (akiṃcit), that they are pure non-existence (abhāva-mātra) and have no real essence (asvabhāva). (365) The argument returns here, for a moment, to the supposition that knowledge is inseparable from the knowable. (366) The term "nihilist" (vaināśika) can be used by Śaṃkara to refer to any Buddhist school. There appear to be references in Buddhist literature to the Ālaya Vijñāna as being in some sense manifest even in dreamless sleep. See Narendradeva, p.464. (367) So that the Advaitin would not then have been able to instance dreamless sleep as an example of knowledge existing in the absence of the knowable. (368) Praśna Bh. VI.2 (369) By the Mīmāṃsaka, who wants to expose as absurd the metaphysical texts of the Upanishads in order to be able to interpret them as figurative, and thus clear the way for expounding his own ritualistic doctrines as the final word of the Veda. (370) The Mīmāṃsaka holds that a word can directly denote only a universal, otherwise its meaning would be different each time it was used and the hearer would not be able to understand it. Its meaning is narrowed down to the universal as residing in a particular individual in a class when it is placed in a sentence and qualified by other words. (371) The Nihilist is made to square his view of negation with that of the P.M., the professional exegetes of the Veda. Cp. Bhatt, p.282, "The function of the word 'not' in a factual statement is to remove ignorance or doubt or to reject a false idea." (372) See above, Vol.I, p.189 f. (373) Chānd. Bh. VI.ii.2 (374) Renou and Filliozat, Vol.II section 2409 (375) Frauwallner, G.I.P. II. p.254 (376) Kumārila's Tantra Vārttika II.iii.12, trans. Jha. Bibliotheca Indica, Vol.I p.234, quoted by von Glasenapp in Schubring (Festchrift) p.80. (376) Frauwallner, G.I.P. II p.275 (377) Hiriyanna, Outlines, p.164. (378) It is a great point in favour of Śaṃkara's interpretation of the B.S. to find the author of the Sūtras himself appealing to

the Law of Contradiction, as this law is Śaṃkara's great weapon against those interpretations of the Sūtras which conflict with his own. (379) See section 4 above.
(380) On the Jaina doctrine, von Glasenapp writes: "Karma expresses itself in eight different ways. (1) It covers over the clear experience of the soul. (2) It covers over the indeterminate experience of the soul. (3) It causes experience of pleasure and pain. (4) It distorts true belief and right behaviour. (5) It brings on a particular mode of existence as god, man, animal or monster in hell. (6) It provides the empirical creature with his particular physical and psychical characteristics and with his destiny or fate. (7) It determines the rank that one attains through birth. (8) It obstructs the energy that belongs to the soul by nature."Einführung, p.298. (381) B.S.Bh. II.ii. 33-36.

LIST OF GENERAL ABBREVIATIONS

In principle, works are referred to under their author's names throughout the Notes, and the abbreviations occasionally used to distinguish between an author's different works should not cause any difficulty. Except for the two entries R.T. and Sac, the following list comprises those abbreviations that are used independently of any author's name. The list excludes the names of Upanishads on which Śaṃkara wrote commentaries, which are listed under his name in the Bibliography of Vol.I and readily identifiable there.

A.B.O.R.I. . Annals of the Bhandarkar Oriental Research Institute, Poona

A.S.S. . . . Ānanda Āśrama Sanskrit Series, Poona

A.Ś.S. . . . Āpastambīyam Śrauta Sūtram, Mysore University

A.V. . . . . Atharva Veda

B.B.V. . . . See Sureśvara in Bibliography to Vol.I

B.B.V.S. . . See Vidyāraṇya in Bibliography to Vol.I

Bh. . . . . . Bhāṣya (i.e. Commentary)

Bh.G.. . . . Bhagavad Gītā, q.v. under Texts of Śaṃkara in Bibliography to Vol.I

B.S. . . . . Brahma Sūtras, see under Śaṃkara in Bibliography to Vol.I

B.S.Bh.. . . See Śaṃkara in Bibliography to Vol.I

B.V.S. . . . i.e. B.B.V.S., see Vidyāraṇya in Bibliography to Vol.I

LIST OF GENERAL ABBREVIATIONS

G.K. . . . . Gauḍapāda's Kārikās on Māṇḍūkya Upanishad. See under Śaṃkara in Bibliography to Vol.I

G.O.S. . . . Gaekwad's Oriental Series, Baroda

G.P. . . . . Gītā Press, Gorakhpur

I.H.Q. . . . Indian Historical Quarterly

I.I.J. . . . Indo-Iranian Journal

J.A. . . . . Journal Asiatique

J.A.O.S.. . Journal of the American Oriental Society

J.B.B.R.A.S. Alternative form of J.R.A.S.B.B., q.v.

J.B.O.R.S.. Journal of the Bihar and Orissa Oriental Society

J.O.I.B. .. Journal of the Oriental Institute, Baroda

J.O.R.M. .. Journal of Oriental Research, Madras University

J.R.A.S.B.B. Journal of the Royal Asiatic Society of Great Britain and Ireland, Bombay Branch

J.U.B. . . . Jaiminīya Upanishad Brāhmaṇa

M.Bh. . . . Mahābhārata. G.P. Mūla-mātra Ed., 4 Vols.

M.V. . . . Method of the Vedanta, see Saccidānandendra in Bibliography

N.S. . . . Nirṇaya Sāgara Press

LIST OF GENERAL ABBREVIATIONS

N.Sū. . . . . Nyāya Sūtras. See Vātsyāyana in Bibliography to Vol.I

P.E.W. . . . Philosophy East and West, Honolulu

P.M. . . . . Pūrva Mīmāṃsā

P.P. . . . . Pañcapādikā, q.v. in Bibliography to Vol.I

R.T. . . . . Rāma Tīrtha (seventeenth century commentator)

R.V. . . . . Ṛg Veda

Sac. . . . . Saccidānandendra Svāmin, modern author, (d.1975) q.v. in Bibliography to Vol.I

Ś.B. . . . . Śatapatha Brāhmaṇa

S.B.E. . . . Sacred Books of the East Series, Oxford, recently re-issued Delhi

T.B.V. . . . See under Sureśvara

U.S. . . . . Upadeśa Sāhasrī. See under Texts of Śaṃkara in Bibliography to Vol.I

V.P. . . . . Viṣṇu Purāṇa, q.v. in Bibliography to Vol.I

W.Z.K.O. . . See W.Z.K.S.O.

W.Z.K.S.O. . Wiener Zeitschrift für die Kunde Süd- und Ostasiens

Y.D. . . . . Yukti Dīpikā, q.v. in Bibliography to Vol.I

Y.S. . . . . Yoga Sūtras. See Patañjali in Bibliography to Vol.I

LIST OF GENERAL ABBREVIATIONS

Z.D.M.G. . . Zeitschrift der Deutschen Morgenländischen Gesellschaft

Z.I.I. . . . Zeitschrift für Indologie und Iranistik

Z.M.R. . . . Zeitschrift für Missionswissenschaft Münster/Westfalen

B I B L I O G R A P H Y

The texts of Śaṃkara here used are those listed in Vol.I of the Śaṃkara Source-Book, Śaṃkara on the Absolute, p.241 f. In regard to the secondary literature, only those works are listed below which did not appear in the Bibliography of Vol.I.

Annambhaṭṭa, *Tarka Saṅgraha* ed. and trans. Athalye, 2nd ed., Bombay 1930

Ārya Deva, *The Catuḥśataka*, ed. V. Bhattacharya, Calcutta, 1931

Belvalkar, S.K., *Brahma Sūtras of Bādarāyaṇa, Chapter II, Quarters 1 and 2*, Poona, 1923-4. For Vedanta Phil., see Vol.I. Bibliog.

Bhatt, G.P., *Epistemology of the Bhāṭṭa School of Pūrva Mīmāṃsā*, Varanasi, 1962

Biardeau, M., *La Démonstration du Sphoṭa par Maṇḍana Miśra*, Pondichéry, 1958

Chatterji, S.K., *Indo-Aryan and Hindi*, 2nd Ed., Calcutta, 1960 reprinted 1969

Das Gupta, S.N., *History of Indian Philosophy*, Vol.V, Cambridge, 1955

Dharmakīrti, *Pramāṇa Vārttikam*, ed. Dvārikādāsa Śāstrī, Varanasi, 1968. See Prajñākara Gupta

Dīgha Nikāya, ed. Rhys Davids and Carpenter, Vol.II, Pali Text Society, London 1966 (reprint)

Foucher A., *Compendium des topiques*, Paris, 1949

Frauwallner, E., *Die Philosophie des Buddhismus*, Berlin, 1958

Gaṃbhīrānanda, Swāmī, *Chāndogya Upanishad with the Commentary of Śrī Śaṅkarācārya*, Calcutta, 1983

Garbe, R., *Die Sāṃkhya Philosophie*, Leipzig, 1917

von Glasenapp, H., *Stufenweg zum Göttlichen*, Baden-Baden, 1948

BIBLIOGRAPHY

Gough, A.E.; see Vaiśeṣika Sūtras

Hiriyanna, M., *Essentials of Indian Philosophy*, London, 1949

—, *Indian Philosophical Studies*, Vol.I, Mysore, 1957

—, *Outlines of Indian Philosophy*, London, 1932

Iyer, K.A. Subramania, *Bhartṛhari*, Poona, 1969

Joshi, L.M., *Studies in the Buddhistic Culture of India*. Delhi, 1967. For Joshi (= Jośī) T.L., see Vol.I, Bibliog.

Kaṇāda; see Vaiśeṣika Sūtras

Kavirāj, Gopināth, *Bhūmikā*, (Introduction to the Acyuta Grantha Mālā ed. of *Brahma Sūtras*), Varanasi, 1942

Keith, A.B., *A History of Sanskrit Literature*, Oxford, 1920

—, *The Sāṃkhya System*, O.U.P., 1924

Kṛṣṇa Miśra, *Prabodha Candrodaya*, ed. and Eng. trans. Sita Krishna Nambiar, Delhi, 1971

Kumārila Bhaṭṭa, *Tantra Vārttika*, ed. Gangadhara Shastri, Benares, 1882-1903; Eng. trans. Ganganath Jha, Bibliotheca Indica, Calcutta, 1903-24. For Ś.V., see under Kumārila, Vol.I, Bibliog.

Kunjunni Raja, K., *Indian Theories of Meaning*, Adyar, Madras, 1963

Matics, Marion L., *Entering the Path of Enlightenment*, London, 1970

Müller, F.Max, *Sacred Books of the East*, Vol.XV, Oxford, 1884

Mus, P., *Barabudur*, Hanoi, 1935

BIBLIOGRAPHY

Nakamura, H., *A History of Early Vedanta Philosophy*, Part One, Delhi, 1983

Narendradeva, *Bauddha-Dharma-Darśana*, Patna, 1956

Prajñākara Gupta, *Pramāṇa Vārtika Bhāṣyam*. ed. Rāhula Sāṃkṛtyāyana, Patna, 1953

Ritter, H., *Das Meer der Seele*, Leiden, 1955

Saccidānandendra, *Method of the Vedanta* (abbreviated M.V), Eng. trans. of *Vedānta Prakriyā Pratyabhijñā*, K.P.I., London, forthcoming

Śānti Deva, *Bodhicaryāvatāraḥ*, ed. P.L. Vaidya, Dharbhanga, 1960

Sogen, Y., *Systems of Buddhistic Thought*, Calcutta, 1912

Stcherbatski, Th., *Buddhist Logic*, Vol.II, Leningrad, 1930

—, *Central Conception of Buddhism*, London 1923

—, *La théorie de la connaissance et la logique chez les Bouddhistes tardifs*, Paris, 1926

Uddyotakara, *Nyāya Vārttikam*, ed. Dvivedin and Dravid, Benares, 1916-7

Upādhyaya, B.S., *Bauddha Darśana Tathā anya Bhāratīya Darśana*, 2 vols, Calcutta, 1954. For Upādhyaya, B.D., see Vol.I, Bibliog.

Vaiśeṣika Sūtras, with Comm. of Śaṅkara Miśra, ed. and Eng. trans. A.E. Gough, Benares, 1873, reprinted Delhi, 1975

—,ed. Jīvānanda, Calcutta, 1886

Vetter, T., *Erkenntnisprobleme bei Dharmakīrti*, Vienna, 1964

BIBLIOGRAPHY

Vijñāna Bhikṣu, *Sāṃkhya Pravacana Bhāṣya,* ed. R. Garbe, Cambridge, Mass, 1895

Warder, A.K., *Outlines of Indian Philosophy,* Delhi, 1971

Yamakami Sogen; see Sogen

Yoga Sūtras; see Patañjali, Vol.I, Bibliog.

CONSPECTUS OF CONTENTS OF THE SIX VOLUMES OF THE ŚAMKARA SOURCE-BOOK

VOLUME I

ŚAṂKARA ON THE ABSOLUTE

CHAPTER

I. SOURCES OF ŚAṂKARA'S DOCTRINE: HIS LIFE & WORKS

1. A Doctrine of Transcendence
2. Vedas: Saṃhitās, Brāhmaṇas, Upanishads
3. The Smṛti: Viṣṇu-worship and Śiva-worship
4. The Bhagavad Gītā
5. The Brahma-Sūtras and their Background: Bhartṛprapañca
6. The true Tradition: Gauḍapāda, Draviḍa, Brahmanandin, Sundara Pāṇḍya
7. Doctrine of illusion before Śaṃkara: Māyā Vāda and Avidyā Vāda
8. Śaṃkara's Date, Life and Works
9. Śaṃkara's School

II. THE DOCTRINE OF NESCIENCE

1. The Nature and Results of Nescience
2. Nescience as Non-comprehension and False Comprehension
3. The Self and the not-self: non-discrimination and mutual superimposition
4. The Standpoint of Nescience and the Standpoint of Knowledge

III. KNOWLEDGE OF THE ABSOLUTE

1. The Absolute is already known in a general way

CONTENTS OF THE ŚAṂKARA SOURCE-BOOK

CONTENTS OF THE ŚAṂKARA SOURCE-BOOK

CONTENTS OF THE ŚAṂKARA SOURCE-BOOK

VOLUME VI

ŚAṂKARA ON THE PATH TO ENLIGHTENMENT

Catalogue of publications
including several translations of
Sanskrit philosophical classics
available on request from the publishers,

SHANTI SADAN
29 Chepstow Villas, London W11 3DR